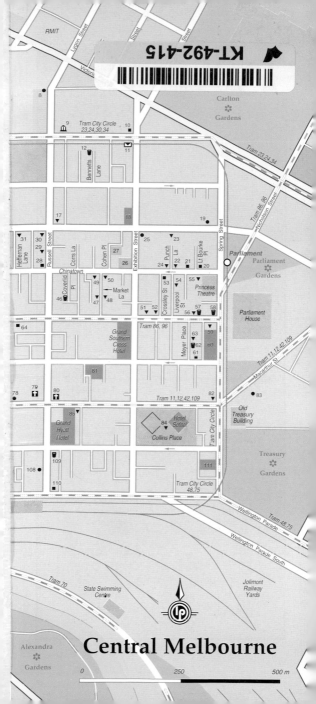

Central Melbourne

SIMON BRACKEN

Melbourne

a Lonely Planet city guide

Mark Armstrong

Melbourne
2nd edition

Published by
Lonely Planet Publications
Head Office: PO Box 617, Hawthorn, Vic 3122, Australia
Branches: 155 Filbert St, Suite 251, Oakland,
CA 94607, USA
10 Barley Mow Passage, Chiswick,
London W4 4PH, UK
71 bis rue du Cardinal Lemoine,
75005 Paris, France

Printed by
Colorcraft Ltd, Hong Kong
Printed in China

Photographs by
Mark Armstrong, Glenn Beanland, Simon Bracken,
Krzysztof Dydynski, Richard I'Anson, Richard Nebesky,
Tony Wheeler, Reimund Zunde

Front cover & title page: The Arts Centre with its distinctive spire
(Simon Bracken)

First Published
March 1993

This Edition
July 1997

Although the authors and publisher have tried to make the information as accurate as possible, they accept no responsibility for any loss, injury or inconvenience sustained by any person using this book.

National Library of Australia Cataloguing in Publication Data

Armstrong, Mark
Melbourne

2nd ed.
Includes index.
ISBN 0 86442 386 1.

1. Melbourne (Vic) – Guidebooks. I. Armstrong, Mark, 1961-
Melbourne city guide. 1st ed. II. Title. III. Title:
Melbourne city guide. 1st ed.

919.45104

Mark Armstrong

Mark was born in Melbourne and completed his tertiary studies at Melbourne University. Among other things, he has worked in computer sales and marketing, as a restorer of old houses, as a fencing contractor and in the hospitality industry. He lived for a while in Barcelona and has travelled in South-East Asia, Europe and North America. Since 1992 he has worked on several LP guides, including *Victoria*, *Queensland*, the Victoria and Queensland chapters of *Australia*, and *Spain*. He researched and wrote the first edition of *Melbourne* as well as updating this edition.

From the Author

Mark would like to thank all the travellers and fellow Melburnians who offered advice about Melbourne's ever-changing face. Special thanks to Rob Kemp, Susan Caudrey, Franny Cox, James Cook, Hilary Guillim, Chris McAsey, Gina Hearndon, Colin Robertson, Susan Rogers, Kerry Armstrong, Mark Croft, John Meckiff, Matthew Nevett and Victoria Cowling for their assistance in the quest to keep up with what's hot and what's not.

From the Publisher

This book was edited by Liz Filleul and proofed by Steve Womersley and Suzi Petkovski. The maps were drawn by Andrew Tudor, and Marcel Gaston was responsible for design and layout. Thanks to David Kemp for designing the cover and to Michelle Lewis and Mary Neighbour for help at layout stage.

Warning & Request

Things change – prices go up, schedules change, good places go bad and bad places go bankrupt – nothing stays the same. So if you find things better or worse, recently opened or long since closed, please write and tell us and help make the next edition even more accurate and useful.

We value all the feedback we receive from travellers. Julie Young coordinates a small team who read and acknowledge every letter, postcard and e-mail, and ensure that every morsel of information find its way to the appropriate authors and publishers.

Everyone who writes to us will find their name in the next edition of the appropriate guide and will also receive a free subscription to our quarterly newsletter, *Planet Talk*. The best contributions will be rewarded with a free Lonely Planet guide.

Exerpts from your correspondence may appear in updates (which we add to the end pages of reprints); new editions of this guide; or in the Postcards section of our Web site – so please let us know if you don't want your letter published or your name acknowledged.

Thanks

Many thanks to Frank Gottschalk, Chris Morcom, Lynn Nicholson and Melanie Osborne, who wrote to us with helpful hints after using the 1st edition.

Contents

Map Contents

Introduction

Melbourne, Australia's second-largest city, was founded and experienced its greatest period of development during the reign of Queen Victoria (1837 to 1901), and the city is in many ways a product of its formative era, both architecturally and socially. It's a traditionally conservative city of elaborate Victorian-era buildings, gracious parks and gardens, and tree-lined boulevards. The first European settlers only arrived in 1835, but within just 50 years Melbourne had been transformed from a small village into a major city, and it remains the youngest city of its size in the world. In 1885, English journalist George Sala described Melbourne as:

...marvellous not merely for its civilisation and its wealth and vigour, but above all for its precocious growth.

The first European settlement was established on Port Phillip Bay at Sorrento in 1803, although within a year it was abandoned and the settlers moved down to Tasmania. In 1835 a group of Tasmanian entrepreneurs returned and established a permanent settlement near the site of today's city centre.

In 1851 the colony of Victoria became independent of New South Wales, and almost immediately the small town of Melbourne became the centre for Australia's biggest and most prolonged gold rush. The immense wealth from the goldfields was used to build a solid and substantial city that came to be known as 'Marvellous Melbourne'. This period of great prosperity lasted until the end of the 1880s, when the collapse of the property market led to a severe depression.

In the years since WWII, Melbourne's social fabric has been greatly enriched by an influx of people and cultures from around the world. Several building booms, most notably that of the 1980s, have altered the city physically so that it is now a striking blend of past and present, with ornate 19th-century buildings sitting alongside towering skyscrapers.

Today Melbourne is perhaps best-known for its trams, its cafes and restaurants, the diversity of its inner suburbs, and events such as the Melbourne Cup and the International Festival of the Arts. It's a vibrant, multicultural city which is characterised by its people rather than any geographical feature. It combines a passion for the arts with an equally healthy passion for sports, food and wine, and 'the good life'.

A recent international survey of the relative living standards of major cities proclaimed Melbourne to be 'one of the world's most livable cities' – and it's also a great place to visit.

Melbourne may lack the physical impact of its more flamboyant northern sister, Sydney, and take a little more time to get to know, but it has much to offer. After all, why else would Lonely Planet, with an entire world to choose from, be based here?

Facts about Melbourne

HISTORY

Early Aboriginal History

It is thought that Aborigines journeyed from South-East Asia to the Australian mainland at least 50,000 years ago.

The Victorian Aboriginal people lived in some 38 different dialect groups (also known as tribal groups) who spoke 10 separate languages, with each of the dialect groups being further divided into clans and sub-clans. Each clan had ownership of a distinct area of land, and the Aborigines' complex traditional culture was largely based on their close spiritual bond with the land they lived in and thrived in.

Their seminomadic existence was a defining feature of their adaptation to the Australian landscape. In Victoria, they were able to cope with the winter climate by sheltering in simple huts, wearing possum-skin cloaks and warming themselves with small fires. The coastal tribes lived on an amazingly wide variety of plants and vegetables, supplementing their diet with fish and turtles from the sea. Shellfish were collected and eaten on the beaches – evidence of these feasts in the form of huge shell middens have been found all along the Victorian coast. Inland tribes were expert game hunters, using nets to catch kangaroos and possums, spears to kill emus, and boomerangs to bring down birds.

The Europeans

While Captain James Cook is popularly credited with Australia's discovery in 1770, Portuguese navigators probably sighted it in the 16th century.

In 1779 the British decided that New South Wales was a fine site for a colony of thieves, and in January 1788, the First Fleet sailed into Botany Bay.

In October 1803, a small party of convicts, soldiers and settlers under the command of Captain David Collins arrived at Sorrento and established Victoria's first European settlement. Less than a year later, unable to find a sustainable supply of fresh water, Collins decided to abandon the settlement.

Facts about Melbourne

Apart from a few whalers' huts along the coastline, Victoria remained unoccupied by the White settlers for years. But as the pastoral runs of New South Wales and Van Diemen's Land became overcrowded, the settlers began to look further afield for fertile lands. In 1824 the explorers Hume and Hovell made the first overland journey southwards from Sydney to the shores of Port Phillip Bay. The arrival of Edward Henty, his family and flock of sheep from Van Diemen's Land at Portland in 1834 marked the beginning of the European invasion – what Richard Broome has called 'the greatest land grab in British imperial history.' Pastoralists and settlers flooded into Victoria from New South Wales and Van Diemen's Land, and within 10 years the Europeans out-numbered the original inhabitants.

In 1836, the colony's surveyor-general, Major Thomas Mitchell, wrote glowing reports of the beautiful and fertile country he had crossed in his explorations of central and western Victoria. He dubbed the region Australia Felix, or 'Australia Fair'. His enthusiasm

MARK ARMSTRONG

Sculptor William Ricketts' work reflects the Aboriginal heritage of the Dandenong Ranges.

encouraged pastoralists to head south from New South Wales and north from Van Diemen's Land to establish pastoral runs throughout Victoria.

Aboriginal Resistance

At a local level, individual Aborigines resisted the encroachment of White settlers. Warriors including Pemulwy, Yagan, Dundalli, Pigeon and Nemarluk were, for a time, feared by the colonists in their areas. Although some settlements had to be abandoned, the effect of such resistance was only to postpone the inevitable.

The Aborigines were generally regarded as savages and a hindrance to the 'civilisation' and settlement of Victoria. Soon after the arrival of the Europeans, their traditional culture was disrupted, they were dispossessed of their lands, and they were massacred in their thousands – firstly by introduced diseases like smallpox, dysentery and measles, and later by guns and poison. Between 1834 and 1849, a humanitarian group called the Port Phillip Protectorate tried to protect some of the rights of the Aborigines, but with little effect. Estimates suggest that around 15,000 Aborigines were living in Victoria in 1834, but by 1860 there were only around 2000 survivors.

Without any legal right to the lands they once lived on, many Aborigines were driven from their lands by force, while others voluntarily left to travel to the fringes of settled areas to obtain new commodities such as steel and cloth, and experience hitherto unknown drugs such as tea, tobacco, alcohol and narcotics.

Founding of Melbourne

Two Tasmanian men, John Batman and John Pascoe Fawkner, are widely acknowledged as the founders of Melbourne.

In 1835 a group of Launceston businessmen formed the Port Phillip Association with the intention of establishing a new settlement on Port Phillip Bay. In May of that year, their representative, John Batman, purchased about 240,000 hectares of land from the Aborigines of the local Dutigalla clan.

The concept of buying or selling land was completely foreign to the Aborigines, but in return for their land they received an assorted collection of blankets, knives, tomahawks, looking-glasses, scissors, handkerchiefs, various items of clothing and 50 pounds of flour. Once the treaty was signed, the other association members joined Batman, and the settlement of Melbourne was established on the north side of the Yarra River.

In October 1835 John Pascoe Fawkner and a group of Tasmanian settlers joined them. The son of a convict, Fawkner grew up in the harsh and fierce environment of a convict settlement. When he was 22, he received 500 lashes for helping seven convicts escape, and all his life he carried with him the scars of the lash and a hatred of the transportation system.

Fawkner was a driving force behind the new settlement – he was a man of vision and worked industriously. He was a self-taught bush lawyer, started several newspapers, and spent 15 years on the Legislative Council of Victoria, where he campaigned vigorously for the rights of small settlers and convicts and for the ending of transportation. By the time of his death in 1869, Melbourne was flourishing and he was known as the 'Grand Old Man of Victoria'. More than 15,000 people lined the streets to bid him farewell at his funeral.

History doesn't remember John Batman as kindly. Within four years of his dodgy deal with the Aborigines, Batman was dead, a victim of his own excesses. The historian Manning Clark described him in *A History of Australia* as '...a man who abandoned himself wantonly to the Dionysian frenzy and allowed no restraint to come between himself and the satisfaction of his desires'.

While the initial treaty with the Aborigines had no legal basis, by 1836 so many settlers had moved to Port Phillip that the administrators of New South Wales had to declare the area open to settlement. The *Advertiser* newspaper wrote on 8 April 1838:

The town of Melbourne is rapidly increasing in population and in building. There are at this present time not less than 10 brick houses in hand, some of them roofed in, and others, the walls partly built...

In 1839 the military surveyor Robert Hoddle drew up the plans for the new city, laying out a geometric grid of broad streets in a rectangular pattern on the northern side of the Yarra River.

By 1840 there were over 10,000 people settled in the area around Melbourne. The earliest provincial towns were established along the south coast at places like Portland, Port Fairy and Port Albert, but gradually the pastoralists explored and opened up the fertile Victorian interior and began clearing land for grazing and agriculture. The earliest inland settlements were sheep stations

– small, self-sufficient communities which housed the sheep farmers and their families and employees. As the new community grew in size and confidence, they began to agitate for separation from New South Wales.

Separation & Gold Rushes

In 1851 Victoria won separation from New South Wales. The colony of Victoria was proclaimed with Melbourne as its capital. In the same year, gold was discovered at Bathurst in New South Wales. Fearing the young city's workers would desert for the northern goldfields, a committee of Melbourne businessmen offered a reward to anyone who found gold within Victoria – but even in their wildest dreams they couldn't have foreseen what would follow. The first gold strike was at Warrandyte in May 1851 and, during the next few months, massive finds followed at Buninyong and Clunes near Ballarat, Mt Alexander near Castlemaine and Ravenswood near Bendigo.

The subsequent gold rush brought a huge influx of immigrants from all around the world. The Irish and English, and later Europeans, Americans and Chinese, began arriving in droves. Within 12 months there were about 1800 hopeful diggers disembarking at Melbourne every week.

Melbourne became a chaotic mess. As soon as ships arrived in the harbour, their crews would desert and follow the passengers to the goldfields. Business in Melbourne ground to a standstill as most of the labour force left to join the search. Shanty towns of bark huts and canvas tents sprung up to house the population (which doubled within a decade). In 1852 the *Sydney Morning Herald* asserted:

...that a worse regulated, worse governed, worse drained, worse lighted, worse watered town of note is not on the face of the globe; and that a population more thoroughly disposed in every grade to cheating and robbery, open and covert, does not exist; that in no other place does immorality stalk abroad so unblushingly and so unchecked...that, in a word, nowhere in the southern hemisphere does chaos reign so triumphant as in Melbourne.

But a generation later, bolstered by the wealth of the goldfields, this ragged city had matured and refined itself into 'Marvellous Melbourne', one of the world's great Victorian-era cities. HM Hyndman, in his *Record of an Adventurous Life*, said of Melbourne in 1870:

TONY WHEELER

Sovereign Hill, Ballarat, re-creates the gold rush which
brought prosperity to Melbourne.

I have been a great deal about the world and I have moved
freely in many societies, but I have never lived in any city
where the people at large, as well as the educated class, took
so keen an interest in all the activities of human life, as in
Melbourne at the time I visited it. Art, the drama, music,
literature, journalism, wit, oratory all found ready appreciation. The life and vivacity of the place were astonishing.

The gold rush produced enough wealth for Victoria to
transform itself from a fledgling colony into a prosper-
ous and independent state, but it also brought with it
tensions that were to lead to significant social and political changes. In the early days of the rush, authorities
introduced a compulsory license fee, but in 1854 a group
of miners at the Ballarat diggings rioted and burnt their
licenses in protest at the inequality of the fees. Twenty-
five miners were killed during what became known as
the Eureka Rebellion, and its aftermath was to change
forever the political landscape in Victoria.

The gold rush years were a period of great prosperity
and flamboyance, leading to a flowering of the arts and

culture. Melburnians took some pride in the fact that theirs was not a convict settlement, and they used their new-found wealth to build a city of extravagant proportions. Among the new migrants came tradespeople from Europe who were well trained in the great traditions of Renaissance building, and the city's architects readily put them to work. Large areas were set aside and planted as public parks and gardens. By the 1880s Melbourne was being referred to as the 'Paris of the Antipodes'.

Similarly, from 1851 onwards provincial Victoria was quickly settled and colonised. The gold-rush wealth was used to build major towns to house the sudden massive increase in the population, and the pastoralists and squatters spread their interests across the state.

This period of great prosperity lasted for 40 years. The 1880s were boom times for Melbourne, but there was an air of recklessness about the place. Money from the goldfields and from overseas was invested in real estate and building works, and speculation led to spiralling land prices that couldn't last. In 1888 Melbourne hosted the Great Exhibition in the opulent Exhibition Buildings. No expense was spared in the construction of the buildings or the exhibition itself, but this flamboyant showing-off to the world was to be the swan song of Marvellous Melbourne.

In 1889 the property market collapsed under the increasing weight of speculation. In 1890 a financial crash in Argentina led to the collapse of several financial institutions in London and, overnight, investment in Australia dried up. The 1890s was a period of severe economic depression. In Melbourne, many buildings that were incomplete at the time of the collapse were never finished, and it was many years before the city recovered.

Federation & After

With federation, on 1 January 1901, Victoria became a state of the new Australian nation. Melbourne became the capital and the seat of government until it was moved to Canberra in 1927. The Federal Parliament sat at the State Parliament Houses, and the State Parliament moved to the Exhibition Buildings. But Australia's loyalties and many of its legal ties to Britain remained. When WWI broke out in Europe, Australian troops were sent to fight in the trenches of France, Gallipoli and the Middle East.

There was more expansion and construction in Victoria in the 1920s, but all this came to a halt with the Great

Depression, which hit Australia hard. In 1931 almost a third of breadwinners were unemployed and poverty was widespread. During the Depression the government implemented a number of major public works programmes and workers were put on sustenance pay. The Yarra Boulevard, the Shrine of Remembrance, St Kilda Rd and the Great Ocean Road were all built by sustenance workers. By 1932, however, Australia's economy was starting to recover as a result of rises in wool prices and a rapid manufacturing revival.

Post WWII

The process of social change was accelerated by WWII, and 'assimilation' became the stated aim of postwar governments. To this end, the rights of Aborigines were subjugated even further – the government had control over everything, from where Aborigines could live to whom they could marry. Many people were forcibly moved to townships, the idea being that they would adapt to the European culture, which would in turn aid their economic development. The policy was a dismal failure.

(The assimilation policy was finally dumped in 1972, to be replaced by a policy of self-determination, which for the first time enabled Aborigines to participate in decision-making processes.)

After WWII the Australian government initiated an immigration programme in the hope that the increase in population would strengthen Australia's economy and contribute to its ability to defend itself. 'Populate or Perish' became the catch phrase. Between 1947 and 1968 more than 800,000 non-British European migrants came to Australia. The majority of migrants came by ships which landed in Melbourne first, and a large percentage of the new arrivals settled there. In the 1970s migrants began arriving from South-East Asia and this still continues. (See the Population & People section for further information on immigration.)

On the political front, Victoria's post-WWII years were dominated by the Liberal party, which governed continuously from 1955 to 1982, when the Labor party under John Cain won office.

During the 1980s Victoria experienced boom times, just as it had 100 years earlier. Land prices rose continuously throughout the decade, and in the competitive atmosphere of the newly deregulated banking industry, banks were queuing up to lend money to speculators and developers. The city centre and surrounds were transformed as one skyscraper sprung up after another, leading some overexcited architects to refer to Melbourne as the 'Chicago of the southern hemisphere'. Even the worldwide stock market crash in 1987 didn't slow things down, but in 1990 the property market collapsed, just as it had 100 years earlier.

By 1991 Australia found itself in recession again, partly as a result of domestic economic policy, but also because Australia is particularly hard hit when demand (and prices) for primary produce and minerals falls on the world markets. Unemployment was the highest it had been since the early 1930s and Victoria was the state hardest hit.

In October 1992, a Liberal/National party coalition led by Jeff Kennett was elected in a landslide victory – ousting the Labor party which had been in power for 10 years. In March 1996 Kennett was re-elected for a second term. The Kennett government has ruled the state with an iron fist. Its policies have succeeded in turning around the state's economy, but at the same time Kennett's belligerence and the government's failure to properly address social-welfare issues have alienated large segments of the community.

GEOGRAPHY

Melbourne's urban sprawl, which extends for more than 50 km from east to west and more than 70 km from north to south, covers a massive 1700 sq km. This is mainly attributable to the Great Australian Dream – where every family wanted to own their own home on their own quarter-acre block. Melbourne's population density is thus a mere 16 persons per hectare, in comparison with cities like Paris (48) and London (56).

All of this results in increasingly greater pressures on urban infrastructure, and planning authorities are doing all they can to encourage higher density housing in both the inner and outer suburbs of the city.

The metropolitan area is predominantly flat. In 1837, the city was laid out in a geometric grid one mile (1.61 km) long and half a mile (805m) wide. This street grid is now at an angle to the main metropolitan grid. Note that long streets often start renumbering addresses at the start of a new suburb.

Melbourne is fairly easy to get around; it has the benefit of many broad, tree-lined avenues and is surrounded by public gardens and parklands. The city centre isn't so much the focal point of Melbourne as the hub of the wheel, surrounded by clusters of interest within the inner suburbs. The Yarra River divides the city geographically and socio-economically. Traditionally the northern and western suburbs are more industrial and working-class, while areas south of the Yarra have been the domain of the more affluent settlers and the setting for the most prestigious housing.

CLIMATE

Victoria's seasons are the opposite of the northern hemisphere's, so that January is the height of summer and July the depths of winter.

Melbourne has four seasons, with no great extremes. It rarely snows, the mercury only rises above 35°C a few times each year, and Melbourne has half the average rainfall of Sydney and Brisbane. In summer, the average temperatures range from a high of 26°C to a low of 14°C; in winter the average maximum is 13°C and the minimum 6°C; while in spring and autumn average highs and lows range from around 20°C to 10°C.

Of course, averages and statistics never paint the true picture. They smooth out the inconsistencies, of which there are plenty. Those four seasons don't always stick to their allocated timeslots, and you are just as likely to have a sunny, blue-sky day in winter and sudden thunderstorms in summer as vice-versa. Or worse still, all four seasons in one day! The saying goes that if you don't like the weather in Melbourne, just wait a couple of minutes. The guiding principle is to expect the unexpected – that way you're prepared for whatever comes over the horizon.

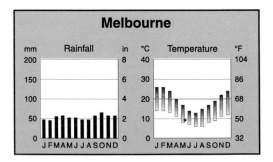

GOVERNMENT & POLITICS

Australian Government

Australia is a federation of six states and two territories, and has a parliamentary system of government based on the Westminister model. There are three tiers of government: federal, state and local.

Australia's two main political groups are the Australian Labor Party (ALP) and the coalition between the Liberal Party and the National Party. In theory, the Australian Labor Party is traditionally socialist, having grown out of the workers' disputes and shearers' strikes of the 1890s; the Liberal Party is traditionally conservative, representing the interests of free enterprise, law and order and family values; and the National Party (formerly the National Country Party) is traditionally the party of rural interests, having originally been formed to represent conservative farmers' unions.

In practice, however, the distinctions between the major parties have become somewhat blurred as political expediency and holding onto office have increasingly taken priority over traditional party values. Particularly since the early 1980s, the ALP and the Liberals have converged on the political middle ground, relinquishing conventional left and right ideology respectively and embracing economic rationalism and the free market.

The Australian Democrats form another important political group (formed, as its first federal leader, Don Chipp, said, to 'keep the bastards honest'), and independent and Green representatives are also playing an increasingly active and important role in national politics.

Australia currently has a Liberal/National coalition government, under the leadership of John Howard.

Victorian Government

Victoria's state government is based in Melbourne and is made up of the Legislative Council (the upper house) with 44 elected representatives and the Legislative Assembly (the lower house) with 88 elected representatives. Elections for the lower house are held every four years. Voting is by secret ballot and is compulsory for everyone aged 18 and over.

The Liberal Party, under the premiership of Jeff Kennett, currently governs in Victoria, having been re-elected for a second term in March 1996.

ECONOMY

Victoria may be Australia's smallest mainland state, but it's also the most densely populated and the most intensively farmed, producing more than 20% of the country's agricultural products.

Victoria has extensive natural resources. The Latrobe Valley has one of the world's largest deposits of brown coal and provides more than 80% of the state's energy requirements, while offshore fields in Bass Strait supply about half of Australia's crude oil and natural gas needs. More than 35% of Victoria is forested, and the timber industry is another major source of income. Most of the timber logged now comes from commercial softwood and hardwood plantations, although some old-growth forests continue to be logged – a matter of great controversy.

Victoria's manufacturing industries contribute around 25% of Australia's Gross National Product. The major industries are clothing and footwear, textiles, automotive and transport equipment, paper, metal, coal and petroleum products.

Around 70% of the state's workforce is employed in the tertiary sector, particularly wholesale and retail trade and community services such as education and health. As with the rest of Australia, the tourism industry is of growing economic importance.

POPULATION & PEOPLE

Melbourne has a population of over three million people, made up of over 60 different nationalities and with almost a quarter of them born overseas. The city is a melting pot for people and cultures from all over the world. The first wave of White settlers were predominantly Anglo-Celtic, coming from England, Scotland and Ireland. During the gold rush, diggers came from all over the world.

After WWII, thousands migrated from Europe. Many were Jewish, survivors of the holocaust who wanted to start again as far away from the horror as possible. Melbourne's large percentage of Greek, Italian and Jewish people date from these times, but many others came from places like Turkey, Lebanon, Malta, Poland and Yugoslavia.

Since the mid-1970s, most immigrants have come from South-East Asia and the Pacific, many being refugees from Vietnam and Cambodia.

Cultural Melbourne

As Australia's cultural capital, Melbourne offers a wide range of music, opera and theatre performances virtually every day of the year.

The Melbourne Symphony Orchestra performs almost every week between February and December, with most performances being held at the Melbourne Concert Hall. If you are visiting in February, their outdoor picnic-style concerts on Wednesday and Saturday nights at the Sidney Myer Music Bowl are a must. The Australian Pops Orchestra also presents a number of performances each year.

The Australian Opera offers up to seven operas in repertoire at the State Theatre from mid-March to mid-May, and the Victoria State Opera presents up to six operas in the second half of each year.

There are also dozens of theatrical productions staged in Melbourne each week, ranging from school plays to the latest Andrew Lloyd Webber extravaganza. The two major theatre companies are the Playbox and the Melbourne Theatre Company – see Theatre in the Entertainment chapter for more details.

The Council of Adult Education (CAE) (☎ 9652 0611), at 256 Flinders St in the city, runs a huge range of short study courses of between one-day and eight weeks' duration. Topics include painting, sculpture, personal development, photography, computer studies, outdoor adventure courses, tai chi, yoga – and just about everything else imaginable. They also run a good English as a Foreign Language (EFL) course geared towards travellers. Call them to find out what's on, or drop in and pick up a programme.

The Royal Society of Victoria (☎ 9663 5259), at 8 Latrobe St in the city, is an interesting place. Their regular meetings (at 8 pm on the second Thursday of each month) are open to the public and topics for discussion include science, medicine and the natural sciences. The building also houses meetings of various 'learned societies' such as the Antique Collectors, the Numerological Society and the Existentialists, whose public meetings (at 8 pm on the first Tuesday of each month) feature guest speakers discussing topics ranging from an analysis of Dostoyevsky's *The Brothers Karamazov* to the existence of UFOs.

Listed under the 'Readings' and 'Hear This' sections in the *EG* in the Friday edition of the *Age* newspaper, you'll also find things like book launches, religious discussions, educational lectures and public debates. ■

Today, one of Melbourne's greatest strengths is the richness of its cultural mix.

There are around 20,000 Koories (as Aborigines call themselves in south-eastern Australia) and Torres Strait Islanders living in Victoria. More than half of these people live in Melbourne, mainly in the inner suburbs.

ARTS

Melbourne is regarded by many people as the cultural capital of Australia. A town that unleashed people as diverse as Barry Humphries, Kylie Minogue, Sir Sidney Nolan, Olivia Newton-John, Nick Cave, Rupert Murdoch, Dame Nellie Melba, Peter Carey and Germaine Greer on the world can't be all beer and horse races.

Aboriginal Art & Culture

There are relatively few traces in Victoria today of the Aboriginal tribes that lived and thrived in the region before White settlement. The Museum of Victoria in Melbourne has an excellent collection of Aboriginal artefacts, and the Koori Heritage Trust (☎ 9669 9061) offers Aboriginal cultural tours of the museum each Thursday at 10 am. The museum is also working to build a centre specifically dedicated to Aboriginal culture.

Also in Melbourne, the National Gallery of Victoria has a collection of contemporary Aboriginal art (guided tours on Thursday at 2 pm) and the gallery shop sells Aboriginal art prints; there is an Aboriginal Resources Walk in the Royal Botanic Gardens; and the City of Melbourne publishes the excellent *Another View Walking Trail* brochure detailing a four to five-hour walking tour through the city that traces the links between Aborigines and the European settlers (available from information booths in the city). There are also numerous commercial galleries in Melbourne that sell Aboriginal art and craft – see the Shopping chapter.

Architecture

Victoria's earliest buildings were built in the Old Colonial style (1788-1840), a simplified version of Georgian architecture. The earliest settled towns such as Portland, Port Fairy and Port Albert are the best examples of this period. In Melbourne few examples remain – St James' Cathedral (1840) in King St is the oldest public building.

Somewhat appropriately, the most prominent architectural style in the state is Victorian (1840-90), which was an expression of the era's confidence, progress and prosperity. It drew on various sources including classical, romantic and Gothic and, as the era progressed, designs became more elaborate, flamboyant and ornamental. Melbourne is widely acknowledged as one of the world's great Victorian-era cities and features many outstanding examples of Victorian architecture in the city centre and inner suburbs such as Carlton, Parkville, East Melbourne, South Melbourne and St Kilda.

With the collapse of Melbourne's land boom in the early 1890s and the subsequent severe economic depression, a new style of architecture which came to be known as 'Federation' evolved. The Federation style was in many ways a watered-down version of Victorian architecture, featuring simplicity of design and less ornamentation. Its evolution was mainly driven by economic necessity, but it was also influenced by the pending federation of Australia (in 1901) and the associated desire to create a more distinctive and suitably 'Australian' style of design.

From around 1910, the most prominent style of residential architecture was a hybrid of the Federation and California Bungalow styles. The Art Deco style was also prominent from the 1920s, but after the Great Depression architecture became increasingly functionalist and devoid of decoration.

In recent years, appreciation of these older styles of architecture has increased to the extent that councils

RICHARD NEBESKY

The splendour of early Victorian architecture, Hawthorn.

have actively encouraged residents to restore houses and buildings in sympathy with the period in which they were built.

Painting

Melbourne's National Gallery houses one of the most comprehensive art collections in the southern hemisphere. The Australian collection contains a significant number of works by Australian impressionists. Based at a bush camp in Heidelberg in the 1880s, Tom Roberts, Arthur Streeton, Frederick McCubbin and Charles Condor were the first local artists to paint in a distinctively Australian style rather than in imitation of the Europeans.

In the 1940s, another revolution in Australian art took place at Heide, the home of John and Sunday Reed in suburban Bulleen. Under their patronage, a new generation of bohemian young artists (including Sir Sidney Nolan, Albert Tucker, Arthur Boyd, Joy Hester and John Perceval) redefined the direction of Australian art. Today, you can visit the Museum of Modern Art at Heide – see the Things to See & Do chapter for details of other galleries in the city.

Music

Melbourne's rich musical heritage covers the spectrum from rock to classical, and the lively rock music scene has been the launching pad for bands like Men at Work, Crowded House and Nick Cave & the Bad Seeds, while two Melburnians who achieved fame on the classical world stage were the singer Dame Nellie Melba and the composer Sir Percy Grainger.

The city hosts a wide range of music festivals throughout the year, featuring everything from jazz and blues to chamber music and alternative rock. Melbourne's music festivals include the Montsalvat Jazz Festival and the Melbourne Music Festival. The Port Fairy Folk Festival and the Wangaratta Jazz Festival are just two of many excellent music festivals held in rural Victoria.

Indigenous music is one of the Australian music industry's great success stories of recent years. Yothu Yindi (from the Northern Territory), with their land rights anthem *Treaty*, is the country's best-known Aboriginal band, but Victoria also has some great indigenous musicians including Archie Roach, Ruby Hunter and Tiddas.

Melbourne's dynamic music scene has consistently produced many of Australia's outstanding bands and musicians, and some local artists well worth checking out include Dave Graney 'n' the Coral Snakes, My Friend the Chocolate Cake, Stephen Cummings, Paul Kelly, Chris Wilson, Rebecca Barnard and Shane O'Mara, the Black Sorrows, Hunters & Collectors, Black Eyed Susans, Dirty Three, and Things of Stone & Wood – to mention but a few. If you're interested in seeing a live performance, check gig guides such as the *EG* in Friday's *Age* newspaper, *Beat* or *Inpress* – otherwise, pick up a few local CDs or tapes to provide the perfect soundtrack for your visit to Melbourne.

Cinema

Melbourne is the birthplace of the Australian film industry, and the base from which Australia began to create a distinctively indigenous style of cinema. Cinema historians regard an Australian film, *Soldiers of the Cross*, as the world's first 'real' movie. It was originally screened at the Melbourne Town Hall in 1901, cost £600 to make and was shown throughout the USA in 1902.

The next significant Australian film, *The Story of the Kelly Gang*, was screened in 1907, and by 1911 the industry was flourishing. Low-budget films were being made in such quantities that they could be hired out or sold cheaply. Over 250 silent feature films were made before the 1930s when the talkies and Hollywood took over.

In the 1950s, the film *On the Beach* was shot in Melbourne. One of its stars, Ava Gardner, was less than enchanted by her surroundings and made the comment that Melbourne was the perfect place to make a film about the end of the world – at the time she may have been right.

With the introduction of government subsidies during 1969 and 1970, the Australian film industry enjoyed a renaissance that came to be known as the New Wave, producing films like *Breaker Morant*, *Sunday Too Far Away*, *Caddie* and *The Devil's Playground*, which appealed to large local and international audiences. Some landmark Victorian productions from this period were *The Adventures of Barry McKenzie*, the *Alvin Purple* series, the *Mad Max* series, *Monkey Grip*, *Picnic at Hanging Rock* and *The Getting of Wisdom*.

Since the 70s, Australian actors and directors like Mel Gibson, Judy Davis, Nicole Kidman, Paul Hogan, Bruce Beresford, Peter Weir, Gillian Armstrong and Fred Schepsi have gained international recognition, as have films like *Gallipoli*, *The Year of Living Dangerously*, *Crocodile Dundee I* and *II*, *The Year My Voice Broke*, *Strictly*

RICHARD NEBESKY

Paul Kelly, one of Australia's leading singer-songwriters.
Born in Adelaide, he now lives in Melbourne.

Ballroom, The Piano, Muriel's Wedding and *Priscilla, Queen of the Desert.*

If you're specifically interested in films made in or about Melbourne, the following are all available on video and well worth seeing: *Malcolm* (a charming film about a simple genius who builds a one-person tram) and *The Big Steal* (about taking revenge on a dodgy used-car dealer), both made by local film makers Nadia Tass and David Parker; *Death in Brunswick*, a black comedy about life in Melbourne's seedy underbelly; *Spotswood*, a nostalgic look at life and industrial relations in Melbourne in the 1950s, set in a moccasin factory; *Proof*, a poignant film about a blind photographer, set in St Kilda and Elwood; *Dogs In Space*, a great portrayal of the punk-grunge side of Melbourne; *Hotel Sorrento*, the story of three sisters and their reunion at a beach house in Sorrento; *Love and Other Catastrophes*, a quirky portrayal of student life set in and around Melbourne Uni; and *Angel Baby*, a tragic love story about a couple of schizophrenics.

Uncompromising local director Geoffrey Wright's films include the savage *Romper Stomper*, about a neo-Nazi skinhead gang based in the Melbourne inner suburb of Footscray, and *Metal Skin*, about teenage boys in Melbourne and their love affairs with fast cars and women. Also, look for the very individual works of local film maker Paul Cox, including *Man of Flowers, Lonely Hearts, My First Wife* and *A Woman's Tale*.

TV Soap Operas

No discussion of culture would be complete without mentioning Victoria's TV soap operas such as *Neighbours* and the now-defunct *Prisoner* (known in the UK as *Prisoner: Cell Block H*), which have reached worldwide cult status and launched the international careers of the likes of Kylie Minogue and Jason Donovan.

Literature

Victoria has produced plenty of outstanding writers. Some of the classic works of Victorian literature are *For the Term of His Natural Life* by Marcus Clarke, *The Getting of Wisdom* by Henry Handel (Florence Ethel) Richardson, *Picnic at Hanging Rock* by Joan Lindsay and *My Brother Jack* by George Johnston. Also, look for the work of Charmian Clift, Hal Porter, Alan Marshall and Frank Hardy. Hardy's first novel, *Power Without Glory*, caused a sensation when it was first published in 1950. It was loosely based on the affairs and dealings of the notorious Melbourne businessman, John Wren, and resulted in Hardy, a member of the Australian Communist Party, being prosecuted for criminal libel.

CJ Dennis' verse story, *The Songs of a Sentimental Bloke*, published in 1915, established him as a national writer with broad appeal. Dennis lived in the small town of Toolangi, north of Melbourne, from 1915 to 1935.

Among Victoria's contemporary writers, the best-known is probably Peter Carey (now living in New York), who won the Booker Prize in 1988 for his novel *Oscar & Lucinda*. Helen Garner's works are mostly set in Melbourne and include *The Children's Bach*, *Postcards From Surfers*, *Cosmo Cosmolino* and *Monkey Grip*. Some other contemporary Melbourne writers to look out for include Kerry Greenwood, Morris Lurie, Carmel Bird, Gerald Murnane and Rod Jones. Barry Dickens' novels are quirky, often hilarious and distinctively Melburnian.

In recent years, Melbourne has produced a new wave of promising young writers, including Andrea Goldsmith, Christos Tsiolkas, Claire Mendes and Fiona Capp.

RELIGION

A shrinking majority of people in Victoria are at least nominally Christian. Most Protestant churches have merged to become the Uniting Church, but the Church of England has remained separate. The Catholic Church is popular (about 30% of Christians are Catholics), with the original Irish adherents boosted by the large numbers of Mediterranean immigrants.

Non-Christian minorities also abound, the main ones being Buddhist, Jewish and Muslim.

LANGUAGE

Melbourne contains many surprises for those who think all Aussies speak some weird variant of English. For a start many Australians don't even speak English – they speak Italian, Lebanese, Vietnamese, Turkish or Greek.

Those who do speak the native tongue are liable to lose you in a strange collection of Australian words. Some have completely different meanings in Australia to the meanings they have in English-speaking countries north of the equator; some commonly used words have been shortened almost beyond recognition. Others are derived from Aboriginal languages, or from the slang used by early convict settlers.

There is a slight regional variation in the Australian accent, while the difference between city and country speech is mainly a matter of speed. Lonely Planet publishes *Australia – a language survival kit*, an introduction to both Australian English and Aboriginal languages. For those wanting to make a more in-depth study of Australian English, the *Penguin Book of Australian Slang (A Dinkum Guide to Oz English)* by Lenie Johansen is a comprehensive and entertaining guide to the Australian vernacular.

Aboriginal Language

At the time the First Fleet arrived to establish the first European settlement in Australia, there were around 250 separate Australian languages spoken by 600 to 700 Aboriginal 'tribes', and these languages were as distinct from each other as English and French. Often three or four adjacent tribes would speak what amounted to dialects of the same language, but another adjacent tribe might speak a completely different language.

It is believed that all the languages evolved from a single language family as the Aboriginal people gradually moved out over the entire continent and split into new groups. There are a number of words that occur right across the continent, such as *jina* (foot) and *mala* (hand). Similarities also exist in the sometimes complex grammatical structures.

Following European contact the number of Aboriginal languages was drastically reduced. At least eight separate languages were spoken in Tasmania alone, but none of these was recorded before the native speakers either died or were killed. Of the original 250 or so languages, many of which were mutually unintelligible, only around 30 are today spoken on a regular basis and taught to children.

There are a number of terms which Aborigines use to describe themselves, and these vary according to the region. The most common term is Koori, used for the people of south-east Australia. Murri is used to refer to the people of Queensland, Nunga for those from coastal South Australia, and Nyoongah is used in the country's south-west.

Facts for the Visitor

WHEN TO GO

The summer months from December to February are Melbourne's busiest times for tourism. Accommodation is heavily booked (and often more expensive) and the popular venues and restaurants are more crowded, but as compensation you can expect to see an amazing variety of sporting events such as test cricket at the Melbourne Cricket Ground (MCG), the Australian Open at the National Tennis Centre, and international golf championships at Royal Melbourne and Huntingdale. You can also expect good beach weather (well, usually) and join in the festivities of events like the Australia Day celebrations and the St Kilda Festival.

The autumn months, particularly March and April, are the best time of year climatically. The days are warm and long and still, perfect for strolling through the gardens or lying on your back on the grass, watching the leaves changing into their autumn colours. Melbourne's fabulous International Comedy Festival is held at this time of year.

In winter, the skies tend to alternate between a soggy grey and a crisp clear blue. Winter temperatures average a maximum of 13°C and a minimum of 6°C – a good time to rug up and head off to see a game of Australian Rules football (the 'footy'), buy a pass to the International Film Festival, or find an open fire somewhere and pull the cork on a bottle of Victorian shiraz.

If you're into skiing, there are good snowfields within two to four hours' drive of the city. The season usually runs from mid-June until mid-September.

Spring in Melbourne, from September until November, means a few different things – the weather is even more unpredictable, the parks and gardens come to life, the world-class Melbourne International Festival begins – and, of course, there's the footy finals. Melburnians are fanatical about their football, and the build-up to the Grand Final, played on the last Saturday in September, is huge. There's also the Spring Racing Carnival, dominated by the horse race the whole country stops for – the Melbourne Cup, run at Flemington on the first Tuesday in November.

RICHARD NERESKY

View of the Yarra River and city centre
from Batman Avenue.

Apart from the climate, it's worth bearing the school-holiday periods in mind. The school year is divided into four terms, and holidays are generally as follows: the longest break is the Christmas holiday during summer from mid-December until the end of January; there are also three two-week holiday periods which vary from year to year, but fall approximately from late March to mid-April, late June to mid-July and mid-September to early October.

ORIENTATION

Melbourne's suburbs sprawl around the shores of Port Phillip Bay, with the city centre sited on the north bank of the Yarra River, about five km inland from the bay. Many of the inner suburbs that surround the city have their own particular character. If you want to get a true feel for Melbourne you'll need to venture beyond the city centre. Most of the places and attractions covered in this book are within the city and inner-suburban areas, and most places are easily accessible by public transport. One of the easiest, cheapest and most enjoyable ways to explore is to take a tram ride – it's also a distinctively 'Melbournesque' experience.

City Centre

The city centre is bordered by the Yarra River to the south, the Fitzroy Gardens to the east, Victoria St to the north and Spencer St to the west. The main streets, running east-west, are Collins and Bourke Sts, crossed by Swanston and Elizabeth Sts, all of which are interspersed with lots of narrower roads and a maze of little alleys and lanes.

If you're arriving in Melbourne by long-distance bus or on the airport bus, you'll arrive in the city at either the Spencer St coach terminal on the west side of town (V/Line, Skybus, Firefly and McCafferty's buses) or at the Melbourne Transit Centre at 58 Franklin St (Greyhound Pioneer Australia and Skybus buses) at the north end of the city.

The City Square is on Swanston Walk, but the true heart of the city is the Bourke St Mall, between Swanston and Elizabeth Sts. On the mall you'll find a tourist information booth, the Myer and David Jones department stores, and, on the corner of Bourke and Elizabeth Sts, the General Post Office.

Swanston St, which runs north-south through the city, is another pedestrian mall. After crossing the Yarra River, Swanston St becomes St Kilda Rd, a tree-lined boulevard which runs all the way south to St Kilda and beyond.

Beside the river on the corner of Swanston and Flinders Sts is Flinders St railway station, the main station for suburban trains. 'Under the clocks' at the station is a popular meeting place. The other major station, for country and interstate services, is the Spencer St railway station at the western end of Bourke St.

Inner Suburbs

Each of the inner suburbs that encircle the city centre has its own particular personality. To the north are North Melbourne, home to the YHA hostels; Carlton, an area known for its gracious Victorian-era architecture and home to Melbourne's Italian community, Melbourne University and the Royal Melbourne Zoo; and the bohemian suburb of Fitzroy, which is Melbourne's arty alternative-lifestyle centre.

East of the city, Richmond is dominated by the local Greek and Vietnamese communities, while to the south-east is stylish South Yarra with its upmarket fashion boutiques and fabulous restaurants.

South of the city, seaside St Kilda is Melbourne's most cosmopolitan and exotic playground. Williamstown, south-west of the city at the mouth of the Yarra River, is a charming seaside suburb with an historic maritime flavour.

Greater Melbourne

The Yarra River wends its way through Melbourne from the Upper Yarra Reservoir (about 90 km east of the city centre) to the head of the bay, dividing the city into two halves.

Most places of interest to travellers are either within the inner-suburban area or beyond the urban fringe. There are a few exceptions, such as the Museum of Modern Art in the north-eastern suburb of Bulleen, but generally there isn't too much that will lure you to the suburbs.

MAPS

Tourist information offices hand out free maps that cover the city and inner suburbs. If you're staying a while, more detailed maps are available from the Royal Automobile Club of Victoria (RACV; free to members), while companies like UBD publish good pocket maps which are available from all newsagencies for around $4.

Comprehensive street directories are produced by Melway, UBD and Gregory's, and are available at book-shops and newsagents. The best option for travellers is probably the *Compact Gregory's* ($14.95). The Melway street directory (around $37) is such a Melbourne insti-tution that places are often located by simply stating the relevant Melway page and grid reference.

Map Land (see Bookshops in the Shopping chapter) has the city's most comprehensive range of maps.

TOURIST OFFICES

Local Tourist Offices

In the city, the best places for information are the city council's three information booths. They have lots of free information as well as maps and monthly calendars of events, and are staffed by friendly, helpful volunteers,

RICHARD NEBESKY

Swanston Walk, a pedestrian mall cutting right through
the city centre.

some of whom are multilingual. The Bourke St Mall and
City Square booths open on weekdays from 9 am to 5 pm
(Friday till 7 pm), Saturday from 10 am to 4 pm and
Sunday from 11 am to 4 pm; the Rialto Observation Deck
booth is open on weekdays from 11 am to 5 pm and on
weekends from 10 am to 4 pm.

In February 1997, the city council launched a new
tourist service – the City Experience Centre (☎ 9658 9658;
9658 9524 AH), Melbourne Town Hall, Swanston St,
provides interactive visitor information in six languages. The City Experience Centre also offers a 'Greeter
Service', in which volunteer tourist guides take visitors
on a three-to-four-hour tour of the city. The centre is
open from 9 am to 7 pm from Monday to Friday, and 9
am to 5 pm on weekends.

The Royal Automobile Club of Victoria (RACV) (☎ 9650
1522) has a tourist information office in the Town Hall on
Swanston Walk – there are plenty of brochures, but it's
mainly a booking office for tours and accommodation.

The Federal Airports Corporation has a tourist information booth (☎ 9339 1805) in the international terminal
at Melbourne airport, which opens to meet all incoming
flights.

For information about Melbourne's public transport,
ring the Met (☎ 13 1638, daily between 7 am and 9 pm)
or visit the Met Shop at 103 Elizabeth St. Another good
spot to visit is Information Victoria at 318 Little Bourke
St, a government-run bookshop which stocks a wide
variety of publications about Melbourne and Victoria. In
the basement is a map shop.

RICHARD I'ANSON

The *Angel* sculpture by Deborah Halpern, outside the
National Gallery

Free Publications

There are a number of free information guides circulated
in Melbourne, most of which are available from the
tourist offices and the RACV. They include booklets like
This Week in Melbourne and *Melbourne Events*, which have
handy 'what's on' listings.

The best giveaways are those produced by Tourism
Victoria. Their *Melbourne & Surrounds Official Visitors'
Guide* has all sorts of helpful information, including a
calendar of events, transport maps, attraction and
accommodation listings, and a useful information
section at the back. They also produce excellent glossy
regional guides to Victoria.

It's worth picking up a copy of the Victorian edition
of *TNT Magazine*, a backpackers' publication which lists
cheap accommodation and eateries, attractions and
events. It's produced bimonthly and is available from
hostels and info centres.

Interstate Tourist Offices

Tourism Victoria has two interstate offices that can
supply you with information about Melbourne and Victoria, book accommodation and advise you on how to
get there:

New South Wales
    403 George St, Sydney 2000 (☎ (02) 9299 2088)
South Australia
    16 Grenfell St, Adelaide 5000 (☎ (08) 8231 4581)

Tourist Offices Abroad

The Australian Tourist Commission (ATC) is the government body established to inform potential visitors about the country. ATC offices overseas have a useful free booklet called *Travellers' Guide to Australia* which is a good introduction to the country, its geography, flora, fauna, states, transport, accommodation, food and so on. They also have a handy, free map of the country. This literature is intended for distribution overseas only; if you want copies, get them before you come to Australia. Addresses of the ATC offices for literature requests are:

Germany
    Neue Mainzerstrasse 22, D6000 Frankfurt/Main 1
    (☎ (069) 274 00 60)
Hong Kong
    Suite 1501, Central Plaza, 18 Harbour Rd, Wanchai
    (☎ 802 7700)
Japan
    Australian Business Centre, New Otani Garden Court Building, 28S 4-1 Kioi-Cho, Chiyoda-Ku, Tokyo 102 (☎ (03) 5214 0720)
    Twin 21 Mid Tower 30, F 2-1-61 Shiromi, Chuo-Ku, Osaka 540 (☎ (06) 946 2503)
New Zealand
    Level 13, 44-48 Emily Place, Auckland 1 (☎ (09) 379 9594)
Singapore
    Suite 1703, United Square, 101 Thomson Rd, Singapore 1130 (☎ 255 4555)
South Africa
    Suite 209 North Block, 75 Maude St, Sandton, Johannesburg 2199 (☎ (011) 784 2579)
UK
    Gemini House, 10-18 Putney Hill, London SW15
    (☎ (0171) 780 2229)
USA
    Suite 1200, 2121 Avenue of the Stars, Los Angeles, CA 90067 (☎ (213) 552 1988)
    25th floor, 100 Park Ave, New York, NY 10017
    (☎ (212) 687 6300)

Canadian travellers should contact the offices in New York or Los Angeles; those from France, Ireland or the Netherlands should contact the London office.

DOCUMENTS

Visas

Australia was once fairly free and easy about who was allowed to visit the country, particularly if you were from the UK or Canada. These days only New Zealanders get any sort of preferential treatment and even they need at least a passport. Everybody else has to have both a passport and a visa.

Visa application forms are available from either Australian diplomatic missions overseas or travel agents, and you can apply either by mail or in person. There are several different types of visas, depending on the reason for your visit.

Tourist Visas Tourist visas are issued by Australian consular offices abroad; they are the most common and are valid for a stay of either three or six months from the date of arrival. After you arrive in Australia, you can apply to extend your visa for a total visit of up to 12 months (see the section on Visa Extensions). If you intend staying less than three months, the visa is free; otherwise there is a processing fee of A$35.

When you apply for a visa, you need to present your passport and a passport photo, as well as sign an undertaking that you have an onward or return ticket and 'sufficient funds'.

Working Visas Young visitors from the UK, Ireland, Canada, Holland, Malta, South Korea and Japan may be eligible for a 'working holiday' visa. 'Young' is fairly loosely interpreted as around 18 to 26 years, and 'working holiday' means up to 12 months. You can work either full-time or part-time and for as much of the 12 months as you want (or are able to), but you can't work for the same employer for more than three months out of the 12. Visitors aged between 26 and 30 years can also apply for a working visa, but the qualifying conditions are much stricter – you have to be able to prove that your working in Australia will be 'mutually beneficial' to both Australia and your own country.

Officially this visa can only be applied for in your home country, but some travellers report that the rule can be bent.

See the section on Work later in this chapter for details of what sort of work is available and where.

Visa Extensions The maximum stay allowed for visitors to Australia is 12 months, including extensions.

Visa extensions are made through Department of Immigration & Multicultural Affairs offices in Australia and, as the process can take some time, it's best to apply about a month before your visa expires. There is a fixed and nonrefundable application fee of $140 – even if they turn down your application they can still keep your money! Some offices are very thorough, requiring things like bank statements and interviews. As a rule of thumb you'll need to have about A$1000 for each month you want to extend your visa by, although if you have statements from friends or relatives who are willing to put you up, this requirement will be relaxed somewhat. In the past, extending visas has been a notoriously slow process, but recently the conditions have been eased and there have been attempts to speed the process up. Since April 1996, a new computerised visa extension system has enabled some people the luxury of extending their visa by phone instead of having to visit the department in person.

If you want to extend your stay, contact the Department of Immigration & Multicultural Affairs (☎ 9235 3999), 2 Lonsdale St, Melbourne.

Other Documents

Foreign driving licenses are valid for the first three months of your visit to Australia. If you're staying for longer, it's worth obtaining an International Driving Permit (IDP) from your local automobile association before you leave – you'll need a passport photo and a valid licence. IDPs are valid for one year.

While you're there, ask your automobile association for a letter of introduction or other proof of membership, which will give you reciprocal rights to the services of the RACV, including free maps, breakdown services and technical advice.

Carrying a student card will entitle you to a wide variety of discounts throughout Victoria. The most common of these is the International Student Identity Card (ISIC), a plastic ID card displaying your photograph. These are issued by student unions, hostelling organisations or 'alternative-style' travel agencies.

It's also worth bringing your youth hostel membership card (HI, YHA etc) if you have one. As well as entitling you to various discounts, your card is also valid for membership of YHA Victoria.

EMBASSIES

Australian Embassies Abroad

Australian consular offices overseas include:

Canada
    Suite 710, 50 O'Connor St, Ottawa K1P 6L2
    (☎ (613) 236 0841); also Toronto and Vancouver
China
    21 Dongzhimenwai Dajie, San Li Tun, Beijing
    (☎ (10) 532 2331)
Denmark
    Kristianagade 21, 2100 Copenhagen
    (☎ 3526 2244)
France
    4 Rue Jean Rey, Paris, 15hme (☎ (01) 40 59 33 06)
Germany
    Godesberger Allee 107, 53175 Bonn 1
    (☎ (0228) 8103173); also in Frankfurt and Berlin
Greece
    37 Dimitriou Soutsou, Ambelokpi, Athens 11521
    (☎ (01) 644 7303)
Hong Kong
    Harbour Centre, 24th floor, 25 Harbour Rd, Wanchai,
    Hong Kong Island (☎ 2827 8881)
India
    Australian Compound, No 1/50-G Shantipath,
    Chanakyapuri, New Delhi 110021 (☎ 688 5637); also in
    Bombay
Indonesia
    JI HR Rasuna Said, Kav C15-16, Kuningan, Jakarta 12940
    (☎ (21) 522 7111); also in Denpasar
Ireland
    Fitzwilton House, Wilton Terrace, Dublin 2
    (☎ (01) 76 1517)
Italy
    Via Alessandria 215, Rome 00198 (☎ (06) 85 2721); also in
    Milan
Japan
    2-1-14 Mita, Minato-ku, Tokyo 108 (☎ (3) 5232 4111); also
    in Osaka
Malaysia
    6 Jalan Yap Kwan Seng, Kuala Lumpur 50450
    (☎ (03) 242 3122)
Netherlands
    Camegielaan 4, 2517 KH The Hague (☎ (070) 310 8200)
New Zealand
    72-78 Hobson St, Thorndon, Wellington (☎ (4) 473 6411);
    also in Auckland
Papua New Guinea
    Independence Drive, Waigani, Port Moresby (☎ 325 9333)

Philippines
   2nd floor, Dona Salustiana, Ty Tower, 104 Paseo de Roxas, Makati, Metro Manila (☎ 817 7911)
Singapore
   25 Napier Rd, Singapore 1025 (☎ 737 9311)
South Africa
   292 Orient St, Arcadia, Pretoria 0083 (☎ 342 3740)
Sweden
   Sergels Torg 12, S-111 57, Stockholm C (☎ (08) 613 2900)
Switzerland
   29 Alpenstrasse, Berne (☎ (031) 351 0143); also in Geneva
Thailand
   37 South Sathorn Rd, Bangkok 10120 (☎ (2) 287 2680)
UK
   Australia House, The Strand, London WC2B 4LA (☎ (0171) 379 4334); also in Manchester
USA
   1601 Massachusetts Ave NW, Washington DC, 20036 (☎ (202) 797 3421); also in Los Angeles, Honolulu, Houston, New York and San Francisco

Foreign Consulates

Most foreign embassies are in Canberra, although many countries also have consulates in Melbourne. They include:

Canada
   123 Camberwell Rd, Hawthorn East (☎ 9811 9999)
Denmark
   Acacia St, Blackburn (☎ 9894 1383)
France
   492 St Kilda Rd, Melbourne (☎ 9820 0921)
Germany
   480 Punt Rd, South Yarra (☎ 9828 6888)
Greece
   34 Queens Rd, Melbourne (☎ 9866 4524)
Indonesia
   72 Queens Rd, Melbourne (☎ 9525 2755)
Italy
   509 St Kilda Rd, Melbourne (☎ 9867 5744)
Japan
   360 Elizabeth St, Melbourne (☎ 9639 3244)
Malaysia
   492 St Kilda Rd, Melbourne (☎ 9867 5339)
Netherlands
   499 St Kilda Rd, Melbourne (☎ 9867 7933)
Norway
   31st Floor, 120 Collins St, Melbourne (☎ 9654 8020)
Spain
   766 Elizabeth St, Melbourne (☎ 9347 1966)
Sweden
   61 Riggall St, Broadmeadows (☎ 9301 1888)

Switzerland
    420 St Kilda Rd, Melbourne (☎ 9867 2266)
Thailand
    277 Flinders Lane, Melbourne (☎ 9650 1714)
UK
    Level 17, 90 Collins St, Melbourne (☎ 9650 4155)
USA
    553 St Kilda Rd, Melbourne (☎ 9526 5900)

Addresses of other foreign consulates can be found in
the Melbourne *Yellow Pages* phone book under 'Consulates & Legations', or in the standard phone book under
'Consuls'.

CUSTOMS

When entering Australia you can bring most articles in
free of duty, provided that customs is satisfied they are
for personal use and that you'll be taking them with you
when you leave. There's also the usual duty-free per-
person quota of 1.125 litres of alcohol, 250 cigarettes and
dutiable goods up to the value of A$400.

With regard to prohibited goods, there are two areas
you need to pay particular attention to. Number one is,
of course, drugs – Australian Customs has a positive
mania about the stuff and can be extremely efficient
when it comes to finding it.

Problem two is animal and plant quarantine. You will
be asked to declare all goods of animal or vegetable
origin – wooden spoons, straw hats, flowers, seeds – and
show them to an official. The authorities are naturally
keen to prevent weeds, pests or diseases getting into the
country. Fresh food is also unpopular, particularly meat,
sausages, fruit and vegetables.

Weapons and firearms are either prohibited or require
a permit and safety testing. Other restricted goods
include products (such as ivory) made from protected
wildlife species, non-approved telecommunications
devices and live animals.

MONEY

Currency

Australia's currency uses the decimal system of dollars
and cents (100 cents to the dollar) and has done since
1966 when the old system of pounds, shillings and pence
was phased out. There are $100, $50, $20, $10 and $5
notes, gold $2 and $1 coins, and silver 50c, 20c, 10c and
5c coins. It can be quite easy to confuse some of the new

KRZYSZTOF DYDYNSKI

KRZYSZTOF DYDYNSKI

Early and modern architecture along Collins St.

plastic notes, which look much more alike than did the old paper ones (which you still sometimes see). The 2c and 1c coins have been taken out of circulation, although prices can still be set in odd cents. Shops should round prices up (or down) to the nearest 5c on your *total* bill, not on individual items.

There are no notable restrictions on importing or exporting currency or travellers' cheques, except that you may not take out more than A$5000 in cash without prior approval.

Exchange Rates

Over the years the Australian dollar has fluctuated quite markedly against the US dollar, but in recent years it seems to have stabilised somewhat, generally fetching between US73c and US68c. Approximate exchange rates are as follows:

Canada	C$1	=	A$0.92
France	FF10	=	A$2.20
Germany	DM1	=	A$0.74
Hong Kong	HK$10	=	A$1.63
Japan	¥100	=	A$1.03
New Zealand	NZ$1	=	A$0.83
Netherlands	Dfl1	=	A$0.66
Singapore	S$1	=	A$0.88
UK	UK£1	=	A$2.00
USA	US$1	=	A$1.26

Changing Money

Changing foreign currency or travellers' cheques is no problem at almost any bank. Normal banking hours are Monday to Thursday from 9.30 am to 4 pm, and Friday from 9.30 am to 5 pm.

There are also foreign-exchange booths at Melbourne's international airport (Tullamarine), which are open to meet all arriving flights. The Westpac Bank also has an exchange booth in the international terminal at the airport. Most of the large hotels will also change currency or cheques for their guests.

You'll also find foreign-exchange booths in the city centre. These places are OK for emergencies – they have more convenient opening hours than the banks – but their rates generally aren't as good.

Thomas Cook (☎ 9654 4222) has four foreign-exchange offices in Melbourne's city centre, including one at 261 Bourke St, which opens Monday to Friday from 8.45 am to 5.15 pm, Saturday from 9 am to 4 pm and Sunday from 10 am to 4 pm. American Express (☎ 9633 6333) has two city offices; the one at 233 Collins St opens Monday to Friday from 8.30 am to 5.30 pm and Saturday from 9 am to noon.

Travellers' Cheques

American Express, Thomas Cook and other well-known international brands of travellers' cheques are all widely used in Australia. A passport will usually be adequate for identification; but it would be sensible to carry a driver's licence, credit cards or a plane ticket in case of problems.

Commissions and fees for changing foreign currency travellers' cheques seem to vary from bank to bank and month to month. It's worth making a few phone calls to see which bank currently has the lowest charges. Different banks charge different fees for different types of cheques and currencies – for example, for American Express travellers' cheques the ANZ charges $6.50 per transaction, the Commonwealth charges $5 per transaction and Westpac don't charge a fee at all.

Buying Australian dollar travellers' cheques is an option worth looking at. These can be exchanged immediately at the bank cashier's window without being converted from a foreign currency and incurring commissions, fees and exchange rate fluctuations.

Credit Cards

The most commonly accepted credit cards in Australia are Visa and MasterCard. American Express and, to a lesser extent, Diners Club are also widely accepted, although some establishments don't (or would rather not) accept them because of the higher fees they charge. The Australian-only Bankcard is also common, although less so in recent years.

Credit cards are a convenient alternative to carrying cash or large numbers of travellers' cheques. With the advent of electronic banking and the proliferation of automatic teller machines (ATMs) throughout the country in recent years, a credit card, preferably linked to your savings account back home, is now the ideal way to organise your money for travelling. Visa, MasterCard and American Express cards are commonly accepted in ATMs – most machines will display the symbols of the credit cards that it accepts. Cash advances are also available over the counter from all banks.

Foreign Banks

Quite a few foreign banks have branches in Melbourne. These include the Banque Nationale de Paris (☎ 9670 9500), 90 William St; the Bank of Singapore (☎ 9612 7588), 565 Bourke St; the Bank of New Zealand (☎ 9618 9200), 395 Collins St; and the Hong Kong Bank (☎ 9618 3888), 99 William St.

Costs

Compared to the USA, Canada and European countries, Australia is cheaper in some ways and more expensive in others. Manufactured goods tend to be more expensive but food is both high quality and low cost. Accommodation is also very reasonably priced.

Tipping

In Australia tipping isn't 'compulsory' the way it is in the USA or Europe. It's only customary to tip in restaurants, and only then if you want to. If you do decide to leave a tip, five to 10% of the bill is considered reasonable. Taxi drivers don't expect tips.

POST & COMMUNICATIONS

Post

The Melbourne General Post Office (GPO), on the corner of Bourke and Elizabeth Sts, is open weekdays from 8.15 am to 5.30 pm, and on Saturday (for stamp sales and poste restante only) from 10 am to 1 pm. The National Philatelic Centre and post office, on the corner of Latrobe and Exhibition Sts in the city, is also open on Saturday from 10 am to 5 pm, as well as Sunday from noon to 5 pm. Other post offices are generally open Monday to Friday from 9 am to 5 pm. You can also get stamps from most newsagents.

Australia's postal services are relatively efficient. It costs 45c to send a standard letter or postcard within Australia, while aerograms cost 70c.

Air-mail letters/postcards cost 75/70c to New Zealand, Singapore and Malaysia; 95/90c to Hong Kong and India; $1.05/95c to the USA and Canada; and $1.20/$1 to Europe and the UK.

Receiving Mail All post offices will hold mail for visitors. The poste restante section at the Melbourne GPO can get fairly hectic, especially in summer, and you may have to wait a while for your mail. The post offices will hold mail for one month before returning it to the sender, although for a small fee you can arrange to have mail forwarded to you. If you have an American Express card or buy Amex travellers' cheques, you can have mail sent to you c/o American Express Travel, 233 Collins St, Melbourne 3000.

Telephone

The STD telephone area code for Melbourne and Victoria is 03. Dial this number first if calling from outside Victoria.

Australia's phone system was until recently owned and run by the government-owned Telstra (formerly Telecom), but these days the market has been deregulated and a second player, Optus, now offers an alternative service for long-distance and international calls. The system is efficient and, equally important, easy to use. Local calls from public phones cost 40c for an unlimited amount of time. You can make local calls from gold or blue phones – often found in shops, hotels, bars etc – and from payphone booths.

It's also possible to make long-distance (Subscriber Trunk Dialling – STD) calls from virtually any public phone. Many public phones accept Telstra Phonecards, which are very convenient. The cards come in $5, $10, $20 and $50 denominations, and are available from retail outlets such as newsagents and pharmacies which display the Phonecard logo. You keep using the card until the value has been used in calls. Otherwise, have plenty of 10c, 20c, 50c and $1 coins ready, and be prepared to feed them through at a fair old rate.

Some public phones are set up to take only bank cash cards or credit cards, and these too are convenient, although you need to keep an eye on how much the call is costing as it can quickly mount up. The minimum charge for a call on one of these phones is $1.20.

Rates for STD calls are charged according to distance, and rates vary depending on when you call. In ascending order, the three different price brackets are:

Economy – from 6 pm Saturday to 8 am Monday; 10 pm to 8 am every night
Night – from 6 to 10 pm Monday to Friday
Day – from 8 am to 6 pm Monday to Saturday

International Calls From most STD phones you can also make international (International Subscriber Dialling – ISD) calls. Dialling ISD you can get through to overseas numbers almost as quickly as you can access local numbers and if your call is brief it needn't cost very much.

All you do is dial 0011 for overseas, the country code (44 for the UK, 1 for the USA or Canada, 64 for New Zealand), the city code (171 or 181 for London, 212 for New York etc), and then the telephone number. Have a Phonecard, credit card or plenty of coins on hand.

All public phones are owned by Telstra, so all calls from these go through Telstra. Private phones are either Telstra or Optus subscribers: to dial overseas from either, you dial normally (0011 etc). But if you want to use

RICHARD NEBESKY

The opulent Hotel Windsor in Spring St.

Optus from a Telstra phone, you need to dial 1456 (or 1 in some areas) *before* the ISD country code or STD area code. Optus is only available from private phones in certain areas.

A standard Telstra call to the USA or UK costs $2.40/$1.60 a minute peak/off-peak from a public phone, or $1.35/$1.03 from a private phone; New Zealand is $2/$1.20 from a public phone, or $1.09/72c from a private phone. Off-peak times, if available, vary depending on the destination – see the front of any telephone book for more details. Sunday is often the cheapest day to ring.

In response to the competition offered by Optus, Telstra often has discount specials to various destinations, although many of these are only available from private phones.

Country Direct Country Direct is a service which gives travellers in Australia direct access to operators in 42 countries, to make collect or credit card calls. For a full list of the countries hooked into this system, check any local telephone book. They include:

Canada (☎ 1800 881 150)
France (☎ 1800 881 330)
Germany (☎ 1800 881 490)
Japan (☎ 1800 881 810)
New Zealand (☎ 1800 881 640)
UK (☎ 1800 881 440)
USA (☎ 1800 881 011 for AT&T, 1800 881 212 for IDB WorldCom, 1800 881 100 for MCI and 1800 881 877 for Sprint).

Operator Assistance Some useful numbers include:

Emergency (free call)
    ☎ 000 from any phone in the country
Directory assistance (free call)
    ☎ 013 for a number in the area you are in;
    ☎ 0175 for a number elsewhere in Australia;
    ☎ 0103 for an overseas number
Reverse Charges – Domestic
    ☎ 0176 from a payphone;
    ☎ 011 from a private phone
Reverse Charges – International
    ☎ 0107 from a payphone;
    ☎ 0101 from a private phone

Telephone Interpreter Service A free translator and interpreter service is available over the telephone in

23 different languages. To access it, call ☎ 13 1450 from anywhere in Australia, 24 hours a day.

Fax

You can send faxes from any post office, either to another fax or to a postal address. Faxes to another fax machine anywhere in Australia cost $4 for the first page and $1 for each subsequent page. Faxes to postal addresses within Australia cost the same, and will be delivered by the postal service, usually the next day. If your fax-post items are urgent, they can be delivered on the same day for $8 if you send them before 1 pm; or within two hours (by courier) for $16 if you send them before 3 pm.

Overseas faxes cost $10 for the first page and $4 for each subsequent page. The same fax-post system is used for overseas postal addresses (this system has replaced international telegrams). International fax-post items cost $16 for each delivery.

As well as from post offices, you can send faxes from many business services, photocopying shops and newsagents – these places are usually much cheaper than post offices.

E-mail

Melbourne has a (rapidly) growing number of 'cyber cafes' – places where you can collect your e-mail or surf the Internet while enjoying a cuppa and a bite to eat. Access charges range from $7 to $12 an hour. They include the following:

Melbourne Internet Cafe, level two of Melbourne Central shopping centre (behind the Shot Tower) in the city (☎ 9663 8410)

Cybernet Cafe, 789 Glenferrie Rd, Hawthorn (☎ 9818 1288)

Cyber Cafe, 541 Church St, Richmond (☎ 9429 1311)

Megabite Internet Cafe, 176 Wellington Parade, East Melbourne (☎ 9250 3050)

Surfnet City Cafe, 140 St Kilda Rd, St Kilda (☎ 9593 9977)

Cafe Wired, 363 Clarendon St, South Melbourne (☎ 9686 9555)

BOOKS

Aborigines

Geoffrey Blainey's award-winning *Triumph of the Nomads* chronicles the life of the country's original inhabitants, and convincingly demolishes the myth that the Aborigines were 'primitive' people trapped on a hostile continent.

For a sympathetic historical account of what's happened to the real Australians since Whites arrived read *Aboriginal Australians*, by Richard Broome.

The Other Side of the Frontier, by Henry Reynolds, uses historical records to give a vivid account from an Aboriginal viewpoint of the arrival and takeover of Australia by Europeans. His *With the White People* identifies the essential Aboriginal contributions to the survival of the early White settlers. *My Place*, Sally Morgan's prize-winning autobiography, traces her discovery of her Aboriginal heritage. In a similar vein is *Over My Tracks* by Evelyn Crawford (as told to Chris Walsh), a remarkable story of life in an Aboriginal family in the 1930s. *The Fringe Dwellers*, by Nene Gare, describes just what it's like to be an Aborigine growing up in a White-dominated society.

Ruby Langford's *Don't Take Your Love to Town* and Kath Walker's *My People* are also recommended reading for people interested in Aborigines' experience.

Australian History

For a good introduction to Australian history, read *A Short History of Australia*, a most accessible and informative general history by the late Manning Clark, the much respected historian. Another good overview of Australian history is *A Shorter History of Australia* by the prolific historian and writer Geoffrey Blainey. Blainey's *The Tyranny of Distance* is a captivating narrative of White settlement, and Robert Hughes' bestselling *The Fatal Shore* is a colourful and detailed account of the history of transportation of convicts.

Finding Australia, by Russel Ward, traces the story of the early days, from the first Aboriginal arrivals up to 1821. It's strong on Aborigines, women and the full story of foreign exploration, not just Captain Cook's role.

Cooper's Creek, by Alan Moorehead, is a classic account of the ill-fated Burke and Wills expedition which dramatises the horrors and hardships faced by the early explorers.

The Fatal Impact, also by Moorehead, begins with the voyages of James Cook, regarded as one of the greatest and most humane explorers, and tells the tragic story of European impact on Australia, Tahiti and Antarctica in the years that followed Cook's great voyages of discovery.

Melbourne History

There are a number of history books that deal specifically with Melbourne. *Old Melbourne Town* by Michael

Cannon is an extensive and detailed history of the city's early years from the time of founding up until the gold rush. Cannon's earlier book, *The Land Boomers*, is a study of Melbourne during the 1880s.

Bearbrass – Imagining Early Melbourne by Robyn Annear is an unconventional and intriguing history – the author 'reinvents' the Melbourne of 1835 to 1851 and integrates the history with her own experiences of contemporary Melbourne.

The Rise and Fall of Marvellous Melbourne by Graeme Davidson takes a look at the city from the time of founding in 1835 until the financial crash of the 1890s.

Fiction

You don't need to worry about bringing a few good novels from home; there's plenty of excellent contemporary Australian literature – see Literature in the Arts & Culture section of the Facts about Melbourne chapter.

Lonely Planet

Apart from the comprehensive guidebook in your hand, Lonely Planet also publishes its *Victoria* and *Australia* guidebooks, both of which have excellent information on all aspects of travel.

Sean & David's Long Drive, a hilarious and offbeat road book by Melbourne writer Sean Condon, is one of the titles in Lonely Planet's new 'Journeys' travel-literature series.

Other Guidebooks

There are various other guidebooks on Melbourne and Victoria. The National Trust publishes *Walking Melbourne*. There's also the comprehensive *Blair's Travel Guide to Victoria & Melbourne*.

Weekend Getaways by Warwick Randall and *Robinson's Guide to B&Bs and Rural Retreats* are good accommodation guides.

There are a couple of good books on the Great Ocean Road: *The Great Ocean Road – A Traveller's Guide*, written, photographed and published by Rodney Hyett, and *Explore the Great Ocean Road* by See Australia Guides. See Australia Guides also publish *Discover Victoria's Goldfield Heritage*, a detailed guidebook to central Victoria.

NEWSPAPERS & MAGAZINES

Melbourne has two major daily newspapers. *The Age* is a quality newspaper which gives reasonable coverage of international news. The Saturday and Sunday editions have several excellent review sections with plenty of weekend reading, and there are other interesting pull-out sections during the week. The *Herald-Sun* is a tabloid-style paper published in several editions throughout the day. *The Australian*, a national daily, is also widely available.

International publications are available at the larger city newsagents such as McGills (☎ 9602 5566), 187 Elizabeth St, opposite the GPO. Papers from the UK, USA and South-East Asia are widely available and typically about three days behind. A large number of foreign-language papers are also published in Melbourne. The *Melbourne Trading Post*, published Thursday, is a good place to look if you want to buy or sell anything – it's available at all corner stores (known in Australia as 'milk bars').

Weekly magazines include an Australian edition of *Time* and the *Bulletin*, a conservative and long-running Australian news magazine which incorporates a condensed version of the US *Newsweek*. International papers such as the *International Herald Tribune*, the *European* and the *Guardian Weekly* are available from larger newsagents.

Gay & Lesbian Publications For an introduction to the gay scene in Melbourne, pick up a copy of the fortnightly *Brother Sister*, or the weekly *Melbourne Star Observer* (MSO). Both are free and available from gay cafes, bars and clubs. Also worth looking out for are *Lesbiana*, a monthly magazine for lesbians, and the handy *Gay & Lesbian Melbourne Map*.

RADIO & TV

Radio

Currently, Melbourne has 26 radio stations, 13 on the AM band and 13 on FM. Most of the commercial stations on the FM band flog the standard 'hits and memories' format.

On the FM band, 3RRR (102.7) and 3PBS (106.7) are both excellent non-commercial stations that feature alternative and independent music, current affairs and talk-show programmes. Triple J (107.5) is the Australian Broadcasting Corporation's (ABC) national 'youth network', which specialises in alternative music and young people's issues and has some interesting talk shows. ABC Classic-FM (105.9) plays classical music as does the non-commercial 3MBS (103.5), while 3ZZZ (92.3) and 3SBS (93.1) are both multicultural stations broadcasting in a variety of foreign languages.

On the AM band, the ABC station Radio National (621) covers a diversity of topics with often fascinating features and has a 10-minute world-news service every hour on the hour, while the Melbourne-based ABC station 3LO (774) has regular talkback programmes, excellent news services on the hour and a world-news feature at 12.10 pm every weekday. 3CR (855) is a non-commercial community radio station, and 3SBS (1224) is another multicultural foreign-language station. 3RG (1593) broadcasts in Italian.

TV

Melbourne has five TV stations. The three commercial networks, channels Seven, Nine and Ten, are just like commercial channels anywhere, with a varied but not particularly adventurous diet of sport, soap operas, lightweight news and sensationalised current affairs, plus plenty of sit-coms (mainly American).

Channel Two is the government-funded, commercial-free ABC station. It produces some excellent current affairs and documentaries as well as showing a lot of sport, slightly heavier news and sit-coms (mainly British). The ABC also has a knack for making good comedy and drama programmes which receive critical acclaim and low ratings.

The best international news service is at 6.30 pm daily on the publicly funded Special Broadcasting Service (SBS, channel 28, UHF). SBS is a multicultural channel which has some of the most diverse and some of the best programmes on TV, including serious current affairs, interesting documentaries, Spanish soap operas, and great films (with English subtitles when necessary).

PHOTOGRAPHY & VIDEO

In the city centre, there's a cluster of photography and video shops along Elizabeth St between Bourke and Lonsdale Sts. Little Bourke St (west of Elizabeth St) is another good area to look for camera gear.

If you need your camera repaired, the Camera Clinic (☎ 9419 5247) at 19 Peel St in Collingwood has an excellent reputation and services all brands except Kodak and Hanimex. In the city, there's the Camera Service Centre (☎ 9602 1820) on the 5th floor at 358 Lonsdale St.

The Melbourne Camera Club (☎ 9696 5445), in South Melbourne on the corner of Ferrars and Dorcas Sts, meets every Thursday night at 8 pm and welcomes visitors.

Kodak (☎ 9286 1011), at 1-19 Hoddle St, will process your slide film within 24 hours provided you hand it in before lunch time.

Film & Taking Photographs

If you come to Australia via Hong Kong or Singapore it's worth buying film there, but otherwise Australian film prices are not too far out of line with those of the rest of the

REIMUND ZUNDE

Cycling along St Kilda Rd.

Western world. Including developing, 36-exposure Kodachrome 64 or Fujichrome 100 slide film costs around $25, but with a little shopping around you can find it for around $20 – even less if you buy it in quantity.

There are plenty of camera shops in Melbourne and standards of camera service are high. Developing standards are also high, with many places offering one-hour developing of print film. While print film is available from just about anywhere, slide film can be harder to find. Camera shops in the larger towns are usually the best bet for Kodachrome or Fujichrome.

Remember that film can be damaged by heat, so allow for temperature extremes and do your best to keep film as cool as possible, particularly after exposure. Other film and camera hazards are dust and humidity.

As in any country, politeness goes a long way when taking photographs or filming; ask before taking pictures of people. Note that many Aborigines do not like to have their photograph taken, even from a distance.

TIME

Australia is divided into three time zones. Victoria is in the Eastern Standard Time zone which is 10 hours ahead of Greenwich Mean Time (GMT/UTC). Tasmania, New South Wales and Queensland are also in this zone.

From the last Sunday in October until the last Sunday in March daylight-saving time comes into operation in Victoria. Clocks are turned forward one hour.

ELECTRICITY

Voltage is 240V and the plugs are three-pin, but not the same as British three-pin plugs (which are bigger). Users of electric shavers or hair dryers should note that, apart from in fancy hotels, it's difficult to find converters to take either US flat two-pin plugs or the European round two-pin plugs. Adaptors for British plugs can be found in good hardware shops, chemists and travel agents.

LAUNDRY

Most accommodation places provide laundry facilities for their guests. There are no self-service laundries in the city centre, but there are quite a few in the inner suburbs. They include the City Edge Laundry at 39 Errol St in North Melbourne (opposite the Town Hall) and the St Kilda Beach Laundrette at 7 Carlisle St in St Kilda. Others are listed in the *Yellow Pages* phone book under 'Laundries – Self-Service'.

WEIGHTS & MEASURES

Australia went metric in the early 70s. Petrol and milk are sold by the litre, apples and potatoes by the kg, distance is measured by the metre or km and speed limits are in km/h. But there's still a degree of confusion: it's hard to think of a six-foot person as being 183 cm tall, and the weight of newborn babies is often given in pounds.

HEALTH

As long as you haven't visited an infected country in the past 14 days (aircraft refuelling stops do not count) no vaccinations are required for entry to Australia.

Medical care is first-class and only moderately expensive. A typical visit to the doctor costs around $35. If you have an immediate health problem, contact the casualty section at the nearest public hospital (see Medical Services later in this chapter for some hospital addresses) or a medical clinic.

Visitors from the UK, New Zealand, Malta, Italy, Sweden and the Netherlands have reciprocal health rights in Australia, and can register at any Medicare office.

Travel Insurance

Ambulance services in Australia are self-funding (ie they're not free) and can be frightfully expensive, so you'd be wise to take out travel insurance. Make sure the policy specifically includes ambulance, helicopter rescue and a flight home for you and anyone you're travelling with, should your condition warrant it. Also check the fine print: some policies exclude 'dangerous activities' such as scuba diving, motorcycling and even trekking. If such activities are on your agenda, you don't want that policy.

Medical Kit

It's always a good idea to travel with a basic medical kit even when your destination is a country like Australia, where most first-aid supplies are readily available. Some of the items that should be included are:

Band-aids, a sterilised gauze bandage, elastoplast, cotton wool, a thermometer, tweezers, scissors, antibiotic cream and ointment, an antiseptic agent, burn cream, insect repellent, Paracetamol or Aspirin, and multivitamins.

St John Ambulance Australia has a selection of first-aid kits for car drivers, motorcyclists and bushwalkers, ranging in price from $45 to $85. They include a first-aid handbook and are well worth considering as a base kit to which you can add some of the above items. They're available at St John offices and at the motoring organisations.

Don't forget any medication you're already taking, and include prescriptions with the generic rather than the brand name (which may not be available locally).

Health Precautions

Travellers from the northern hemisphere need to be aware of the intensity of the sun in Australia. Those ultraviolet rays can leave you burnt to a crisp even on an overcast day, so if in doubt wear protective cream, a wide-brimmed hat and loose-fitting cotton clothing that gives maximum skin coverage. Australia has the world's highest incidence of skin cancer, a fact directly connected to exposure to the sun. Be careful.

The contraceptive pill is available on prescription only, so a visit to a doctor is necessary. Doctors are listed in the *Yellow Pages* phone book or you can visit the outpatients section of a public hospital. Condoms are available from chemists, many convenience stores and often from vending machines in pub toilets.

Basic Rules

Heat Victoria has its fair share of hot weather during the summer months with an average daily maximum of over 30°C in some areas. The sensible thing to do on a hot day is to avoid the sun between mid-morning and mid-afternoon. Infants and elderly people are most at risk from heat exhaustion and heat stroke.

Water People who first arrive in a hot climate may not feel thirsty when they should; the body and 'thirst mechanism' often need a few days to adjust. The rule of thumb is that an active adult should drink at least four litres of water per day in warm weather, more when walking or cycling.

Melbourne has one of the highest standards of tap water in the world. Tap water is safe to drink in most

MARK ARMSTRONG

The Yarra River and city skyline from Southgate.

other parts of Victoria, but in the more remote areas it may be bore water that's unfit for human consumption – check with the locals.

Sexually Transmitted Diseases

There are numerous sexually transmitted diseases, for most of which effective treatment is available. If you suspect anything is wrong, go to the nearest public hospital or visit the Melbourne Sexual Health Centre (☎ 9347 0244) at 580 Swanston St in Carlton – visits are free and confidential, and don't require a referral.

The AIDS Line (☎ 9347 6099 or 1800 133 392 toll-free) provides information on AIDS and AIDS-related illnesses.

Medical Services

The Traveller's Medical & Vaccination Centre (☎ 9602 5788), Level 2, 393 Little Bourke St in the city, is open weekdays from 9 am to 5 pm (Monday and Thursday till 9 pm) and Saturday from 9 am to 1 pm. It has excellent information on the latest vaccinations needed for most countries. Appointments are necessary.

The Melbourne Sexual Health Centre (☎ 9347 0244), 580 Swanston St, Carlton, provides free checkups and other medical services. The Victorian AIDS Council & Gay Men's Health Centre (☎ 9865 6700), 6 Claremont St, South Yarra, provides education, information and support for AIDS sufferers and operates a health centre for gays. The Positive Living Centre (☎ 9525 4455), 46

Acland St, St Kilda, provides support services for people with HIV or AIDS.

Melbourne's major public hospitals are:

The Alfred
　　Commercial Rd, Prahran (☎ 9276 2000)
Royal Children's
　　Flemington Rd, Parkville (☎ 9345 5522)
Royal Melbourne
　　Grattan St, Parkville (☎ 9342 7000)
Royal Women's
　　132 Grattan St, Carlton (☎ 9344 2000)
St Vincent's
　　41 Victoria Pde, Fitzroy (☎ 9288 2211)

See Dangers & Annoyances later in this chapter for information on emergency services.

WOMEN TRAVELLERS

Melbourne is generally a safe place for women travellers, although you should avoid walking alone, especially late at night. Sexual harassment is rare, although the Aussie male culture does have its sexist elements. Don't tolerate any harassment or discrimination. Female hitchhikers should exercise care at all times. The following organisations offer advice and services for women:

Royal Women's Hospital Sexual Assault Centre (☎ 9344 2000), 132 Grattan St, Carlton
Women's Health Resource Service (☎ 9670 0669), Level 3, 373 Little Bourke St, Melbourne
Women's Information & Referral Exchange (☎ 9654 6844), 247 Flinders Lane, Melbourne
Women's Refuge Referral Service (☎ 9329 8433)

GAY & LESBIAN TRAVELLERS

The attitude in Victoria towards gays and lesbians is, on the whole, open-minded and accepting. This is particularly the case in Melbourne, which has a high-profile gay community. The highlight of the local calendar is the Midsumma Festival held each January/February, which showcases a wide range of theatrical, musical and artistic productions and events like the Midsumma Carnival, the 'Fur Ball' and the Pride Ride, a gay pride march that ends at Luna Park with funfair rides. Other major events are Red Raw, a dance party (attended by 6000 in 1997) held on the docks on the Saturday of the Australia Day weekend, and the Melbourne Queer Film & Video Festival.

Homosexuality has been decriminalised in Victoria since 1981, and the age of consent, equal to that for heterosexuals, stands at 16.

Police relations with the gay community were just starting to rebuild following a disastrous raid in 1994 on the Tasty nightclub, when in early 1997 the Victorian Police Minister spoke out against gay and lesbian members of the force. In regional Victoria there's still a strong streak of homophobia, and violence against homosexual people, in particular gay men, is not unknown.

Melbourne has an increasingly lively gay and lesbian scene, with numerous bars, cafes, nightclubs and accommodation places in the inner-city suburbs of Fitzroy, Collingwood, Prahran, South Yarra and St Kilda. Around the state, places such as Daylesford and Hepburn Springs, Phillip Island, Bright, the Mornington Peninsula, Echuca and Lorne have accommodation catering for gays and lesbians.

The following organisations offer a range of advice and services for gays and lesbians. Bookshops are also useful sources of information and contacts (See the Bookshops section of the Shopping chapter).

Gay & Lesbian Switchboard, which operates nightly between 6 and 10 pm (Wednesday from 2 to 10 pm), is a telephone information service with trained counsellors who offer advice and counselling; or you can just ring for a chat (☎ 9510 5488).

Gay & Lesbian Switchboard Information Service is a 24-hour recorded service that covers the entertainment scene as well as social and support groups (☎ 0055 12504).

DISABLED TRAVELLERS

Victoria provides an exciting range of accessible attractions. Highlights include the Penguin Parade (☎ 5956 8691) at Phillip Island, *Puffing Billy* (☎ 9754 6800) in the Dandenong Ranges, Healesville Sanctuary (☎ 5962 4022) and the Twelve Apostles along the Great Ocean Road.

Easy Access Australia – A Travel Guide to Australia, available from PO Box 218 Kew, Vic 3101 ($24.85), has a chapter devoted to Victoria.

For information on useful organisations, equipment hire, libraries, accommodation and transport for disabled travellers see the relevant sections in this chapter; see also the Places to Stay and Getting Around chapters.

The following organisations offer a range of services for disabled people:

National Industries for Disability Services, operating through the Australian Council for the Rehabilitation of the Disabled (ACROD) , 75 Buckhurst St, South Melbourne, produces information sheets for disabled travellers, including lists of state-level organisations, specialist travel agents, wheelchair and equipment hire and access guides (☎ 9690 2266).

Disabled Persons Information Bureau can refer you to a specific service (☎ 9616 7704).

Paraplegic & Quadriplegic Association of Victoria (Para Quad) can provide advice on access, equipment hire and attendant care (☎ 9415 1200 or freecall 008 805 384).

Assist Travel is a travel agent specialising in travel for people with disabilities (☎ 1800 809 192 toll-free, or write c/o PO Box 83, Lara 3212).

Victorian Deaf Society (☎ 9657 8111).

Association for the Blind (☎ 9598 8555).

Independent Living Centre, 52 Thistlewaite St, South Melbourne, hires wheelchairs and other equipment for disabled people (☎ 9254 5400).

Traveller's Aid Society (☎ 9670 2873) is at Spencer St railway station and level two, 169 Swanston St Walk where the Support Centre (☎ 9654 2690) has accessible toilets, lounge, phone, and can supply assistance and information.

LIBRARIES

The historic State Library of Victoria is at 328 Swanston St in the city. Other public libraries in the inner suburbs include the Port Phillip Library at 150 Carlisle St in St Kilda; the Braille & Talking Book Library at 51 Commercial Rd in South Yarra; the Carlton Library on the corner of Newry and Rathdowne Sts; the Fitzroy Library at 201 Napier St; the East Melbourne Library at 122 George St; and the Port Melbourne Library at 147 Lidiard St.

CAMPUSES

Major universities within Melbourne's inner suburbs include Melbourne University (☎ 9349 8400) at 200 Leicester St in Carlton, the Royal Melbourne Institute of Technology (RMIT; ☎ 9662 0611) at 124 Latrobe St in the city, and the Victoria University of Technology (☎ 9248 1000) at 300 Flinders St in the city.

Melbourne's other two major universities are both about half an hour's drive from the city: Monash University (☎ 9905 4000) is on Wellington Rd in Clayton, and La Trobe University (☎ 9479 1111) is on Kingsbury Drive in Bundoora.

DANGERS & ANNOYANCES

Emergency

In the case of a life-threatening emergency, telephone ☎ 000. This call is free from any phone, and the operator will connect you to either the police, ambulance or fire brigade. Otherwise, you can call these services direct:

Police (☎ 11 444)
Ambulance (☎ 11 440)
Fire Brigade (☎ 11 411)

In the city centre, there's a police station at 637 Flinders St (up the Spencer St end) which is staffed 24 hours a day.

The Travellers' Aid Support Centre (☎ 9654 2600), on the 2nd floor at 169 Swanston St in the city, offers assistance for stranded travellers, information, advice, showers, toilets and, if you're in need, a cup of coffee and a sandwich. There's a youth worker on staff, and also support services for disabled and aged people. The service is free (open on weekdays from 8 am to 5 pm and Saturday from 10 am to 4 pm).

Some other useful emergency numbers include:

Accidents
    State Emergency Service (☎ 9696 6111)
Chemist
    David Crouch Pharmacy (☎ 9386 1000), 28 Sydney Rd, Coburg (9 am to midnight)
    Leonard Long Pharmacy (☎ 9510 3977), corner of Williams Rd and High St, Prahran (8 am to midnight)
Dentist
    Dental Emergency Service (☎ 9341 0222)
Interpreter Service
    Translating & Interpreting Service, 24 hours (☎ 13 1450 or 9416 9999)
Life Crisis
    Crisis Line (24 hour telephone counselling) (☎ 9329 0300)
    Lifeline Counselling (24 hours, six languages; ☎ 13 1114 or 9662 1000)
Mechanical Breakdown
    Accident Towing Service (☎ 13 1176)
    RACV Emergency Roadside Service (☎ 13 1111)
Poisons
    Poisons Information Centre (☎ 13 1126)

Theft

Melbourne is a relatively safe place to visit, but you should still play it safe and take reasonable precautions. Don't leave hotel rooms or cars unlocked, and don't leave money, wallets, purses or cameras unattended or in full view through car windows, for instance. Most accommodation places have a safe where you can store your valuables.

If you are unlucky enough to have something stolen, immediately report all details to the nearest police station. If your credit cards, cash card or travellers' cheques have been taken, notify your bank or the relevant company immediately (most have 24-hour 'lost or stolen' numbers listed under 'Banks' or 'Credit Card Organisations' in the *Yellow Pages*).

Trams

In Melbourne, passengers should be *extremely* cautious when stepping on and off trams – a lot of people have been hit by passing cars, so don't step off without looking both ways. Pedestrians in Bourke St Mall and Swanston Walk should watch for passing trams too.

Car drivers should treat Melbourne trams with caution (see the Getting Around chapter). Cyclists should be careful not to get their wheels caught in a tram track and motorcyclists should take special care when tram tracks are wet.

Swimming & Boating

Port Phillip Bay is generally safe for swimming – the closest you're likely to come to a shark is in the local fish & chip shop (shark is euphemistically called 'flake'). The blue-ringed octopus is sometimes found hiding under rocks in rockpools on the foreshore. Its sting can be fatal, so don't touch it under any circumstances! Many of the bay and coastal beaches are patrolled by life-savers in summer – patrolled beaches have a pair of red and yellow flags which you should always swim between. Boating on Port Phillip Bay can be hazardous, as conditions can change dramatically and without warning.

If you happen to get caught in a rip when swimming and are being taken out to sea, try not to panic. Raise one arm until you have been spotted, and then swim parallel to the shore – *don't* try to swim back against the rip; you'll only tire yourself.

Spiders

Victoria's most dangerous spider is the redback. It's a small black spider with a red stripe and a very painful bite – apply ice and seek medical attention. The white-tailed spider should also be avoided. Some people have an extreme reaction to this spider's bite and gangrene can occur.

Insects

In summer, you'll have to cope with flies and mosquitoes. An insect repellent like Rid or Aerogard will help, but at times you might have to resort to the 'Great Australian Wave' to keep them at bay. Stingose is a very good spray for relieving the sting of mosquitoes or sunburn.

BUSINESS HOURS

Standard shop trading hours are Monday to Thursday from 9 am to 5.30 pm, Friday 9 am to 9 pm, and Saturday 9 am to 12.30 pm. Many shops in Melbourne's city centre and other major shopping centres also stay open until at least 9 pm on Thursday and until 5 pm on Saturday – especially the larger retailers. Most retail shops close on Sunday, although many shops in tourist precincts like Acland St (St Kilda), Chapel St (Prahran), Lygon St (Carlton) and Brunswick St (Fitzroy) are open every day. Places such as delicatessens, milk bars and bookshops often stay open late and on weekends. Many supermarkets are open until late at night, and some stay open 24 hours a day.

Most offices and businesses open Monday to Friday from 9 am to 5.30 pm, although some government departments close at 4.30 or 5 pm. Normal banking hours are Monday to Thursday from 9.30 am to 4 pm, and Friday from 9.30 am to 5 pm. Pub bottleshops generally stay open until 11 pm from Monday to Saturday, but close by 8 pm on Sunday.

PUBLIC HOLIDAYS & SPECIAL EVENTS

Melbourne has festivals all year round, with themes ranging from film, comedy, arts, theatre, sports, food and wine, multiculturalism or just simple celebrations of life.

'What's on' lists are available from tourist information offices. Tickets to most major events can be booked through the Bass agency – both the enquiries line (☎ 11 566) and credit-card booking line (☎ 11 500) operate Monday to Saturday from 9 am to 9 pm and Sunday from 10 am to 5 pm.

Summer

December The outdoor evening performances of plays such as *A Midsummer Night's Dream* and *Romeo & Juliet* in the Royal Botanic Gardens are a special summer highlight. Christmas in Melbourne is always celebrated with Carols by Candlelight, when 30,000 people head to the Sidney Myer Music Bowl to sing under the stars. You'll need to book for both of these through Bass, and don't forget a rug, a candle and insect repellent.

If you're into cricket, head for the Melbourne Cricket Ground (MCG) on Boxing Day, when thousands turn up for the traditional first day of the international Test match.

January Each January, the Australian Open Grand Slam tennis championship is held at the Melbourne Park Tennis Centre. The Summer Music Festival is based at the Victorian Arts Centre and features everything from the classics to rock music.

Australia Day is celebrated in all sorts of ways, including street parades, food fairs and fireworks at Albert Park Lake. For jazz lovers, the eclectic Montsalvat Jazz Festival is held over three days at a picturesque artists' colony in Eltham and various other venues around town. If you want to get out of town for Australia Day, pack a picnic basket and head to the rustic Hanging Rock Horse Races, held yearly since the 1870s.

February During February, the St Kilda Festival is a week-long celebration of local arts and culture – food, art, music and writing. Also in February, the Australian Matchplay and the Australian Masters golf tournaments are held on the great sandbelt courses, while Vietnamese culture is celebrated with the Victoria St Festival. At the marvellous Harvest Picnic out at Hanging Rock, you can enjoy the pick of the crop of Victorian produce. Chinatown comes to life with the celebration of Chinese New Year and the Asian Food Festival. The Melbourne Music Festival is also held in February, and showcases local musicians at various venues.

REIMUND ZUNDE

Government House, one of Melbourne's many National
Trust buildings.

Autumn

March March sees the staging of the Formula One Grand
Prix motor race at Albert Park. The 10-day Moomba festival is one of Melbourne's favourite family events, with
carnivals, fireworks and an outdoor art show, as well as
water-skiing, a Dragon Boat Festival and the zany
Birdman Rally, all on the Yarra River. The Aboriginal
meaning of Moomba is 'getting together and having fun'.

March is also the time for the Antipodes Festival –
devoted to Greek art, culture and music, and held in
Melbourne's small Greek quarter in Lonsdale St,
between Swanston and Russell Sts – as well as the Great
Melbourne Bike Ride (from the MCG, over the West Gate
Bridge and back) and the horticultural show Garden
Week, held in the Fitzroy Gardens. The Yarra Valley
Grape Grazing Festival and the Red Hill Wine & Food
Festival feature the fine local products from the Yarra
Valley and Mornington Peninsula respectively. Oh, and
the football season kicks off in March too!

April It seems like almost everyone's a comedian in
Melbourne, but in April when the brilliant International
Comedy Festival takes over the town, the locals are
joined by a swag of fabulous international acts.

On a more serious note, the National Trust runs Heritage Week during April, devoted to increasing the
appreciation of Melbourne's rich architectural heritage.

Anzac Day, commemorating those who fell in war, is always held on 25 April, the date that the Australian and New Zealand combined forces landed at Gallipoli during WWI. The day begins with a dawn service at the Shrine of Remembrance, followed by a march along St Kilda Rd into the city. The play *The One Day of the Year* by Alan Seymour gives a marvellous insight into the mixed feelings with which different generations of Australians view this 'celebration' of war.

Easter is pretty quiet in Melbourne – half the population heads to the countryside in pursuit of various activities, such as tennis carnivals in country towns, the

RICHARD NEBESKY

Getting together and having fun – Moomba in Melbourne.

Easter Fair in Bendigo or to watch the world's best surfers rip, tear and lacerate at Bells Beach in the Bells Beach Surfing Classic held just south of Torquay.

Winter

June June brings the Queen's Birthday weekend, when all ski resorts go into party mode to herald the official opening of the ski season (weather permitting!). At the same time, the International Film Festival opens and runs for two weeks, featuring the newest and the best in local and international film – luckily, Melbourne is one of the cappuccino centres of the world, so you can always top up on caffeine to get through the next session or two.

August August sees yet more food and wine shows in Melbourne – the Exhibition of Victorian Winemakers and the Sip 'n' Sup Wine & Food Festival in Sunbury.

Spring

September The Australian Football League (AFL) Finals series builds up to an extravagant, colourful and noisy climax when the Grand Final is played on the last Saturday in September.

Also in September, the Royal Melbourne Show is when the country comes to town. Held at the Royal Melbourne Showgrounds in Flemington, it's a large-scale agricultural fair with a carnival atmosphere – livestock judging, equestrian events, wood-chopping competitions, rides and showbags (bags containing novelties, samples and confectionery) – and attracts 800,000 visitors yearly.

October Melbourne International Festival combines the best of the performing arts, visual arts and music, and incorporates the Melbourne Writers Festival and the Melbourne Fringe Arts Festival – don't miss the weird and wild street party in Brunswick St.

Once the cows and ducks have gone home, the Royal Melbourne Showgrounds are filled up with beer tents for the three-day Oktoberfest, styled on the Bavarian festival of the same name. The Spring Racing Carnival runs through October and November, and the two feature horse races are the Caulfield Cup and the Melbourne Cup. October also features two professional cycling races, the Herald-Sun Tour 10-day event and the race most riders refer to as the 'Holy Grail' – the Melbourne to Warrnambool Classic.

November The Melbourne Cup horse race is always run on the first Tuesday in November. During Cup Week, Melbourne gets caught up in something called 'Spring Fever', which manifests itself as a frenzy of partying, gambling, social intercourse and high fashion.

For the Italian Lygon St Festa in November, the street is blocked to traffic and filled with food stalls, bands and dancers; the entertainment also includes the manic waiters' race.

Also in November is the Hispanic Community Festival when Melbourne's small Spanish and South American communities take over Johnston St for a lively celebration of Latin culture.

Holidays

See the earlier When to Go section for details on school holiday periods in Victoria. On public holidays, government departments, banks, offices, large stores and post offices are closed. On Good Friday and Christmas Day newspapers are not published and about the only stores you will find open are the 24-hour convenience stores. Also note that some consulates close for 10 days over the Christmas-New Year period.

Victoria has the following nine public holidays:

New Year's Day
   1 January
Australia Day
   celebrated on 26 January
Labour Day
   first or second Monday in March
Easter
   Good Friday and Easter Saturday and Monday: usually falls in late March or early April
Anzac Day
   25 April
Queen's Birthday
   second Monday in June
Melbourne Cup Day
   first Tuesday in November
Christmas Day
   25 December
Boxing Day
   26 December

When the proclaimed date falls on a weekend, the following Monday is declared a holiday (with the exception of ANZAC Day and Australia Day).

WORK

If you come to Australia on a 12-month 'working holiday' visa you can officially work for the entire 12 months, but can only stay with the one employer for a maximum of three months. On the other hand, working on a regular tourist visa is strictly *verboten*. Some travellers do find casual work, but with an unemployment rate around 10% and youth unemployment rates much higher, it's becoming more difficult to get a job – legal or otherwise.

To receive wages you must have a Tax File Number, issued by the Taxation Department. Application forms are available at all post offices, and you must show your passport and visa. Finding work will usually be tough, and those who succeed are very determined but not too choosy about what they do. The more common jobs found by travellers include factory work, bar work, waiting or washing dishes, nursing and nanny work, telephone sales, fruit picking and collecting for charities.

The staff at the Department of Employment, Education & Training (DEET) Job Centres can advise you on how to go about looking for work and what's available – but be prepared for long queues. Try the classified section of the daily papers under 'Situations Vacant', especially on Saturday and Wednesday. The staff and notice boards at some of the backpackers' hostels can also be good sources of information.

LUGGAGE

There are luggage lockers on the ground and 1st floors of the international terminal at Melbourne airport, which cost $4 a day.

In the basement at Spencer St railway station, left-luggage lockers cost $2 per day and the cloakroom costs $3.50 per item per day. There are also left-luggage facilities at the Elizabeth St entrance of Flinders St railway station.

Getting There & Away

AIR

Melbourne's airport services both domestic and international flights. The airport is in Tullamarine, 22 km north-west of the city centre – about a 30-minute drive, although you should allow longer in peak-hour traffic.

While plenty of international airlines have direct flights into Melbourne, many flights still stop off in Sydney. Sydney's airport is stretched way beyond its capacity and flights are frequently delayed on arrival and departure. Furthermore, the Customs and Immigration facilities are cramped, crowded and too small for the current visitor flow, so even after you've finally landed you may face further long delays. It's a wise idea to organise your flights to avoid Sydney if you can.

A departure tax of $27 is payable by everyone leaving Australia: the tax is generally added onto the price of your air ticket.

Discount Tickets

Rule number one if you're looking for a cheap ticket is to go to an agent, not directly to the airline. The airline can usually only quote you the regular fare, but an agent can offer all sorts of special deals, particularly on competitive routes.

What's available and what it costs depends on what time of year it is, what route you're flying and who you're flying with. The high season for flights to/from Australia is generally between December and February. If you're flying on a popular route (like from Hong Kong) or one where the choice of flights is very limited (like from South America or Africa), the fare is likely to be higher or there may be nothing available but the official fare.

Similarly, the dirt-cheap fares are likely to be less conveniently scheduled, and to go by less convenient routes or with less popular airlines.

Things to consider when choosing a ticket are its validity, the number of stopovers (generally, the cheaper the ticket the fewer stopovers allowed), and whether you have to change planes on the way. Sometimes paying a bit more for a ticket is worthwhile to avoid hanging around a foreign departure lounge for hours on end.

In Melbourne, two travel agents to try for discounted airline tickets are STA (☎ 9347 4711), at 222 Faraday St, Carlton, or Flight Centres International (☎ 9663 1304), at 317 Swanston St, in the city centre. Both have a number of other offices around Melbourne. The YHA travel office (☎ 9670 7991), at 205 King St in the city centre, is another good place to try.

Cheap international flights are also advertised in *The Age* each Saturday, in the travel section of the *Saturday Extra*. International airlines with offices in Melbourne are listed in the *Yellow Pages*.

Round-the-World Tickets

Round-the-World (RTW) tickets have become very popular and many will take you through Australia. Airline RTW tickets are often real bargains and, since Australia is pretty much on the other side of the world from Europe or North America, it can work out to be no more expensive, or even cheaper, to keep going in the same direction right round the world rather than U-turn when you return.

Official airline RTW tickets are usually put together by a combination of two airlines and permit you to fly anywhere you want on their route systems, so long as you do not backtrack. Other restrictions are that you (usually) must book the first sector in advance, and cancellation penalties then apply. There may be restrictions on how many stops you are permitted, and usually the tickets are valid from 90 days up to a year. Typical prices for South Pacific RTW tickets start from around £800 or US$1900.

An alternative type of RTW ticket is one put together by a travel agent using a combination of discounted tickets from a number of airlines. A UK agent like Trailfinders can put together interesting London-to-London RTW combinations including Australia for £750 to £950.

Circle Pacific Tickets

Circle Pacific fares are a similar idea to RTW tickets, using a combination of airlines to circle the Pacific – combining Australia, New Zealand, North America and Asia. Examples would be Qantas-Northwest, Canadian Airlines International-Cathay Pacific, and so on. As with RTW tickets, there are advance purchase restrictions and limits to how many stopovers you can take. Typically, fares range between US$1750 and US$2200. A possible Circle Pacific route is Los Angeles/Hawaii/Auckland/Melbourne/Sydney/Singapore/Bangkok/Hong Kong/Tokyo/Los Angeles.

The UK

The cheapest tickets in London are from the numerous 'bucket shops' (discount ticket agencies) which advertise in magazines and papers like *Time Out*, *Southern Cross* and *TNT*. The magazine *Business Traveller* also has a great deal of good advice on air-fare bargains, and the *Evening Standard*'s travel section is also worth perusing. Most bucket shops are trustworthy and reliable, but the occasional sharp operator appears – *Time Out* and *Business Traveller* give some useful advice on precautions to take.

Trailfinders (☎ (0171) 938 3366) at 46 Earls Court Rd, London W8, and STA Travel (☎ (0171) 581 4132) at 74 Old Brompton Rd, London SW7, and 117 Euston Rd, London NW1 (☎ (0171) 465 0484), are good, reliable agents for cheap tickets.

Cheap London to Melbourne bucket-shop tickets start from about £400 one way or £650 return. Britannia Airlines runs a charter flight between London and Melbourne from November to March, with prices as low as £499 return. Its returns from Melbourne to London during this period cost around $1,600 return. Otherwise, such prices are usually only available if you leave London in the low season – March to June. In September and mid-December fares go up about 30%, while for the rest of the year they are somewhere in between.

From Melbourne you can expect to pay at least A$1000 one way and A$1600 return to London and other European capitals, with stops in Asia on the way.

North America

There are a variety of connections across the Pacific from Los Angeles, San Francisco and Vancouver to Australia, including direct flights, flights via New Zealand, island-hopping routes or more circuitous Pacific rim routes via nations in Asia. Qantas, Air New Zealand and United all fly USA/Australia, while Qantas, Air New Zealand and Canadian Airlines International all fly Canada/Australia.

If flying via Hawaii, it might pay to fly with Qantas or Air New Zealand. If you fly with a US airline, you might find that the west coast to Hawaii sector is treated as a domestic flight (this means that you have to pay for drinks and headsets, goodies that are free on international sectors).

To find good fares to Australia, check the travel ads in the Sunday travel sections of papers like the *Los Angeles Times*, *San Francisco Chronicle-Examiner*, *New York Times* or *Toronto Globe & Mail*. The straightforward return excursion fare from the US west coast is around US$1100, depending on the season, but plenty of deals are available. Return fares from the US east coast range from US$1200 to US$2100. You can typically get a one-way ticket from US$800 (west coast) or US$1000 (east coast). In the USA, good agents for discounted tickets are the two student travel operators, Council Travel and STA Travel, both of which have lots of offices around the country. Canadian west-coast fares out of Vancouver will be similar to the US west coast. From Toronto, fares go from around C$1650 return.

If Pacific island-hopping is your aim, check out the airlines of Pacific island nations, some of which have good deals on indirect routes. Qantas can give you Fiji or Tahiti along the way, while Air New Zealand can offer both and the Cook Islands as well. See the Circle Pacific Tickets section for more details.

Sample return fares from Melbourne to North America include: Los Angeles A$1500, New York A$1950, Vancouver A$1550 and Toronto $1950. Note that these are low-season fares.

New Zealand

Air New Zealand and Qantas operate a network of trans-Tasman flights linking Auckland, Wellington and Christchurch to Melbourne. Typical fares range from NZ$550/750 one way/return. One-way fares are not much cheaper than return fares but there is a lot of competition on this route – and with United Airlines also flying it, there is bound to be some good discounting going on.

From Melbourne, the cheapest return fares to Auckland start from about A$450, and to Wellington and Christchurch from A$610.

Asia

Ticket discounting is widespread in Asia, particularly in Singapore, Hong Kong, Bangkok and Penang. There are a lot of fly-by-nights in the Asian ticketing scene, so a little care is required. Also, the Asian routes fill up fast.

Flights between Hong Kong and Australia are notoriously heavily booked, while flights to or from Bangkok and Singapore are often part of the longer Europe to Australia route, so they are also sometimes very full. Plan ahead. For much more information on South-East Asian travel and on to Australia, see Lonely Planet's *South-East Asia on a shoestring*.

Typical return fares to Sydney or Melbourne from Hong Kong cost around A$1000, and from Singapore they're around A$800. You can also pick up some interesting tickets in Asia to include Australia on the way across the Pacific. Air France was first in this market, but Qantas and Air New Zealand are also offering discounted trans-Pacific tickets.

From Melbourne, return fares start from A$1100 to Hong Kong, from A$800 to Singapore, from A$950 to Kuala Lumpur and from A$750 to Bangkok.

Africa & South America

The flight possibilities from these continents are not so varied and you're much more likely to have to pay the full fare. There are only a handful of direct flights each week between Africa and Australia, and then only between Perth and Harare (Zimbabwe) or Johannesburg (South Africa). In many cases, the cost of your connecting flight to/from Melbourne will be partially or even fully absorbed in the ticket price. Return fares between Melbourne and Harare or Johannesburg start from A$1800 to A$2100. A cheaper alternative from East Africa may be to fly from Nairobi to India or Pakistan and on to South-East Asia, and then to connect from there to Australia.

Two routes now operate between South America and Australia. The long-running Chile connection involves a Lan Chile flight Santiago/Easter Island/Tahiti, from where you fly Qantas or another airline to Australia. Alternatively, there is a route which skirts the Antarctic circle, flying Buenos Aires/Auckland/Sydney; this is operated by Aerolineas Argentinas.

Sydney to Santiago or Buenos Aires costs about A$2200 return; again, the cost of your connecting flight to/from Melbourne will be partially or fully absorbed.

Domestic Flights

Australia's major domestic carriers are Qantas, which is the international flag-carrier, and Ansett. Both have flights between Melbourne and all the Australian capital cities.

You don't have to reconfirm domestic flights, but you should phone on the day of your flight to check the details. For Ansett, call ☎ 13 1515; for Qantas, call ☎ 13 1223.

Fares Ticket prices on all domestic flights within Australia are determined by the airlines, so travel agents will quote you exactly the same fare as the airlines themselves. Given this, the quickest and easiest approach is to book directly through the airlines, then pay for and collect your ticket from your nearest travel agent. Alternatively, if you have a credit card and you book more than three days in advance, the airline can forward your ticket to you by express post. Both carriers have toll-free reservations numbers: for Ansett, call ☎ 13 1300; for Qantas, call ☎ 13 1313.

Some examples of full economy one-way fares from Melbourne include Sydney $276, Hobart $240, Adelaide $260, Brisbane $432, Cairns $642, Darwin $669, Perth $623 and Canberra $222. See the following sections for details of discounted fares.

Discounted Fares Although full economy fares are quoted in this book, in practice very few people pay full fare on domestic travel, as the airlines offer a wide range of discounts. Discounted fares depend on various factors, including your age, whether you're studying, where you're going to and how far in advance you book your ticket. Note that the following discounts apply only to the full economy fare, and in many cases it will be cheaper to take advantage of advance purchase fares (see the next section).

Full-time tertiary students get 25% off the regular economy fare on production of student ID or an ISIC card. Children (between the ages of three and 14) and secondary students qualify for a 50% discount, 'seniors' (travellers over the age of 60) qualify for discounts of up to 70%, and international travellers get a 25 to 40% discount (by presenting their international ticket when booking).

Advance Purchase Fares In many cases, the cheapest fares available are advance purchase deals, which offer up to 33% off full one-way fares and up to 60% off full return fares. The basic rule is that the further ahead you book, the cheaper the fare, but certain conditions apply. There are restrictions on changing flights – you can reschedule your flight at any time (subject to availability) but you can't change your route, and you usually have to stay away at least one Saturday night. The other major disadvantage is that advance purchase tickets are nonrefundable, so you lose 100% of the ticket price if you cancel, although you can buy health-related cancellation insurance.

As an example of how advance purchase fares work, the full economy return fare from Melbourne to Sydney costs $552. If you book the same ticket seven days in advance, the fare drops to $307; if you book 14 days in advance, it's $245; and if you book 21 days in advance, it's $215. The full economy one-way Melbourne to Sydney fare is $276; if you book five days in advance it's $235.

Within Victoria Because of the state's compact size, scheduled flights within Victoria are somewhat limited. Kendall Airlines (book through Ansett on ☎ 13 1300) operates daily services from Melbourne to Mildura ($165 one way), Portland ($136) and Albury-Wodonga ($129), as well as to destinations in New South Wales including Merimbula, Wagga Wagga and Cooma.

Southern Australia Airlines (book through Qantas on ☎ 13 1313) also flies between Melbourne and Mildura ($165). Hazelton (book through Ansett on ☎ 13 1300) flies from Melbourne to Albury-Wodonga ($129); from Albury-Wodonga to Sale ($114) and Traralgon ($114); and from Melbourne to Merimbula in New South Wales ($181).

BUS

Travelling by bus is the cheapest way to get around Australia, and you get to see more of the wide red-brown land than if you fly. But don't forget that it's a big country – bus travel can be slow and tedious.

There is only one truly *national* bus network – Greyhound Pioneer Australia (☎ 13 2030), which consists of the former Greyhound, Pioneer and Bus Australia companies.

McCafferty's (☎ 13 1499) is Australia's next biggest operator, with services all along the east coast as well as the loop through the Centre from Adelaide, Alice Springs and Darwin to Townsville. There are also a few smaller companies, such as Firefly (☎ 03 9670 7500), which operate discounted bus trips between Melbourne, Sydney and Adelaide.

You can book directly with the bus companies, although it's often worth checking with travel agents and fare brokers such as the Bus Booking Centre (☎ 9629

3848) at 44 Flinders St and the Backpackers' Travel Centre (☎ 9654 8477) at Shop 19 Centre Place, 258 Flinders Lane – both in Melbourne's city centre.

There are basically two types of fares for bus travel – express fares and bus passes (ask the bus companies for more information). Students, backpackers (YHA and VIP card holders) and pensioners get discounts of at least 10% off most express fares and bus passes.

Note that the majority of bus services within country Victoria are operated by V/Line – see Within Victoria section under Train.

Alternative Bus Tours & Networks

If you're travelling between Melbourne and either Sydney or Adelaide, you'll miss some great countryside if you fast-track down the main highways. The Wayward Bus (☎ toll-free 1800 882 823) explores the natural attractions of the Great Ocean Road and coastal route between Melbourne and Adelaide, stopping at Port Fairy and Beachport overnight. It also operates a Melbourne-Sydney bus.

Straycat (☎ toll-free 1800 800 840) operates between Melbourne and Sydney via the High Country or the coast. Contact the bus companies for details of current prices.

Oz Experience (☎ 1300 300 028) is basically a backpackers' bus line. It has frequent bus services up and down the east coast and through central Australia to all the major destinations, with off-the-beaten-track detours. Again, contact the company for price details.

TRAIN

Australia's railway system is less comprehensive than the bus networks, and train services are less frequent and more expensive. However, interstate trains are now as fast or faster than buses and in recent years the railways have cut their prices in an attempt to be more competitive with both bus fares and reduced air fares. Somewhat confusingly, the individual states run their own railway services – Victoria has V/Line, Queensland has Queensland Rail, NSW has Countrylink and Western Australia has Westrail.

As the railway booking system is computerised, any station (other than those on metropolitan lines) can make a booking for any journey throughout the country. For reservations telephone ☎ 13 2232 from anywhere in Australia; this will connect you to the nearest booking agent. Hours for this service vary slightly from state to state. In Victoria, the hours are 7 am to 9 pm daily; in Queensland, they're 6 am to 8.30 pm; and in NSW, they're 6.30 am to 10 pm.

Fares & Conditions

There are three standard fare levels for rail travel – economy, 1st class and sleeping berths, although sleeping berths aren't available on all trains. Ticket prices are set by V/Line, so you can't get better deals by shopping around. Depending on availability, a limited number of discounted fares are offered on most trains. These cut 10 to 40% off the standard fares, and if you book early or travel at off-peak times, you'll usually qualify for one of these cheaper fares. There are also half-price concession fares available to children under the age of 16, secondary students and Australian tertiary students, but unfortunately there are no discounts for backpackers.

On interstate journeys you can make free stopovers – you have two months to complete your trip on a one-way ticket and six months on a return ticket.

There are no discounts for return travel – a return ticket is just double the price of a one-way ticket.

Interstate Services & Fares

Interstate railway services basically operate between the capital cities. That means that while there are direct services from Melbourne to Sydney, if you want to go from Melbourne to Brisbane you have to go via Sydney, and if you want to go from Melbourne to Perth you have to go via Adelaide. Fares are also calculated on each sector; for example, to go from Melbourne to Brisbane you'll pay the Melbourne to Sydney fare *plus* the Sydney to Brisbane fare.

Countrylink runs daily XTP (express) trains between Melbourne and Sydney. The Melbourne-Sydney service operates during the day and Sydney-Melbourne overnight. The trip takes 10¾ hours, and standard fares are $90 in economy, $125 in 1st class and $215 for a 1st-class sleeper, although discounts of between 10 and 40% apply for advance bookings.

To get to Canberra from Melbourne by rail you take the daily *Canberra Link*, which involves a train to Wodonga on the Victoria-New South Wales border and then a bus from there. This takes about eight hours and costs $45 in economy or $59.60 in 1st class.

The *Overland* operates between Melbourne and Adelaide every night of the week. The trip takes 12 hours and costs $50 in economy, $104 in 1st-class or $170 for a

1st-class sleeper – you can get a discount of up to 20% off 1st-class fares for advance bookings. You can transport your car on the *Overland* for $80. There's also the *Daylink* to Adelaide, which involves a train to Bendigo and a bus from there. This trip takes 11 hours and costs $47 in economy, $54.80 in 1st class.

To get to Perth by rail from Melbourne you take the *Overland* to Adelaide and then the popular *Indian-Pacific* (which comes through Adelaide from Sydney). The Melbourne to Perth trip takes two days and three nights, and fares are $270 for an economy seat, $518 for a 'holiday fare' (seat to Adelaide, sleeper to Perth) or $892 for a 1st-class sleeper (all meals included). Between July and January only, you can get a discount of between 10 and 30% off holiday and 1st-class fares for advance bookings.

Rail Passes There are a number of rail passes (available from major railway stations, travel agents or the V/Line Travel Centre at 589 Collins St in Melbourne) which allow unlimited rail travel, but these passes are now only available to international visitors – you need to show your passport or return ticket.

Within Victoria

Extensive train and bus services within country Victoria are operated by V/Line. The major centres are serviced by trains, with buses filling in the gaps and doing the cross-country runs between towns.

On return tickets, V/Line offers special off-peak fares called 'Super Savers', which give you a nearly 30% discount. For 'inter-urban services' (generally shorter trips), Super Saver fares are available every weekday, although you mustn't arrive in Melbourne before 9.30 am or leave Melbourne between 4 and 6 pm. For 'intercity services' (generally longer trips), Super Saver fares are available on Tuesday, Wednesday or Thursday. V/Line's 'Victoria Pass', which is only available to international visitors, gives you seven days unlimited travel on V/Line trains and buses within the state for $75, or two weeks unlimited travel for $130.

In Melbourne, all long-distance trains operate out of the Spencer St railway station on the western side of the city centre. Long-distance buses operate out of the Spencer St coach terminal, 100m north of the railway station.

Out of Melbourne, the principal train routes and connecting bus services are as follows:

South-west to Geelong then across to Warrnambool; a daily
bus service runs along the Great Ocean Road from
Geelong through Lorne ($10.40) and Apollo Bay ($16.80),
continuing through to Warrnambool on Friday (also on
Monday during summer).
North-west to Ballarat, Stawell, Horsham and on to Adelaide
($50); buses connect from Stawell to Halls Gap in the
Grampians.
North through Bendigo to Swan Hill; buses continue from
Bendigo to Echuca.
North to Shepparton and Cobram.
North along the Hume Highway to Albury-Wodonga, and on
to Sydney; buses run from Wangaratta to Beechworth and
Bright.
East through Traralgon and Sale to Bairnsdale; buses connect
from Bairnsdale to Lakes Entrance, Orbost, Cann River
and Merimbula.

One-way economy fares are quoted throughout this
book; 1st-class fares (available on trains only) are around
30% more than economy fares, and return fares are
double the one-way fare. See the 'One-way V/Line Fares
from Melbourne' chart for details of some fares on
V/Line's regional services.

CAR & MOTORCYCLE

See the Getting Around chapter for details of road rules,
driving conditions and information on buying and
renting vehicles.

The main road routes into Victoria are as follows:
between Sydney and Melbourne you have a choice of
either the Hume Highway (870 km, and freeway most of
the way) or the coastal Princes Highway (1039 km, much
longer and slower but also a hell of a lot more
scenic).There's a similar choice if you're travelling
between Adelaide and Melbourne, with either the fairly
direct Western Highway (730 km) or the slower Princes
Highway coastal route (894 km), the first section of
which is known as the Great Ocean Road.

If you're travelling between Brisbane and Melbourne,
the quickest route is via the Newell Highway (1890 km).

BOAT

Crewing on Yachts

It is quite possible to make your way round the Australian coast, or even to/from other countries like New
Zealand, Papua New Guinea or Indonesia, by hitching
rides or crewing on yachts. Ask around at harbours,

marinas or yacht clubs. It's often worth contacting the secretaries of sailing clubs and asking whether they have a notice board where people advertise for crews – some of the major Australian clubs even run waiting lists for people wanting to crew on yachts. Look under 'Clubs – Yacht' in the *Yellow Pages* telephone directory. It obviously helps if you're an experienced sailor, but some people are taken on as cooks (not very pleasant on a rolling yacht).

Cargo Ship

If you like the idea of travelling the high seas as a paying passenger on a cargo ship, a Sydney-based company called Freighter Travel (☎ (02) 9484 6100) can book you on a slow boat from Melbourne to New Zealand, Europe or the USA. You'll be up for about $6000 to Europe (51 days), $4500 to the east coast of the USA (33 days), $3500 to the west coast of the USA (23 days, via New Zealand and either Fiji or Honolulu) and $1100 to New Zealand (nine days).

Tasmania

Operating regular services across Bass Strait to Tasmania is the *Spirit of Tasmania* (☎ 13 2010 toll-free) car and passenger ferry. There are dozens of different fares available; prices depend on the type of sleeping quarters and the time of year, and all include breakfast and dinner. Cheapest are the 'hostel fares' at $99/120 per person each way in the low/high season. The next level up costs $145/160 for a two or four-berth cabin, with the most expensive option being $225/280 for a luxury suite. Return fares are just double the one-way fares, and high-season prices apply during the Christmas school holidays and at Easter.

The *Spirit of Tasmania* takes a leisurely 14.5 hours to cross Bass Strait, and leaves Station Pier in Port Melbourne at 6 pm every Monday, Wednesday and Friday and returns from Devonport at 6 pm every Tuesday, Thursday and Saturday. The ship arrives into both ports at 8.30 am.

For more information on other ways of getting to the Apple Isle, fly/drive packages etc, telephone or visit the Tasmanian Travel Centre (☎ 9206 7922) at 256 Collins St.

WARNING

The information in this chapter is particularly vulnerable to change: prices for international travel are volatile, routes are introduced and cancelled, schedules change, rules are amended and special deals come and go. Get opinions, quotes and advice from as many airlines and travel agents as possible before you part with your hard-earned cash. The details given in this chapter should be regarded only as pointers and cannot be any substitute for your own careful, up-to-date research.

Getting Around

THE AIRPORT

Melbourne airport is at Tullamarine, 22 km north-west of the city centre. It's a modern airport with a single terminal: Qantas at one end, Ansett at the other, international in the middle. There are two information desks at the airport: one on the ground floor in the international departure area and another upstairs next to the duty-free shops.

If you're driving, the Tullamarine Freeway runs from the airport almost into the city centre, finishing in North Melbourne. A taxi between the airport and city centre costs about $25.

The Skybus (☎ 9662 9275) operates frequent shuttle-bus services between the airport and the city centre, costing $9 for adults and $4.50 for children. Skybus has two city terminals: Bay 30 at the Spencer St coach terminal, with departures about every half-hour between 5 am and 10.45 pm (6 am and 10.05 pm on weekends); and the Melbourne Transit Centre at 58 Franklin St, with departures about every 30 minutes between 7 am and 11 pm (10 pm on weekends). Buy your ticket from the driver; bookings are not usually necessary. You can take your bicycle on the Skybus, but the front wheel must be removed.

There is also a fairly frequent bus operated by Gull Airport Services (☎ 5222 4966) between the airport and Geelong. It costs $20 one way. The Geelong terminus is at 45 McKillop St. Other airport buses operate services to the Mornington Peninsula and other outer areas. The airport information desks can provide travellers with details.

Public transport between the city and the airport is limited. The Skybus is by far the best bet, but if you can't afford the $9 you could always take tram No 59 from Elizabeth St to the Moonee Ponds Junction – from there, Tullamarine Bus Lines (☎ 9338 3817) runs bus Nos 478 and 479 to the airport around seven times a day. You can do this trip on a zone 1 & 2 Met ticket ($6.80).

There's also a cycling track following the Moonee Ponds Creek from the city almost to the airport. The track starts on the west side of the Tullamarine Freeway and finishes in Westmeadows. From there, follow Mickleham Rd south under the freeway and turn right into Melrose Drive.

PUBLIC TRANSPORT – THE MET

Melbourne's public transport system, the Met, incorporates buses, trains and the famous trams. There are about 750 trams and they operate as far as 20 km out from the centre. They're frequent and a fun way to get around. Buses take routes where the trams do not go, and replace them at quiet weekend periods. Trains radiate out from the city centre to the outer suburbs.

There's quite an array of tickets, and the Met has a glossy *Travel Guide* brochure which describes them all. You can buy tickets on board trams and buses, from railway stations and from retail outlets like newsagents, milk bars and chemists. The same ticket allows you to travel on trams, trains *and/or* buses. The most common tickets are based on a specific period of travelling time – either two hours, one day, one week, one month or one year – and allow you unlimited travel during that period and within the relevant zone.

The metropolitan area is divided into three zones, and the price of tickets depends on which zone(s) you will be travelling in and across. Zone 1 covers the city and inner-suburban area, and most travellers won't venture beyond that unless they're going right out of town – on a trip to the Healesville Sanctuary, for example, or down the Mornington Peninsula. The fares are as follows:

Zones	2 Hours	All Day	Weekly
1	$2.20	$4.30	$18.60
2 or 3	$1.60	$2.90	$12.80
1 & 2	$3.80	$7.00	$31.40
1, 2 & 3	$5.20	$9.40	$38.40

Monthly and yearly tickets are also available.

Note that if you buy a weekly, monthly or yearly Zone 1 ticket, it also allows you unlimited travel in Zones 1, 2 and 3 on weekends. If you're heading into the city by train from Zone 2 or 3, you can get off-peak tickets for use after 9.30 am which take you into the city and then allow unlimited travel on trams and buses within the city area.

There are also Short Trip tickets ($1.60) which allow you to travel two sections on buses or trams in Zone 1, or you can buy a Short Trip Card ($12.50) which gives you ten short trips. There are numerous other deals but we don't want to make this too complicated, do we!

For trams/buses, buy your ticket on board from the conductor/driver. For trains, you must buy your ticket at the station *before* you board. Most services operate between 5 am and midnight Monday to Saturday and from 8 am to 11 pm on Sunday.

For information on public transport, phone the Met Information Centre (☎ 13 1638), which operates daily from 7 am to 9 pm. The Met Shop at 103 Elizabeth St in the city (open weekdays from 8.30 am to 5.15 pm and Saturday from 8.30 am to 12.30 pm) also has transport information and sells souvenirs and tickets. It also has a 'Discover Melbourne' kit. If you're in the city it's probably a better bet for information than the telephone service, which is usually busy. Railway stations also have some information.

Disabled Travellers

Melbourne's excellent *Mobility Map* is available from tourist information booths in the Bourke St Mall and Rialto Towers, and from the Melbourne City Council's information desk (☎ 9658 8679) on the corner of Swanston Walk and Little Collins St (ring and they will post one to you).

Victoria's Public Transport Corporation (PTC) publishes *Disability Services for Customers with Specific Needs* and provides accessible rail services on V/Line Sprinter trains to the major rural centres of Geelong, Ballarat, Bendigo, Seymour and Traralgon. Hoist-equipped buses then link other centres and also Adelaide (via Ballarat). Contact V/Line's Disability Services section on (☎ 9619 2354 or ☎ 13 2232). Melbourne's accessible suburban rail network is operated by the Met and all trains carry a portable ramp in the driver's compartment. Just wait at the end of the platform where the front of the train will be.

See the Taxi and Car Rental sections for further information.

TRAM

Melbourne's trundling trams are one of the city's most distinctive features. Trams are a great way to get around, but you might need to exercise a little patience. Tram travel is something from another era, an era when people weren't so concerned with matters like efficiency and speed.

Tram routes cover the city and inner suburbs quite extensively. The majority of routes operate as back-and-forwards shuttle services, with the city centre acting as the hub of the wheel and the tram routes as the spokes. This makes it a good system if you want to get to somewhere from the city centre, but not so good if you

KRZYSZTOF DYDYNSKI

The old 'W' class tram – still going strong.

RICHARD NEBESKY

Tram stop at MacArthur Street, East Melbourne.

want to travel across from one suburb to another. All tram stops are numbered out from the city centre.

Most trams are the traditional green and yellow, but some trams have been illustrated by local artists, and others are mobile billboards. For the total 'tram experience', the old W-class trams can't be beaten, but the modern trams are generally faster and more comfortable.

There are also 'light rail' services to some suburbs – these modern express trams are a sort of hybrid between a train and a tram.

In theory, trams run along most routes about every six to eight minutes during peak hour and every 12 minutes at other times. Unfortunately, trams have to share the roads with cars and trucks, so the reality is that they are often subject to delays. It's not uncommon to wait 20 minutes for a tram – then see two or three arrive at once. Be patient – trams are only (almost) human, and some are faster than others! Services are less frequent on weekends and late at night.

Be extremely careful when getting on and off a tram: by law, cars are supposed to stop when a tram stops to pick up and drop off passengers, but that doesn't always happen.

See the Tram Tours section for details on the free City Circle tram service.

TRAIN

Melbourne has an extensive train network that covers the city centre and suburban areas. The trains are generally faster and more convenient than trams or buses, but they don't go to many inner suburbs like Fitzroy, Carlton, St Kilda or South Melbourne.

Flinders St railway station is the main terminal, and each suburban line has a separate platform there. The famous row of clocks above the entrance on the corner of Swanston and Flinders Sts indicate when the next train will be departing from each line. There's an information booth just inside the entrance.

Weekdays, trains on most lines start at 5 am and finish at midnight and should run every three to eight minutes during peak hour, every 15 to 20 minutes at other times, and every 40 minutes after 7 pm. On Saturday they run every half-hour from 5 am to midnight, while on Sunday it's every 40 minutes from 7 am to 11.30 pm. Of course, these are just rule-of-thumb times. In a perfect world (or if Mussolini were transport minister) all of the above would be accurate. In reality, expect deviations, plus the odd strike.

The city service includes an underground City Loop which is a quick way to get from one side of town to the other. The stations on the loop are Parliament, Melbourne Central, Flagstaff, Spencer St and Flinders St.

Bicycles can be carried free on trains during off-peak times and weekends.

BUS

Melbourne's bus network is ancillary to the trains and trams – it fills in the gaps. Generally, buses continue from where the trains finish, or go to places, such as hospitals, universities, suburban shopping centres and the outer suburbs, not reached by other services. If you find you can't get somewhere by train or tram, ring the Met – chances are they will have a bus going that way.

CAR

You can get around Melbourne and between the main country centres easily enough by train and bus, but many of Victoria's finest features – the national parks, the remote beaches, the mountain regions, the back-road country towns are not readily accessible by public transport. So if you're planning to explore Victoria in intimate detail or just want to get off the beaten track, you'll need your own set of wheels – and for many visitors, that means buying a car or renting one.

Car Rental

All the big car-rental firms operate in Melbourne. Avis (☎ 1800 225 533), Budget (☎ 13 2727), Hertz (☎ 13 3039) and Thrifty (☎ 1800 652 008) have desks at the airport, and you can find plenty of others in the city. The offices tend to be at the northern end of the city or in Carlton or North Melbourne.

The major companies all offer unlimited km rates in the city, and in country areas it's a flat rate plus so many cents per km. One-day hire rates are around $70 for a small car, $90 for a medium car or $100 to $110 for a big car – obviously, the longer the hire period, the cheaper the daily rate.

For disabled travellers Avis and Hertz provide hand-controlled rental vehicles while Norden Transport Equipment (☎ 9793 1066) has a self-drive van, equipped with a lift, available for long or short-term rentals.

Melbourne also has a number of budget operators, renting older vehicles at lower rates. Their costs and conditions vary widely, so it's worth making a few enquiries before going for one firm over another. Be sure to ask whether rates include insurance and about the excess, km charges and so on. Beware of distance restrictions; many companies only allow you to travel within a certain distance of the city, typically 100 km.

Some places worth trying are Delta (☎ 13 1390), Astoria (☎ 9662 2166) and RealCheap (☎ 9662 2166) (all of which have branches around Melbourne), and Airport Rent-a-Car (☎ 1800 331 220): rates are around $50 a day.

If you're after a real cheapie (around $30 a day) try one of the 'rent-a-wreck' operators like Rent-a-Bomb (☎ 9428 0088) in Richmond and Ugly Duckling Rent A Car (☎ 9525 4010) in St Kilda. The *Yellow Pages* lists lots of other firms under 'Car &/or Minibus Rental', including some reputable local operators who rent newer cars but don't have the nationwide network (and overheads) of the big operators.

4WD Renting a 4WD vehicle costs from around $75 a day for a Suzuki Vitara soft-top to around $140 a day for a Toyota Landcruiser (plus a hefty deposit which you get back if you do no damage to it). Companies with 4WDs for hire out of Melbourne include Hertz (☎ 13 3039), Budget (☎ 13 2727), Thrifty (☎ 1800 652 008), Delta (☎ 13 1390) and Off Road Rentals (☎ 9543 7111).

Buying a Car

Shopping around for a used car involves much the same rules as anywhere. Firstly, used-car dealers in Melbourne are just like used-car dealers from Los Angeles to London – they'd sell their mother into slavery if it turned a dollar. You'll generally get a car cheaper by buying privately through newspaper ads – try *The Age* classifieds on Wednesday or Saturday, or the weekly *Trading Post* – rather than through a car dealer, although if you buy through a dealer and spend more than $3000 you get a warranty of at least 3000 km or two months.

In Australia third-party personal-injury insurance is always included in the vehicle registration cost, but you'd be wise to extend that to at least third-party property insurance as well – minor collisions with Rolls Royces can be surprisingly expensive.

In Victoria a car has to have a compulsory safety check (Road Worthiness Certificate – RWC) before it can be registered in the new owner's name. *Don't* let yourself be talked into buying a vehicle without a RWC or registration – it almost *always* turns into a nightmare. Stamp duty has to be paid when you buy a car and, as this is based on the purchase price, it's not unknown for buyer and seller to agree privately to understate the price! It's much easier to sell a car in the same state that it's registered in, otherwise it has to be re-registered in the new state.

For a fee ($85, or $115 for nonmembers), the RACV will check over a used car and report on its condition before you agree to purchase it. Most mechanics and garages offer a similar service. Arranging a mechanical test might seem like a hassle at the time, but it's a sensible investment that could save you a bundle of money and much heartache.

Royal Automobile Club of Victoria

The RACV provides an emergency breakdown service, literature, excellent maps and detailed guides to accommodation. They can advise you on regulations you should be aware of and give general guidelines about buying a car. The RACV's head office (☎ 9790 2755) is at 550 Princes Highway in Noble Park, although they also have three offices in the city centre – at 422 Little Collins St, 230 Collins St and 123 Queen St.

If you're a member of the AAA in the USA or the RAC or AA in the UK, you can use any of the RACV's facilities. But bring proof of membership with you.

Road Rules

Australians drive on the left-hand side of the road. Although overseas licences (preferably with photo-ID) are acceptable in Australia, an International Driving Permit is even more acceptable.

The speed limit in residential areas is 60 km/h, rising to 75 or 80 km/h on some main roads and dropping to 40 km/h in specially designated areas such as school zones. On highways the speed limit is generally 100 km/h (roughly 60 miles per hour), while on many freeways it rises to 110 km/h.

Speed and red-light cameras operate throughout Victoria and police cars are equipped with radar for speed checks. Be warned.

The wearing of seat belts is compulsory, and small children must be belted into an approved safety seat. Motorcyclists must wear a helmet at all times when riding.

Don't drink and drive – Victoria's blood-alcohol limit of 0.05% is strictly enforced by the police. Random breath-tests occur throughout the state and penalties are severe, including losing your licence and having to pay a heavy fine. Probationary and learner drivers must display 'P' and 'L' plates and maintain a blood-alcohol reading of zero.

Cars & Trams

Car drivers should treat Melbourne trams with caution – trams are about half the weight of an ocean liner and seldom come off second best in accidents. You can only overtake a tram on the left and must *always* stop behind a tram when it halts to drop off or collect passengers (except where there are central 'islands' for passengers).

Melbourne has a notoriously confusing road rule, known as the 'hook turn', for getting trams through the city centre without being blocked by turning cars. To turn right at certain intersections, you have to pull to the left, wait until the light of the street you're turning into changes from red to green, then complete the turn. These intersections are identified by the black-and-white hook sign that hangs down from the overhead cables.

Parking

If you're lucky enough to find an on-street parking space in the city centre, the meters take 20c, $1 and $2 coins. Check parking signs for restrictions and times, and watch out for clearway zones which operate during peak hours.

There are over 70 car parks in the city, and the Melbourne City Council produces a map-and-brochure guide to city parking – it's available from Melbourne Town Hall. Hourly rates vary depending on the car-park's location, but you'll pay around $3 to $6 an hour or $12 to $25 a day during the week – less on weekends.

MOTORCYCLE

If you want to bring your own motorcycle into Australia you'll need a *carnet de passage*, and when you try to sell it here you'll get less than the market price because of bureaucratic problems in registering vehicles without Australian approval markings.

One option is hiring, though there aren't many places where you can do this and it often costs less to hire a car. Garner's Hire-Bikes (☎ 9326 8676) at 179 Peel St (on the corner of Queensberry St) in North Melbourne has Victoria's biggest range of trail bikes and large road bikes for rent, with prices ranging from $70/140/350 per day/weekend/week for a Suzuki TS185 trail bike all the way up to $230/400/980 for a Harley-Davidson Softail

Custom; prices include insurance and unlimited km.
Victorian Motorcycle Hire & Sales (☎ 9817 3206) at 606
High St in East Kew also has a wide range of bikes for
rent, ranging from a Kawasaki ZR250 for $75 a day to a
Honda CBR1000 for $130 a day.

If you want wheels for more than a few weeks, you
might want to look at buying. Australian newspapers
and the lively local motorcycle press have extensive
classified advertisement sections where $2500 gets you
something that will easily take you around Australia if
you know a bit about bikes. But you'll have to sell it
again afterwards.

An easier option might be a buy-back arrangement
with a large motorcycle dealer (Elizabeth St near Franklin St in Melbourne is a good hunting ground). They're
keen to do business, and basic negotiating skills allied
with a wad of cash (say, $4000) should secure a good
second-hand bike with a written guarantee that they'll
buy it back in good condition minus 25% after your
three-month tour. Shop around.

See the previous Car section for details of road rules
etc.

BICYCLE

Melbourne's a great city for cycling. It's reasonably flat,
so you're not pushing and panting up hills too often, and
there are some great cycling routes throughout the metropolitan area. Two of the best are the bike path which
runs around a section of Port Phillip Bay from Port
Melbourne to Brighton, and the bike path which follows
the Yarra River out of the city for more than 20 km,
passing through lovely parklands along the way. There
are numerous other bicycle tracks, including those along
the Maribyrnong River and the Merri Creek.

Discovering Melbourne's Bike Paths ($14.95), has excel-
lent maps and descriptive routes of the city's bicycle
paths. The *Melway Greater Melbourne* street directory is
also useful for cyclists. Note that bicycles can be taken
on suburban trains for free during off-peak times (and if
you strike a friendly tram driver and the tram is fairly
empty, on trams too). One note of caution: tram tracks
are a major hazard for cyclists in Melbourne. Every
cyclist has their own 'wheel-in-a-track' horror story.

Quite a few bike shops and companies have bikes for
hire, and a good mountain bike, helmet and lock will
cost about $20 a day. The following places are all worth
trying: St Kilda Cycles (☎ 9534 3074), 11 Carlisle St, St
Kilda; Bob's Boards (☎ 9537 2118), 17 Fitzroy St, St Kilda;
Cycle Science (☎ 9826 8877), 320 Toorak Rd, South Yarra;

REIMUND ZUNDE

Bicycle path along the Yarra River.

Bicycles for Hire (☎ 018 580 809), below Princes Bridge on the south side of the Yarra; and Borsari Cycles (☎ 9347 4100), 193 Lygon St, Carlton.

TAXI

Taxis in Melbourne have a large dome light on their roof (lit up when they're available for hire) and a narrow strip of chequered yellow and green running along their flanks.

There are plenty of taxi ranks in and around the city. The main ones in town are outside the major hotels, outside Flinders and Spencer St railway stations, on the corner of William and Bourke Sts, on the corner of Elizabeth and Bourke Sts, in Lonsdale St outside Myer and outside Ansett in Franklin St.

Flagfall is $2.60, and the standard tariff is 89c per km. There is a $1 charge for telephone bookings between midnight and 6 am, and most cabs only take either cash, American Express or Diners Card. Tipping is not expected, but always appreciated.

If you want to book a taxi, the major companies include Silver Top (☎ 13 1008), Arrow (☎ 13 2211), Black Cabs (☎ 13 2227) and Embassy (☎ 13 1755).

WALKING

There are some wonderful walking areas in and around Melbourne. Some of the most popular city destinations include the Yarra River parklands, the Kings Domain, the Botanic Gardens, Royal Park, Albert Park Lake and around Port Phillip Bay. See the Things to See & Do chapter for details of our suggested Walking Tour of Melbourne.

There are also plenty of great places just beyond the city outskirts, including the Dandenong Ranges, the Yarra Valley, the Brisbane Ranges National Park and Anakie Gorge, the You Yangs, the Kinglake National Park and the Mornington Peninsula (particularly the Point Nepean National Park and Cape Schanck Coastal Park).

See the Walking Tours section of Things to See & Do for details of some of the walking tours on offer in Melbourne.

BOAT

Williamstown Bay & River Cruises (☎ 9397 2255) operates two ferry services across to Gem Pier in Williamstown; one from the city, the other from St Kilda. The *Williamstown Seeker* runs between Southgate and Williamstown, stopping at the Casino, the World Trade Centre and the Scienceworks museum, daily between January and March and on weekends and public holidays during the rest of the year. The one-way/return fare is $10/18.

The company also operates the *John Batman* ferry between St Kilda Pier and Williamstown, which runs year round on weekends and public holidays and costs $6/10. For details on departure times and other fares, call the above number or the recorded information

RICHARD NEBESKY

Port of Williamstown

number (☎ 9506 4144). The same company also operates a range of cruises.

Between October and May the restored 1933 steam tug *Wattle* (☎ 9328 2739) runs a ferry service on Sunday between Station Pier in Port Melbourne and Gem Pier in Williamstown. It leaves from Station Pier at 10.30 am, noon, 1.30 and 3 pm, and returns from Williamstown at 11.30 am, 1, 2.30 and 4 pm; the return fare costs $10 for adults and $7 for children.

See the Excursions chapter for details of the ferry services between Sorrento, Portsea and Queenscliff.

ORGANISED TOURS

There's a huge array of tours on offer in and around Melbourne. Ask at the tourist information centres in the city if you're looking for something in particular.

City Bus Tours

Companies like Australian Pacific, AAT King's and Down Under Day Tours run conventional city bus tours, as well as day trips to the most popular tourist destinations like Sovereign Hill, Healesville Sanctuary, Phillip Island and the Great Ocean Road.

London Transport Bus Tours (☎ 9563 9788) also operates several popular double-decker bus tours around Melbourne. Their City Explorer does a continuous circuit around the city and inner suburbs, with 16 stops including the Royal Melbourne Zoo, the Meat Market Craft Centre, the Queen Victoria Market, the Shrine of Remembrance and the Victorian Arts Centre. The City Wanderer does a similar circuit around the inner-city area, as well as heading over the West Gate Bridge to the Scienceworks museum and Williamstown. One-day passes for either bus cost $15 for adults, $8 for children or $30 for a family of five. Tickets for both buses get you discounts on entry to various attractions, and you can get on and off all day from 10 am to 5 pm.

Tram Tours

In the city centre, the free City Circle trams travel on a fixed route along Flinders, Spring and Nicholson Sts to Victoria Pde and then back along Latrobe and Spencer Sts. Designed primarily for tourists, and passing many city sights along the way, the trams run daily between 10 am and 6 pm, every ten minutes or so. There are eight refurbished W-class (built between 1936 and 1956) trams operating on this route. Built in Melbourne, they have all been refurbished and painted a distinctive deep burgundy and gold.

You can even dine on board a tram while taking a scenic night cruise around Melbourne's streets – see the boxed aside on the Colonial Tramcar Restaurant in the Places to Eat chapter.

There's also a restored 1920s tourist tram that runs from the city to the Melbourne Zoo on Sunday. This service leaves from the Flinders St end of Elizabeth St at 9, 10 and 11 am and noon each Sunday – phone the Met to confirm times.

River Cruises

Melbourne River Cruises (☎ 9614 1215) offers regular cruises along the Yarra River, departing every half-hour from Princes Walk (on the north bank of the river, east of Princes Bridge) and from Southgate. You can take a one-hour cruise either upstream or downstream ($13 for adults, $6.50 for children) or combine the two for a 2½-hour cruise ($25/13). Southgate River Tours (☎ 9818 6870) offers a 1½-hour cruise in the old *Queen Mary* ferry from Southgate up-river past the mansions of Toorak. The cost is $17.50 for adults, $8 for kids, including a barbecue lunch. There are also half-hour cruises ($7/3.50) and one-hour cruises ($12/6.50).

Maribyrnong River Cruises (☎ 9689 6431) has 2½-hour cruises up the Maribyrnong River to Avondale Heights, with a stopover at the interesting Living Museum of the West, costing $14 for adults and $4 for children. There are also one-hour cruises down to the West Gate Bridge and docklands ($7/4). Departures are from the end of Wingfield St in Footscray.

You can also take a cruise to the penguin colony at St Kilda pier – see the St Kilda section of the Things to See & Do chapter for details.

Walking Tours

Melbourne Heritage Walks (☎ 9827 1085) conducts informative and interesting walking tours of Melbourne. Focusing on fine arts, history and architecture, the two-hour walks operate on Wednesday from 10 am to noon ($20 per person) and Sunday from 2 to 4 pm ($25 per person).

Art & About (☎ 9696 0591 or 11 500) runs the popular Arts City Backstage tours, taking you behind the scenes and into the rehearsal rooms and costume departments of the Australian Ballet, Opera Australia and the Victorian Arts Centre. The tour departs from the Victorian

Arts Centre forecourt (under the spire) every Tuesday at 10.30 am and costs $25 ($19 concessions) – you can book ahead or just turn up.

Savetime Service (☎ 9654 2535) offers an interesting and unusual variety of themed walks, including the Chocolate Indulgence Walk (every Saturday at 12.30 pm, $20), Melbourne's Fabulous Food Walk (every second Wednesday at 10 am, $29), the Made In Melbourne Walk (every second Wednesday at 1 pm, $20), and the Just Desserts Walk (every Saturday at 2.30 pm, $19).

The Melbourne Town Walking Tour (☎ 9415 8017) is a two-hour discovery tour of some of the city's hidden treasures. The tour departs most days at 10 am from the Exhibition Buildings fountain, and the cost of $25 includes refreshments.

Things to See & Do

HIGHLIGHTS

Rating attractions and activities is of course totally subjective – one person's paradise is another person's purgatory, as they say – but the following list covers some of the more popular and unusual things to see and do while you're in Melbourne, and includes some quintessentially 'Melbournesque' experiences:

- A beer, a band and a bite at the Espy (St Kilda's Esplanade Hotel)
- A picnic on the lakeside lawns at the Royal Botanic Gardens
- The No 8 tram ride from the city along Toorak Rd – actually, any tram ride will do
- Afternoon tea at The Windsor Hotel
- Ferry rides from St Kilda or Southgate to Williamstown
- Exploring Brunswick St in Fitzroy – preferably with an appetite and time on your hands
- Going to the footy at the MCG (and seeing Collingwood lose by one point, preferably with a kick after the siren)

RICHARD NEBESKY

A north-eastern view of Melbourne at night from
Rialto Towers.

- Clothes shopping and people-watching in Chapel St
- Early dinner at Southgate (followed by one of Charmaine's ice creams) before heading to a show at the Victorian Arts Centre nearby
- A late lunch at Caffe e Cucina in Chapel St
- Cycling, strolling, running or in-line skating along the foreshore between St Kilda and Albert Park
- Devonshire tea at the Studley Park Boathouse or Fairfield Boathouse, followed by a (wet) paddle along the Yarra River
- Shopping at, or just wandering around, the Queen Victoria Market
- Eating out in Melbourne's 'Little Saigon' – Victoria St in Richmond
- Breakfast at Mario's in Brunswick St, Fitzroy
- Visiting the National Gallery of Victoria
- Spending Boxing Day at the Test cricket match at the MCG
- Cult movies at the old Astor cinema
- The open-air Moonlight Cinema and live theatre performances in the Botanic Gardens during summer
- Sunday morning yum cha in Chinatown
- Dinner on the Colonial Tramcar Restaurant
- Exploring the delicatessens at the Prahran Market
- Leisurely cycling excursions around the Yarra River bike paths
- Sunday lunch at The Stokehouse in St Kilda
- Twilight Jazz sessions at the Royal Melbourne Zoo

There are also some great things to see and do just beyond the city outskirts – see the Excursions chapter for details.

WALKING TOURS

The following walking tour (Map 1) is a good way to introduce yourself to the city centre and some of its attractions (although to really get to know Melbourne you'll need to jump on a tram or two and explore beyond the city – see the Melbourne inner-suburbs sections later).

This walking tour starts at the intersection of Flinders and Swanston Sts, home to three of Melbourne's best-known landmarks. The grand old **Flinders St railway station** is the main railway station for suburban trains. Built in 1899 on the site of Melbourne's first fish market, the station is quite impressive with its domes, towers and rows of clocks, and is splendidly lit at night. Across the road is one of Melbourne's best-known pubs, **Young & Jackson's**, which is famed mainly for the painting of *Chloe* hanging in the upstairs bar. Judged indecent at the Melbourne Exhibition of 1880, she has gone on to win affection among generations of Melbourne drinkers. The third landmark on this corner, **St Paul's Cathedral**, is a masterpiece of Gothic Revivalist architecture, and the interior is particularly noteworthy for its detailed tiled floors, stained-glass windows, restored organ and stonework.

Stroll up Swanston St, which has been closed to cars to create **Swanston Walk**, a tree-lined boulevard which pedestrians share with trams and commercial vehicles. In the block between Flinders Lane and Collins St is the **City Square**, with its fountains and ponds, a statue to the ill-fated explorers Burke and Wills (on the Collins St side), and an information booth nearby. Across Collins St is the **Melbourne Town Hall**, built between 1870 and 1880.

Continue up to Bourke St and take a left into the **Bourke St Mall**. Like Swanston Walk, it's difficult for a pedestrian mall to work with 30-tonne trams barrelling through the middle of it every few minutes, but despite the tram threat the mall has become something of a focus for city shoppers, with its buskers, missionaries and big department stores.

Collect your mail from the GPO at the Elizabeth St end of the mall, then return to Swanston Walk and head north again. Across Little Lonsdale St you'll pass the **State Library** and the **National Museum of Victoria** on your right, and in the next block is the **Royal Melbourne Institute of Technology**, with its rather bizarre architectural facades. Take a right into Franklin St, right into Victoria Pde and then another right into Russell St, and head down past the **Old Melbourne Gaol**. Continue

---

Chloe
Painted by the French artist Jules Lefebre, she was one of the first nudes exhibited in Australia and the painting caused an uproar when shown in Melbourne at the Great Exhibition of 1880. The model, aged 14 when Lefebre immortalised her, committed suicide a couple of years later by consuming a cocktail of match heads and champagne. She had fallen in love with the artist, but he had spurned her and gone off with her sister instead. The Young & Jackson pub bought the painting in 1908, and *Chloe* has been a part of Melbourne ever since, winning the affections of generations of drinkers. ■

MARK ARMSTRONG

The controversial *Chloe*, still cheering drinkers at Young & Jackson's Hotel.

down Russell St and when you get to Little Bourke St, turn left and you've entered Melbourne's **Chinatown**. This narrow lane was a thronging Chinese quarter even back in the gold-rush days and it's now a crowded couple of blocks of excellent Chinese restaurants, Asian supermarkets and shops.

At the top end of Little Bourke St, turn right into Spring St, which has some of Melbourne's most impressive old buildings, including the lovely **Princess Theatre**, the gracious **Windsor Hotel** and the **Parliament House of Victoria**. Built with gold-rush wealth, this building served as the national parliament while Canberra was under construction. There are free tours of both houses (see the Spring St section of this chapter).

Farther down Spring St opposite Collins St, the **Old Treasury Building** is one of the finest 19th-century buildings in the city. The building now houses the Melbourne Exhibition with displays on Melbourne's past and future, which opens daily from 9 am to 5 pm. You can also tour the gold vaults daily at 1 and 3 pm.

Cross Spring St into Collins St, and on your left you'll see the soaring towers of Collins Place, which house Melbourne's five-star **Sofitel**. The hotel's toilets on the 35th floor are well worth a visit – they boast spectacular views over the MCG, parkland and shimmering suburbs of Melbourne, and are one of the city's prime (unofficial) attractions. While you're up there, you could have a drink in the hotel's ritzy Atrium Bar.

Back on ground level, head around to Flinders Lane (south of Collins Place). The **'top end' of Flinders Lane**, between Spring and Swanston Sts, is said to be the closest thing Melbourne has to New York's Soho, and was once the focal centre of Melbourne's rag trade. It's an interesting area to explore, with numerous fine-art

---

Market Tours & Tasting Trips

Food is something of an obsession for many Melburnians, and if you're interested in exploring behind the scenes a couple of local operators offer walking tours through two of Melbourne's most interesting food precincts – the Queen Victoria Market and Richmond's Victoria St.

Mira Freedman (☎ 9348 2221) has been taking people on 'discovery tours' in Victoria St, Richmond – known as Melbourne's 'Little Saigon' – since the early 1990s. Her tours offer a wonderful insight into this fascinating area, with its cluttered grocery shops, exotic fruits, vegies, sauces, pastries, other Vietnamese delicacies, and dozens of restaurants. Tours run every Wednesday from 10 am to 12.45 pm, about an hour of which is taken up by lunch. The cost is $40 which includes a 'showbag', which you fill up with samples and recipes along the way. Mira takes a maximum of 12 people, so book ahead.

Queen Victoria Market Walking Tours (☎ 9658 9601) runs great two-hour tours around the market every Tuesday, Thursday, Friday and Saturday. You get to visit all sorts of different stalls, meet a fascinating bunch of characters, and taste a variety of interesting goodies – great fun! The 'Magical History' tour starts at 10.30 am and costs $10 including morning tea. The 'Foodies Dream' tour starts at 10 am and costs $15 – it's great if you're specifically interested in food, and you get to try weird and wonderful things like emu sausages and wallaby pies. Tours depart from the market's Visitor's Centre, and bookings are essential. ∎

galleries (see Commercial Art Galleries in the Shopping chapter), fashion warehouses and offices, restaurants and cafes.

Continue down Flinders' Lane as far as Swanston Walk and take a left. Continue past Flinders St railway station, then turn right just before the river and stroll along the riverside. An arched footbridge takes you across the river to the **Southgate** complex, with its excellent restaurants, bars and cafes. South of Southgate is Melbourne's **Arts Precinct**, and across St Kilda Rd are the parklands of the **Kings Domain** – a marvellous area to wander through and explore, if you still have the energy.

Other Walking Tours

The City of Melbourne publishes a series of *Heritage Walk* brochures which are available from the council's information booths. The National Trust's *Walking Melbourne* booklet is particularly useful if you're interested in Melbourne's architectural heritage.

See the Organised Tours section in the Getting Around chapter for details of other walking tours.

TRAM TOURS

When you tire of walking, consider buying yourself a Zone 1 daily ticket and continuing your exploration of Melbourne by tram. For $4.30, you can spend the entire day travelling around the city and inner suburbs by tram – a bargain, and a great way to get a feel for Melbourne. The same ticket lets you use trains and buses too.

Try a ride on tram No 8. It starts off along Swanston St in the city, rolls south down St Kilda Rd beside the Kings Domain and continues up Toorak Rd through South Yarra and Toorak. Another popular tram ride is on No 16 which cruises all the way down St Kilda Rd to St Kilda.

CITY CENTRE

Swanston St

Swanston St (Map 1) runs through the heart of the city. Formerly a major traffic artery, it was closed to cars early in 1992 to create Swanston Walk, a boulevard lined with trees and street cafes and shared by pedestrians, trams and commercial vehicles. Despite the winds of change, many of Swanston St's more impressive buildings remain, and Swanston Walk has provided a welcome facelift to the city's main thoroughfare.

On the corner of Swanston and Collins Sts, the **Manchester Unity** building is easily missed, but if you raise your eyes above street level you'll see a marvellous example of a Gothic 1930s building. One of Melbourne's earliest skyscrapers, it had the city's first escalators, and the original ventilation system was cooled in summer by tons of ice!

The **Melbourne Town Hall**, opposite the Manchester Unity building, is another fine building. The administration office (☎ 9658 9462) has a range of brochures, maps and information, and if you ring in advance the staff can arrange a tour of the main hall with its notable organ.

Opposite Melbourne Town Hall at No 113 is the **Capitol Theatre**, built in 1925-27. Local architect and writer Robin Boyd called the theatre 'possibly the finest picture theatre ever built anywhere'. Unfortunately, the facade was demolished for an arcade 20 years ago, but if you ignore the trashy exterior and wander inside, you'll see what he meant. The ceiling, designed by the team of Marion Mahony Griffin and her husband Walter Burley Griffin (the architects of Canberra), is a kaleidoscopic creation that glitters like illuminated crystals. The Capitol is now a Chinese cinema.

Farther north, in the block between Little Lonsdale and Latrobe Sts, are the State Library and the National Museum of Victoria (see the following sections).

The next block north along Swanston St is dominated by what local architect Dimity Reed once called 'a concrete building in the neo-Stalinist style of the 1960s' – the **Royal Melbourne Institute of Technology**. In recent years the RMIT buildings have been radically transformed by the addition of striking post-modernist facades – well worth checking out.

On the corner of Swanston and Victoria Sts, the **Melbourne City Baths** were built in 1903, and to quote Reed again, 'the design is a flamboyant but disciplined extravaganza of towers and domes and red-and-white striped brickwork'.

State Library

The State Library (Map 1), with its classical revival facade facing Swanston St, was built in various stages from 1854. When it was completed in 1913, the reinforced concrete dome over the octagonal **Reading Room** was the largest of its kind in the world. If you want somewhere peaceful to write letters or just contemplate life, the Reading Room is one of the most serene rooms in Melbourne. In 1871, Marcus Clarke wrote much of *For the Term of His Natural Life* in this room. The book is an Australian masterpiece about transportation and the penal system.

The library's collection of more than a million books and other reference material is notable for its coverage of the humanities and social sciences, as well as art, music, performing arts, Australiana and rare books dating back to a 4000-year-old Mesopotamian tablet. The collection also includes the records from the Burke & Wills expedition, and various interesting items are periodically displayed in glass cabinets.

This same building also houses the National Museum of Victoria.

National Museum of Victoria

The National Museum of Victoria (Map 1), housed in the State Library building on the corner of Swanston and Latrobe Sts, is bursting at the seams with a massive collection of over 12 million items, gathered since it was founded as the Museum of Natural History in 1854. Only a small (but fascinating) proportion of the museum's collection is on display.

The museum is due to close in mid to late 1997 to allow staff the chance to move all these items to the museum's new home in the Carlton Gardens. The museum should reopen in the new premises early in the year 2000.

Collins St

Collins St (Map 1) is Melbourne's most elegant street-scape, although much of its original grandeur and history was lost during short-sighted periods of 'development'. Collins St has a fashionable end and a financial end. The west end (from Elizabeth St) is home to bankers and stockbrokers, while the east or top end is mostly five-star hotels and exclusive boutiques. The top end was once known as the 'Paris End' because it was lined with plane trees, grand buildings and street cafes. The trees remain (and are beautifully lit at night by fairy lights), but many of the finer buildings are gone.

The top end of Collins St is the place to be if you're weighed down by too much money – there's an assortment of very expensive boutiques, specialist shops and galleries that will be more than happy to lighten your load.

In between Russell and Swanston Sts are two of Melbourne's most historic churches, **Scots Church** (1873), at No 140, the exterior of which has recently been cleaned, and the adjacent **St Michael's Church** (1866). **Kay Craddock's Antiquarian Bookshop** at No 156 is a marvellous place for book lovers. The **Athenaeum Theatre**, at No 188, dates back to 1886 and was recently refurbished. There's a general library on the 1st floor which is open to the public. Across the road is the **Regent Theatre**, which sat slowly decaying for years, but after a major restoration project the theatre re-opened in late 1996 to host Melbourne's run of the musical *Sunset Boulevard*. The theatre will be a venue for both theatre and film. The Plaza Ballroom lies beneath the theatre.

Just across Swanston St, the **Sportsgirl Centre** is one of the city's best shopping centres, with a spacious, well-planned layout and an excellent food court on the 3rd floor.

The section of Collins St between Swanston and Elizabeth Sts contains some interesting examples for students of 1930s architecture, a period in which the emphasis lay more on facades and external ornamentation than on integrated design. Some of the better buildings are the former **Wertheim's Lyric House**, at No 248, **Kodak House**, at No 252, and **Newspaper House**, at No 247 – an 1880s warehouse which received a new facade in 1932.

The **Block Arcade**, which runs between Collins and Elizabeth Sts, was built in 1890 and is a beautifully intact 19th-century shopping arcade. Its design was inspired by the Galleria Vittorio in Milan and features intricate mosaic tiled floors, marble columns, Victorian window surrounds and the magnificently detailed plasterwork of the upper walls. The arcade has been fully restored, and houses some exclusive specialist shops selling things like lingerie, crystal and glass, and designer clothing. Taking tea in the old-fashioned **Hopetoun Tearooms** is an elegant step back in time.

The financial sector begins across Elizabeth St, but this area isn't all banks and brokers. **Henry Buck's**, at No 320, is a gentlemen's outfitter of distinction and a great place if you're in the market for classic menswear, and at No 338, **Hardy Brothers** is one of Australia's most famous jewellers.

The financial sector also has some of Melbourne's best-preserved old buildings. The original facade of the **CBA Bank building** at No 333 was one of the most extreme examples of classicism of its time, but unfortunately the bank decided to 'update' its image in 1939, and the new facade represents the austerity of between-the-wars architecture. The interior is another matter, and you can wander inside to enjoy the restored magnificence of the domed foyer.

The three buildings on the corner of Collins and Queen Sts are fine examples of the extravagance of late Victorian architecture during Melbourne's land boom period, and you should wander into all three chambers and feast your eyes. The **Gothic Bank** is at No 376, the former **National Mutual Life building** at No 395 and the former **Bank of Australasia** at No 396.

The block between William and King Sts provides a striking contrast between the old and the new. The Gothic facade of the three **Olderfleet buildings**, at No 471-477, has been well preserved, and **Le Meridien Hotel**, at No 497, is an imaginative five-star hotel behind the facades of two marvellous old Venetian Gothic buildings, with the original cobbled laneway between them covered as an internal atrium. These older buildings are dwarfed by the soaring Rialto Towers, Melbourne's tallest office building. The semi-reflective glass exterior looks stunningly different under varying light – it's something of a city Ayers Rock. See the following section on the Rialto's Observation Deck.

At the **Stock Exchange** building, at No 530, you can wander through the impressive central foyer and check out the glass-fronted lifts running up the outside of the atrium. Since the computerisation of the exchange there's not much to see in the public gallery apart from a big screen and some public terminals.

Rialto Towers Observation Deck

This popular lookout is on the 55th floor of Melbourne's tallest building, the Rialto Towers (Map 1) on Collins St. The lookout platform offers spectacular 360° views of Melbourne's surrounds, and there's a cafe if you want to linger. It's open daily from 11 am to 11.30 pm; entry costs $6, or $8 if you want to watch a 20-minute film on the development of Melbourne.

Bourke St

The area in and around the centre of Bourke St (Map 1) is the shopping heart of the city, and the mall section between Swanston Walk and Elizabeth St is closed to traffic – like Swanston Walk, pedestrians share the Bourke St Mall with trams (share and beware!).

The north side of the mall is dominated by the frontages of the Myer and David Jones department stores, and the tower-topped **GPO** on the corner of Elizabeth St. This elaborate and elegant building was built in stages, and if you look closely at the designs on the columns, you'll see that the three levels feature the classical Doric, Ionic and Corinthian forms respectively. On the other side of the mall, the **Royal Arcade** is lined with souvenir, travel, food and jewellery shops, but if you look up you'll see the fine detail of the original 19th-century arcade. At the Little Collins St end, the tall figures of **Gog & Magog** stand guard. These mythological giants were modelled on the original figures in London's Guildhall, and have been striking the hour on the clock here since 1892.

The east end of the street beyond the mall has some great cafes and restaurants, interesting book and music shops, mainstream cinemas and more fashion boutiques.

Spring St

Standing at the eastern end of Collins St beside the Treasury Gardens, the **Old Treasury Building** (Map 1) is appropriately solid and imposing. It was built in 1858 with huge basement vaults to store much of the £200 million worth of gold that came from the Victorian goldfields, and was designed by the 19-year-old government draftsman JJ Clark, who went on to become one of the city's finest architects. See the earlier Walking Tour section for details of exhibitions here.

At 103 Spring St, between Bourke and Little Collins Sts, the **Windsor Hotel** is a marvellous reminder of the 19th-century era. Built in 1883, it was extensively restored during the 1980s and is the city's grandest historic hotel. A visit to the Windsor should be on every traveller's agenda.

Opposite, the **Parliament House of Victoria** building was started in 1856, when the two main chambers, the Lower House (Legislative Assembly/House of Representatives) and the Upper House (Legislative Council/Senate), were built. The library was built in 1860, Queen's Hall in 1879, and the original plans also included a dome over the entrance. The dome is still on the drawing board, and the side facades were never completed to plan. Despite being incomplete, this structure is still the city's most impressive public building. Australia's first federal Parliament sat here from 1901 before moving to Canberra in 1927.

The interiors are superb and well worth seeing – free half-hour tours through both houses and the library are given when Parliament is in recess, every weekday at 10 and 11 am, noon and 2, 3 and 3.45 pm. Ask about the story behind the second ceremonial mace that went missing from the Lower House in 1891 – rumour has it that it ended up in a brothel! The tour guide points out

RICHARD NEBESKY

Old and new – the Olderfleet buildings dwarfed by Rialto
Towers, Collins Street.

some fascinating design aspects and explains the symbolism underlining many of the ornamentations. Another way to see the houses is to visit when Parliament is sitting. The public galleries of both houses are open to the public – phone ☎ 9651 8568 to find out when Parliament is in session.

The small and pretty **gardens** behind Parliament House are open to the public, as are the **Parliament Gardens** to the north. The steps of Parliament House give great views of Bourke St, the Windsor Hotel and the elaborate facade of the restored **Princess Theatre**.

At the top of Spring St, the building of the **Royal Australasian College of Surgeons** stands alone, a marvellous and restrained example of 1930s architecture, which is unfortunately not open to the public.

Chinatown

Little Bourke St (Map 1) has been the centre for Chinese people in Melbourne since the days of the gold rush. It's a fascinating walk along the section from Spring St to Swanston St.

This is the only area of continuous Chinese settlement in the country, as well as one of Melbourne's most intact 19th-century streetscapes. In the 1850s, the Chinese set up their shops alongside brothels, opium dens, boarding houses and herbalists, but nowadays it's mainly restaurants and discount traders.

The **Po Hong Trading Company**, on the corner of Cohen Place, is famous for its huge assortment of Chinese nick-nacks. It is housed in the former Chinese Mission Hall, built in 1894 by a Chinese evangelist.

The **Museum of Chinese Australian History** (Map 1), 22 Cohen Place, was established in 1985 to document the history of Chinese people in Australia. The ground-floor gallery has a few artefacts on display and is the home of Dai Loong, the long Chinese dragon who comes out to party on Chinese New Year. The 1st floor displays an audiovisual history and the 2nd floor is an exhibition gallery for the works of Chinese artists. It's open daily from 10 am to 4.30 pm (Saturday from noon); admission is $5 (children $3). The museum also conducts two-hour walking tours around Chinatown every morning, and these cost $15, or $28 including lunch at a Chinatown restaurant. Phone ☎ 9662 2888 for bookings.

There are many well-preserved old buildings and warehouses in Little Bourke St and the narrow cobbled lanes that run off it, and it can be fun just to wander around, especially if you're hungry. Sunday-morning yum cha is very popular with the Chinese, and this is the busiest and most lively time to visit.

Old Melbourne Gaol

This gruesome old gaol and penal museum (Map 1) is at the top end of Russell St. It was built of bluestone in 1841 and was used until 1929. In all, over 100 prisoners were hanged in the jail. It's a dark, dank, spooky place. The museum displays include death masks and histories of noted bushrangers and convicts, Ned Kelly's armour, the very scaffold from which Ned took his fatal plunge and some fascinating records of early 'transported' convicts, indicating just what flimsy excuses could be used to pack people off to Australia's unwelcoming shores. It's an unpleasant reminder of the brutality of Australia's early convict days. It is open from 9.30 am to 4.30 pm daily, and admission is $6.50 (children $3.50, family $18, students $4.50). There are also tours of the gaol on Wednesday and Sunday nights at 8.45 pm, costing $15 for adults, $8 for children – book in advance on ☎ 9663 7228.

Victoria Police Museum

Nearby on Latrobe St, down from the corner of Russell St, the Victoria Police Museum (Map 1) is open on weekdays from 10 am to 4 pm. Entry is free and the museum has a small but interesting collection of police history – old uniforms and caps, communications and fingerprinting equipment, and various displays including one of the four original sets of the Kelly gang's armour.

National Philatelic Centre

The National Philatelic Centre (Map 1) at 321 Exhibition St has an outstanding collection of stamps. It's open daily from 8 am to 5 pm (Saturday from 10 am, Sunday from noon).

Queen Victoria Market

This market (Map 1), on the corner of Victoria and Peel Sts, is equally popular with Melburnians and visitors. The market has been on the site for more than 100 years, and many of the sheds and buildings are registered by the Historic Buildings Council. It's a link with the past, but also a great place to buy just about anything or just wander around and soak up the atmosphere.

See Markets in the Shopping chapter for details of opening hours, and see the boxed aside on Market Tours & Tasting Trips earlier in this chapter for details of walking tours around the market.

Other Historic Buildings

Melbourne is an intriguing blend of the soaring new and the stately old, and a few places manage to combine the two sympathetically. The **Melbourne Central** shopping and office complex (Map 1), on Latrobe St between Elizabeth and Swanston Sts, manages just that. The centrepiece is an old **shot tower**, which was built on the site in 1889. The complex was built around the tower, which is now enclosed in a 20-storey-high cone-shaped glass tower which is worth a visit. When you walk in you'll see lots of people looking up – when you look up, you'll see why.

The city's other historic buildings are too numerous to mention here. However, some of the more notable ones (Map 1) include the **Old Customs House** (1858-70) on Flinders St between William and Market Sts, which dates back to the days when ships sailed up the Yarra as far as the former Queen's Wharf at the end of Queen St; the simple Georgian **John Smith's House** (1848) at 300 Queen St; the massive structure of the **Law Courts** buildings (1874-84) in William St between Little Bourke and Lonsdale Sts; the **Old Royal Mint** (1872) in William St, adjacent to the Flagstaff Gardens; and **St James Old Cathedral** (1842), which was moved to its present site at 419 King St in 1913, and is Melbourne's oldest building.

Victoriana enthusiasts may also find some very small Melbourne buildings of interest – scattered around the city are a number of very fine cast-iron men's urinals (like French *pissoirs*). They mainly date from 1903 to 1914, and the one on the corner of Exhibition and Spring Sts is classified by the National Trust.

SOUTHBANK

South across the river from the city centre, the area known as Southbank (Map 1) is a former industrial wasteland that was brilliantly transformed in the early 1990s by the Southgate development. An arched foot-bridge crosses the Yarra River from behind Flinders St railway station, linking the city centre to the Victorian Arts Centre, the National Gallery and Southgate itself. Parisian-style riverside walks flank the river on both sides, and where you once would have seen bellowing chimney stacks and saw-toothed roofs you'll now see dozens of people happily promenading along the riverside.

The Southgate complex houses three levels of restaurants, cafes and bars, all of which enjoy a marvellous outlook over the city skyline and the river. There's also an international food hall, an upmarket shopping galleria with some interesting speciality boutiques, and a collection of specially commissioned sculptures and other artworks that are well worth seeing. On the ground level is the **Southgate Aquarium**, a 12m-long aquarium suspended from the ceiling by chains; entry costs $3 for adults, $2 for children and $8 for a family.

Behind Southgate is the impressive five-star Sheraton Towers Hotel, as well as several office towers. And, of course, just a hop, skip and a jump away from Southgate

RICHARD I'ANSON

The shot tower inside the glass cone
of Melbourne Central.

are the theatres and galleries of the Arts Precinct. See the Places to Eat chapter for details of Southgate's restaurants.

ARTS PRECINCT

This small area (Map 1), on St Kilda Rd across the Yarra River from Flinders St railway station, makes up the cultural heart of Melbourne. It contains the National Gallery of Victoria, the Concert Hall and theatres of the Victorian Arts Centre, the Victorian College of the Arts, the Malthouse Theatres and the new Southgate complex.

National Gallery of Victoria

The National Gallery of Victoria was the first part of the arts complex to be completed, back in 1968. While the 1960s isn't too many people's favourite period of architecture, the gallery is one of its better examples. The building was designed by Sir Roy Grounds and is constructed from bluestone and concrete. The stark, imposing, fortress-like facade with its moats and fountains has been enlivened by the addition of Deborah Halpern's quirky two-headed and three-legged sculpture *Angel*, which stands in one of the moats looking a bit like a mutated antipodean Loch Ness Monster.

The internationally renowned European section has an impressive collection of the works of European masters including Rembrandt, Picasso, Turner, Monet, Titian, Pissarro and van Dyck. The sculpture courtyard and gallery has some fine works including sculptures by Auguste Rodin and Henry Moore. The gallery also has a good collection of contemporary Aboriginal art, large collections of Chinese art, an excellent photography collection, a display of period costumes, jewellery, prints, ceramics and much more. The gallery's full collection is too large for permanent displays, so many exhibits are featured temporarily.

The fine collection of Australian painters includes the work of the modernists Sir Sidney Nolan, Arthur Boyd, Fred Williams, Albert Tucker and John Perceval, and Australian impressionists including the Heidelberg School's Tom Roberts, Frederick McCubbin, Charles Condor and Arthur Streeton. Female Australian artists represented at the gallery include the impressionists Jane Sutherland and Clara Southern, Margaret Preston and, in contemporary art, Rosalie Gascoigne, Bea Maddock and Janet Davison.

The **Great Hall** is a highlight, and the best way to see its best feature is to lie on your back on the floor. Melbourne artist Leonard French spent five years creating the amazing stained-glass ceiling. The Gallery Shop is a good place to buy souvenirs, posters, books and postcards, and there's also a good restaurant here (see Places to Eat).

The gallery is open daily from 10 am to 5 pm and admission to the general collection is now free. The gallery also regularly features special exhibitions, for which an entry fee of between $6 and $12 is charged (children and students half-price). Note that on Monday only the ground and 1st floors of the gallery are open. Free guided gallery tours are given on weekdays at 11 am, 2 and 3 pm, Saturday at 2 pm and Sunday at 11 am and 2 pm. The 2 pm tour each Thursday focuses on the Aboriginal art collection. Between January 1 and February 2, tours only operate on weekdays at 11 am. (Note that the gallery is due to be renovated shortly. This may mean that it will be closed to the public for some part of 1999.)

Felton Bequest

Some people might think that Melbourne's most famous artist is Felton Bequest. So many of the National Gallery of Victoria's major works carry an acknowledgment to the bloke that after a while, you start to wonder how anybody could be so prolific and gifted. Actually, Alfred Felton was a wealthy businessman who left his fortune to the gallery when he died in 1904, and it was with his money that many of the most important works were purchased. ∎

Victorian Arts Centre

The Victorian Arts Centre is made up of two separate buildings – the Melbourne Concert Hall and the Theatres Building – which are linked to each other and the gallery by a series of landscaped walkways.

The **Melbourne Concert Hall**, the circular building closest to the Yarra, is the main performance venue for major artists and companies, and the base for the Melbourne Symphony Orchestra. The **Theatres Building** is topped by the distinctive spire, underneath which are housed the State Theatre, the Playhouse and the George Fairfax Studio. The stylish interiors of both buildings are quite stunning, and are well worth visiting in their own right, although you should try and see a performance at the centre. Both buildings feature the works of prominent Australian artists, and in the Theatres Building the **Westpac Gallery** and the **Vic Walk Gallery** are free gallery spaces with changing exhibitions of contemporary works.

There are one-hour tours of the complex ($9) at noon and 2.30 pm each weekday and at 10.30 am and noon each Saturday. On Sunday, Backstage Tours (☎ 9281 8000) runs 1½-hour backstage tours ($12) at 12.15 and 2.15 pm.

The **Performing Arts Museum** is at ground level in the Concert Hall building, on the riverside. It's a small space that has changing exhibitions on all aspects of the performing arts – it might be a display of rock musicians' outfits or an exhibit on horror in the theatre. Opening hours are weekdays from 11 am to 5 pm and weekends from noon to 5 pm; admission is $5 ($3.50 for children). Next door is the **Alfred Brash Soundhouse**, a public-access recording studio.

PARKS & GARDENS

Melbourne is surrounded by an array of public parks and gardens, thanks to the foresight of the city's founders.

Royal Botanic Gardens

Certainly the finest botanic gardens in Australia and arguably among the finest in the world, these gardens form one of the best spots in Melbourne (Map 9). There's nothing more genteel than a Devonshire tea by the lake on a Sunday afternoon. The beautifully laid out gardens are right beside the Yarra River; indeed, the river once actually ran right through the gardens, and the lakes are the remains of its curves, cut off when the river was straightened to lessen the annual flood damage.

There's a surprising amount of wildlife in the gardens, including water fowl, ducks, swans, cockatoos, rabbits and possums. A large contingent of fruit bats, usually found in the warmer climes of north Queensland, has taken up residence for the last 10 summers or more – look for them high in the trees of the fern gully.

You can pick up guide-yourself leaflets at the park entrances; these are changed with the seasons and tell you what to look out for at the different times of year. There are various entrance gates around the gardens, but the visitor centre is in the National Herbarium inside Gate F on Birdwood Ave. Free guided tours depart from the visitor centre most days at 10 and 11 am. The gardens are open daily from sunrise to sunset and no admission fee is charged. The tearooms and kiosk beside the lake are open daily from 9 am to 5 pm (4.30 pm in winter).

Kings Domain

The Royal Botanic Gardens form a corner of the Kings Domain (Maps 6 & 9), a park which also contains the Shrine of Remembrance, Governor La Trobe's Cottage and the Sidney Myer Music Bowl. The domain is bordered by St Kilda Rd, Domain Rd, Anderson St and the Yarra River.

The whole park is encircled by the **Tan**, a four-km-long former horse-exercising track, now Melbourne's favourite venue for joggers. The track has an amusing variety of exercise points – a 'mixture of the stations of the Cross and miniature golf', someone once said.

Beside St Kilda Rd stands the massive **Shrine of Remembrance** (Map 9), built as a memorial to Victorians killed in WWI. Its design is partly based on the Temple of Halicarnassus, one of the seven ancient wonders of the world, and it wasn't completed until 1934. The inner crypt is inscribed with the words:

This holy place commemorates Victoria's glorious dead. They gave them all, even life itself, that others may live in freedom and peace. Forget them not.

These words are heeded every Anzac Day, held on 25 April, when a dawn service at the shrine is attended by thousands, and also on Remembrance Day at the 11th hour of the 11th day of the 11th month – the time at which the Armistice of 1918 was declared. At this moment, a shaft of light shines through an opening in the ceiling to

RICHARD I'ANSON

Royal Botanic Gardens

illuminate the Stone of Remembrance. The forecourt, with its cenotaph and eternal flame, was built as a memorial to those who died in WWII, and several other war memorials surround the shrine.

It's worth climbing to the top as there are fine views from the balcony to the city along St Kilda Rd and towards the bay. The shrine is open daily from 10 am to 5 pm.

Across Birdwood Ave from the shrine is **Governor La Trobe's Cottage** (Map 9), the original Victorian government house sent out from the mother country in prefabricated form in 1840. The simple little cottage is open Monday and Wednesday from 10 am to 4 pm, weekends from 11 am to 4 pm, and admission is $4 (children $2, families $10).

The cottage provides a dramatic contrast with the more imposing **Government House** (Map 9) where Victoria's Governor resides. It's a copy of Queen Victoria's palace on England's Isle of Wight, and was built in 1872. There are guided tours on Monday, Wednesday and Saturday for $6 per person – you need to book on ☎ 9836 7246 (no tours from mid-December to the end of January).

On either side of La Trobe's humble cottage are the **Old Melbourne Observatory** (Map 9) and the **National Herbarium** (Map 9). On some nights the Old Observa-

Statues

There are some fine statues throughout the city and its parkland. Many of them commemorate significant figures in the history of Melbourne. These are just a few.

In the forecourt of the National Mutual building, 447 Collins St, stand statues of the two founders of Melbourne, John Pascoe Fawkner and John Batman. Beside St Paul's Cathedral is Charles Gilbert's statue of a young Matthew Flinders, who, during his voyage of 1802-3, became the first person to circumnavigate Australia and chart its coastline. The Burke & Wills Memorial in the City Square was Melbourne's first public monument, erected in 1865 to commemorate the tragic expedition that first crossed the continent from south to north.

A fine statue of the poet and horseman Adam Lindsay Gordon stands opposite the Windsor Hotel in Spring St. Gordon shot himself on Brighton Beach in 1870 after reading a review of his most recent book of poetry. Near the Shrine of Remembrance is the statue of Simpson and his donkey. It was erected in memory of Private John Simpson Kirkpatrick for his bravery during the Allied landing at Gallipoli in WWI when he helped wounded soldiers from the front line. Kirkpatrick was killed less than a month after the landing, aged 22.

The Queen Victoria Monument, in the Queen Victoria Gardens, shows the monarch accompanied by four female figures which represent her birth, marriage, reign and death. ■

tory is open to the public for a free view of the heavens between 8 and 10 pm, but it is usually booked out months in advance. Phone the Museum of Victoria (☎ 9669 9942) for details.

The National Herbarium, just inside the Royal Botanic Gardens, was established by Baron von Mueller in 1853 as a centre for identifying plant specimens. Among other things, the staff test suspected marijuana samples to decide if they really are the dreaded weed.

Across the road from the herbarium, on Dallas Brooks Drive, is the **Australian Centre for Contemporary Art** (Map 9; see Other Art Galleries later). Up at the city end of the park is the **Sidney Myer Music Bowl** (Map 6), a functional outdoor performance area in a natural amphitheatre. It's used for all manner of concerts in the summer months, although of late not rock concerts, due to too much trouble afterwards. In winter it's turned into a skating rink.

The small section of park across St Kilda Rd from the Victorian Arts Centre is the **Queen Victoria Gardens**

(Map 6), containing a memorial statue of the good Queen herself, a statue of Edward VII astride his horse, and a huge floral clock, as well as several more contemporary works of sculpture.

Fitzroy & Treasury Gardens

The leafy Fitzroy Gardens (Map 6) divide the city centre from East Melbourne. With their stately avenues lined with English elms, these gardens are a popular spot for wedding photographers – on Saturday afternoons there's a continuous procession of wedding cars pulling up for the participants to be snapped.

Governor La Trobe's nephew designed the original layout in 1857 which featured paths in the form of the Union Jack. James Sinclair, the first curator, was landscape gardener to the Russian Tsar Nicholas I until the Crimean War cut short his sojourn. Sinclair amended and softened the original design, and the gardens are now a rambling blend of elm and cedar avenues, fern gullies, flower beds and lawns.

In the centre of the gardens are ferneries, fountains and a kiosk. By the kiosk is a miniature **Tudor village** and the **Fairy Tree**, carved in 1932 by the writer Ola Cohn. The painted carvings around the base of the tree depict fairies, pixies, kangaroos, possums and emus.

In the north-west corner of the gardens is the **People's Pathway** – it's a circular path paved with individually engraved bricks and is quite the nicest bit of whimsy in any park in Melbourne.

Captain Cook's Cottage (Map 6) is actually the former Yorkshire home of the distinguished English navigator's parents. It was dismantled, shipped to Melbourne and reconstructed stone by stone in 1934. The cottage is furnished and decorated as it would have been around 1750, complete with handmade furniture and period fittings. There is an interesting exhibit on Cook's life and achievements during his great exploratory

---

Possums

Both the Fitzroy and Treasury gardens have a large resident population of common ring-tail and common brush-tail possums. These possums are fairly tame and are used to being fed by people. The best time to turn up is at dusk, when they come out to feed for a couple of hours (especially in warmer weather), and they have a preference for fruit. ■

voyages of the southern hemisphere. The cottage is open daily from 9 am to 5 pm and admission is $2.50 (children $1.20).

Nearby, the **Conservatory** (Map 6), built in 1928, contains glorious floral displays and a tropical-rainforest atmosphere – well worth the $1 admission.

The smaller Treasury Gardens (Map 6), a popular lunch time and barbecue spot, contain a memorial to John F Kennedy and are the site of the *Herald-Sun* Outdoor Art Show held annually as part of the Moomba Festival.

Other Parks & Gardens

The **Flagstaff Gardens** (Map 1), near the Queen Victoria Market, were first known as Burial Hill – it's where most of the early settlers ended up. As the hill provided one of the best views of the bay, a signalling station was set up here – when a ship was sighted arriving from Britain, a flag was raised on the flagstaff to notify the settlers. Later, a cannon was added and fired when the more important ships arrived, but once newspapers started publishing regular information about shipping, the signalling service became redundant. Free lunch-time concerts are now a frequent feature in the gardens, particularly in warmer weather.

The **Carlton Gardens** (Map 1) surround the historic **Royal Exhibition Building** (☎ 9270 5000), a wonder of the southern hemisphere when it was built for the Great Exhibition of 1880. Later it was used by the Victorian Parliament for 27 years, while the Victorian parliament building was used by the National Legislature until Canberra's parliament building was finally completed. It is still used as a major exhibition centre today, and the building has been restored and is gradually regaining the appreciation it deserves. At night it is brilliantly lit in the same ceremonial manner as at the turn of the century. Ring for details of exhibitions.

ALONG THE YARRA RIVER

Melbourne's prime natural feature, the 'muddy' Yarra River, is the butt of countless jokes but is actually a surprisingly pleasant river. It is slowly but surely becoming more of an attraction as new parks, walks and buildings appear along its banks. Despite being known as 'the river that flows upside down', it's just muddy, not particularly dirty.

This hasn't always been the case. During the gold-rush period, the Yarra River was everything from a water supply to an open drain. Raw sewage was emptied into the river until 1900, and industrial wastes from tanneries, soap works and, later on, chemical companies were dumped into it as well. In recent years efforts have been made to clean up the river and beautify its surrounds, and the result is now looked upon with some pride by Melburnians.

When rowing boats are gliding down it on a sunny day, or you're driving towards the city on a clear night, the Yarra can really look quite magical. There are some beautiful old bridges across the river, and the riverside boulevards provide delightful views of Melbourne by day or night.

As it winds its way into the city, the Yarra River is flanked by tree-lined avenues – Batman Ave along the north bank and Alexandra Ave on the south. Farther east, the Yarra Blvd follows the river in several sections from Richmond to Kew – like the Great Ocean Road, the Yarra Blvd was a relief-work project of the Great Depression.

Boat cruises along the river depart from Princes Walk (below Princes Bridge) and from Southgate. A series of bike paths (see the Bicycle heading in the Getting Around chapter for more details) start from the city and follow the Yarra River, and bikes can be hired from various places. Studley Park Boathouse and Fairfield Park Boathouse are both popular spots where you can hire a canoe and paddle around, enjoy a leisurely Devonshire tea or have a walk beside the river.

Polly Woodside Maritime Museum

The Polly Woodside Maritime Museum is on the riverfront, close to the Spencer St bridge, across the river from the World Trade Centre and adjacent to the Melbourne Exhibition Centre. The *Polly Woodside* is an old iron-hulled three-masted sailing ship. She was built in Belfast in 1885, and spent the first part of her working life carrying coal and nitrate between Europe and South America. She made the rounding of Cape Horn 16 times. She ended her career as a coal hulk, but was bought by the National Trust in the 1970s and restored by volunteers.

The *Polly Woodside* is now the centrepiece of a maritime museum park, and floats proudly in a dry dock in the centre of the park – a 'memorial to a breed of ships and men the world will not see again.' The park has a souvenir shop, kiosk, lighthouse, theatrette, a flying fox, an old pump house, a museum with maritime displays and a workshop where you can watch boat builders at work.

The ship and museum are open every day of the week from 10 am to 4 pm, and admission is $7 for adults and $4 for children.

Yarra Bend Park

North-east of the city centre, the Yarra River is bordered by the Yarra Bend parkland (Maps 4 & 7), much loved by runners, rowers, cyclists, picnickers and strollers. To get there, follow Johnston St through Collingwood and turn into the scenic drive of Yarra Blvd or, better still, hire a bike and ride around the riverside bike paths – a leisurely 40-minute roll. By public transport, take tram No 42 from Collins St east along Victoria St to stop No 28, then walk up Walmer St and over the footbridge; or take bus No 201 or 203 from Flinders St railway station, both of which go up Studley Park Rd.

The park has large areas of natural bushland (not to mention two golf courses, numerous sports grounds and a hospital) and there are some great walks. In parts of Studley Park you could be out in the bush; with the songs of bellbirds ringing through the trees and cockatoos screeching on the banks it's hard to believe the city's all around you. At the end of Boathouse Rd is the **Studley Park Boathouse** (☎ 9853 1972), open daily from 9.30 am to sunset. These timber buildings on the riverbank date back to the 1860s, and you can enjoy a Devonshire tea or a light snack here – there are also boats

RICHARD NEBESKY

Studley Park Boathouse, Yarra River, Kew

and canoes available for hire. Kanes suspension bridge takes you across to the other side of the river, and it's about a 20-minute walk from here to Dights Falls at the confluence of the Yarra River and Merri Creek, with some great views along the way. You can also walk to the falls along the southern riverbank. On the way is the **Pioneer Memorial Cairn**, which commemorates Charles Grimes (the first European to discover the Yarra River, in 1803) and the first settlers to bring cattle from Sydney to Melbourne (in 1836).

Farther around the river, Fairfield Park is the site of the **Fairfield Amphitheatre**, a great open-air venue used for concerts and films among other things.

The **Fairfield Park Boathouse & Tea Gardens** (☎ 9486 1501) on Fairfield Park Drive, Fairfield, is a restored turn-of-the-century boathouse with broad verandahs and an outdoor garden restaurant serving meals like grills, salads, fresh juices, scones and tea. It's open from 9.30 am to 5.30 pm on weekdays and from 9.30 am to sunset on weekends. (From May to September it only opens on weekends.)

YARRA PARK

Yarra Park (Map 6) is the large expanse of parkland to the south-east of the city centre. It contains the Melbourne Cricket Ground, the Melbourne Park National Tennis Centre, Olympic Park and several other sports ovals and open fields. Unfortunately, the park is bisected by the ugly Jolimont Railway Yards – one of Melbourne's most enduring eyesores.

Melbourne Cricket Ground

The Melbourne Cricket Ground (MCG) is the temple in which sports-mad Melburnians worship their heroes and heroines. There are sports stadiums and there are sports stadiums, but the MCG is one of the world's great sporting venues, imbued with an indefinable combination of tradition and atmosphere. The first game of Australian Rules Football was played where the MCG and its car parks now stand in 1858, and in 1877 the first Test cricket match between Australia and England was played here. The MCG was also the central stadium for the 1956 Melbourne Olympics, and in 1992 the Great Southern Stand was opened, providing spectators with a greatly improved standard of facilities.

The Melbourne Cricket Club (MCC), founded in 1838, manages the MCG and in return retains a section of the ground for the exclusive use of its members. The **Members' Pavilion** is the oldest stand and, if you're interested in sports, you can lose hours wandering through the pavilion's creaking corridors of sporting history. Its walls are lined with a collection of fascinating old sporting photos. The pavilion also houses the famous Long Room (members only!) and the MCC Cricket Library & Museum, which has thousands of items of sporting memorabilia, books, records and ancient equipment. The pavilion, library and museum are open on weekdays from 10 am to 4 pm (except on match days) and admission is free. Guided tours are also offered – see following section.

Australian Gallery of Sport & Olympic Museum

In front of the members' entrance to the MCG (near the corner of Jolimont St and Jolimont Terrace) is the Australian Gallery of Sport & Olympic Museum, a museum dedicated to Australia's sporting passions. It has three levels: the foyer and souvenir shop are on the ground floor, the 1st floor houses special exhibitions and topical displays, and the 2nd floor houses the permanent collection with 10 separate sporting sections and the Olympic Museum. It's open from 10 am to 4 pm every day, and the admission – $8 adults, $5 children, $20 families – includes a tour of both the MCG and the museum.

Melbourne Park National Tennis Centre

A footbridge links the Melbourne Park National Tennis Centre (formerly Flinders Park) with the MCG, crossing the Jolimont Railway Yards from the members' car park. Opened in 1988, the centre hosts the Australian Open championship each January, and is also used as a concert venue. The centre court area is covered with a retractable roof. The centre has five indoor and 23 outdoor tennis courts available to the public (see Tennis in the Activities section later).

EAST MELBOURNE

East Melbourne (Map 7) is a small residential pocket of elegant Victorian town houses, mansions and tree-lined avenues. Clarendon, Hotham and Powlett Sts are all

RICHARD I'ANSON

RICHARD I'ANSON

Melbourne Cricket Ground

worth a wander if you're interested in seeing some of Melbourne's most impressive early residential architecture.

Tasma Terrace, in Parliament Place behind Parliament House, is a magnificent row of six attached Victorian terraces. The three-storey terraces were built in 1879 for a grain merchant, a Mr Nipper, and are decorated with enough cast-iron lace to sink a small ship. They also house the office of the **National Trust**, an organisation dedicated to preserving Australia's heritage. It's worth visiting the office – it has a range of information on National Trust properties, and the interior of the reception office is a great example of over-the-top Victoriana. The terrace next door has also been restored, and if you ask nicely they will show you the parlour and sitting room with its original Victorian furniture and artworks. The last terrace houses the **Victorian National Parks Association** (☎ 9650 8296), a lobby group for conservation and the promotion of national parks. They also host regular bushwalks and nature walks in and around Melbourne – ring for details.

St Patrick's Cathedral, placed behind Parliament House in Cathedral Place, is said to be one of the world's finest examples of Gothic Revival architecture. It was designed by William Wardell, begun in 1863 and built in stages until the spires and west portal were added in 1939. The imposing bluestone exterior is floodlit to great effect by night.

Diagonally across Gisborne St from the cathedral is the Eastern Hill Fire Station. The Old Fire Station building on the corner of Gisborne St and Victoria Pde was built in 1891. Its ground floor now houses the **Fire Services Museum of Victoria**, which has an historic collection of fire-fighting equipment – fire engines, helmets, uniforms, medals and photos – and is open on Friday from 9 am to 3 pm and on Sunday from 10 am to 4 pm; admission is $3 (children $1). Facing Albert St, the unattractive facade of the newer building has been brightened up with a mural designed by Harold Freedman, the same bloke responsible for the murals at Spencer St railway station and the Australian Gallery of Sport. The mosaic mural depicts the history and legends of fire.

The **WR Johnston Collection** (☎ 9416 2515) is a private museum of the decorative arts of 18th-century England, displayed in the collector's former home, Fairhall, at 152 Hotham St. Tours are held on weekdays and cost $10 ($5 concessions), and you have to ring in advance to book.

CARLTON & PARKVILLE

Up this end of town you'll find a cosmopolitan area that blends the intellectual with the gastronomic, the sporting with the cultural – and you'll also see some of the city's finest Victorian residential architecture.

These two suburbs are divided by the tree-lined Royal Pde. In Parkville there's Melbourne University and the Royal Melbourne Zoo; in Carlton there's the Melbourne General Cemetery and some great restaurants in the Italian quarter around Lygon, Drummond and Rathdowne Sts.

Royal Park

Royal Park (Map 2), a large expanse of open parkland, contains a number of sports ovals and open spaces, large netball and hockey stadiums, a public golf course and the Royal Melbourne Zoo. In the corner closest to Mel-

bourne University is a garden of Australian native
plants, and a little farther north, just before MacArthur
Rd, a memorial cairn marks the spot from which the
Burke & Wills Expedition set off in 1860 on its fateful
crossing of the interior.

Royal Melbourne Zoo

Melbourne's zoo (Map 2) is one of the city's most
popular attractions, and deservedly so. Established in
1861, this is the oldest zoo in Australia and the third
oldest in the world. In the 1850s, when Australia was
considered to be a foreign place full of strange trees and
animals, the Acclimatisation Society was formed for 'the
introduction, acclimatisation and domestication of all
innoxious animals, birds, fishes, insects and vegetables'.
The society merged with the Zoological Society in 1861,
and together they established the zoo on its present site.

Set in spacious and attractively landscaped gardens,
with broad strolling paths leading from place to place,
the zoo's enclosures are simulations of the animals'
natural habitats. The walkways pass through the enclosures – you walk through the bird aviary, cross a bridge
over the lions' park, enter a tropical hothouse full of
colourful butterflies and walk around the gorillas' very
own rainforest. There's also a large collection of native
animals in a native bush setting, a platypus aquarium,
fur seals, lions and tigers, plenty of reptiles and lots more
to see. You should allow at least half a day. There's also
a good selection of not-too-tacky souvenirs, as well as
quite a few snack bars and two bistros.

The zoo is open daily from 9 am to 5 pm; admission
is $12.60 adults, $9.50 concessions, $6.30 children and
$34.50 for families. (During January and February, the
zoo stays open from Thursday to Sunday until 7 pm,
then jazz bands play until around 9 pm – see Jazz & Blues
in the Entertainment chapter for details.) To get to the
zoo from the city, take tram No 55 or 56 from William St,
or an Upfield-line train to Royal Park railway station (no
trains on Sunday!).

Melbourne University

Melbourne University (Map 2) is well worth a visit. The
university was established in 1853, and a wander around
the campus will reveal an intriguing blend of original
Gothic-style stone buildings and some incredibly
unattractive brick blocks from more recent, less noteworthy 'functionalist' periods of architecture. The

college buildings, to the north of the campus, are particularly noteworthy for their fine architecture.

The grounds are sprinkled with open lawns and garden areas and, during term, there's always something going on. There are often bands playing in North Court (behind Union House), or you could sit in on a lecture, go book browsing in the Baillieu Library, inspect the rare plants in the System Garden (between the Botany and Agriculture & Forestry buildings) or visit one of several free galleries and museums.

The **Sir Ian Potter Gallery**, in the Physics building on the corner of Swanston St and Tin Alley, features contemporary exhibitions and opens Wednesday to Saturday from noon to 5 pm (closed in January). The **University Gallery** in the former Physics building has a small but interesting collection of Australian art, and is open at the same times. On the Royal Pde side (next to the Conservatory of Music), the **Percy Grainger Museum** is dedicated to the life and times of Percy Grainger (1882-1961), an eccentric composer who lived an extraordinary life and travelled the world collecting and recording folk music on an old Edison recording machine. Grainger set up the museum before his death, and it contains his collections, instruments, photos, costumes and other interesting personal effects. The museum is open weekdays from 10 am to 4 pm and admission is free.

Lygon St

Carlton is Melbourne's Italian quarter, and Lygon St (Map 3) its backbone. Many of the thousands of Italian immigrants who came to Melbourne after WWII settled in Carlton, and Lygon St became the focal point of their community. Over the ensuing years, the street has gradually evolved into what is now referred to as Melbourne's Via Veneto.

Lygon St is the most highly 'developed' example of the multicultural evolution of Melbourne's inner suburbs. A fondness lingers for the older, less glamorous version, but as they say, you can't stop progress. The developers moved in and, with their out-with-the-old and in-with-the-new philosophy, gave Lygon St a facelift that didn't necessarily improve its looks. Lygon St lost its offbeat appeal and the bohemian element moved on to Brunswick St, Fitzroy and beyond.

But not all of the old Lygon St was lost. In among the tourist restaurants and exclusive fashion boutiques, you'll still find a few of the oldies: Readings Bookstore is still there, albeit in a new shop; places like Tiamo, Papa Cino's and Jimmy Watson's have resisted the winds of

MARK ARMSTRONG

Strolling down Lygon Street, Carlton.

change; you can still see art-house films at the Carlton Movie House (the 'bug house') or play pool at Johnny's Green Room; and La Mama, the tiny, experimental theatre started by Betty Burstall in 1967 and now run by Liz Jones, is still going strong in Faraday St.

Lygon St is one of Melbourne's liveliest streets. Day and night it is always filled with people promenading, dining, sipping cappuccinos, shopping and generally soaking up the atmosphere. Every November, Lygon St hosts the lively Lygon St Festa, a four-day food-and-fun street party.

Other Attractions

Two attractive and broad tree-lined avenues, **Drummond St** (Map 3) and **Royal Pde** (Map 3), contain outstanding examples of 19th-century residential architecture. Drummond St in particular, from Victoria St to Palmerston St, is one of the most impressive and intact Victorian streetscapes in the city. **Rathdowne St** (Map 3), north of Princes St, has a great little shopping area and some good cafes and restaurants. Head up into North Carlton and Brunswick (Sydney Rd and the top ends of Lygon and Nicholson Sts) to see the less commercial face of this cosmopolitan area.

Princes Park (Map 3), to the north of Melbourne University, has a number of sports grounds including the Carlton Football and Cricket clubs' main ground, as well as a 3.2-km fun-and-fitness exercise circuit. A visit to the **Melbourne General Cemetery**, next to Princes Park, is a sombre reminder that no matter how many laps of the fun-and-fitness circuit you do, you can't avoid the inevitable. The earliest gravestones date back to the 1850s, and the cemetery is a graphic and historic portrait of the wide diversity of countries from which people have come to settle (permanently) in Australia.

FITZROY & COLLINGWOOD

Fitzroy (Map 3) is where Melbourne's bohemian subculture moved to when the lights got too bright in Carlton. It's a great mixture of artistic, seedy, alternative and trendy elements, and one of Melbourne's most interesting suburbs to live in or to visit.

In Melbourne's early years Fitzroy was a prime residential area, and the suburb contains some fine terrace and row houses from the mid-Victorian era, the most notable of which is **Royal Terrace** (1854) on Nicholson St, opposite the Exhibition Building. Later on, the suburb became a high-density working-class stronghold with a large migrant population. The inner-city location and cosmopolitan atmosphere has attracted students, artists and urban lifestylers, creating the lively blend that now exists.

Brunswick St (Map 3) is Fitzroy's and probably Melbourne's most vibrant, extreme and lively street, and you shouldn't visit the city without coming here. This is where you'll find some of the best food, the weirdest shops, the most interesting people, the wildest clothes and the wackiest waiters. In particular, the blocks on either side of the Johnston St intersection have a fascinating collection of young designer and retro clothes shops, bookshops, galleries, nurseries, antique dealers and, of course, more cafes and restaurants than you can poke a fork at. (See the Places to Eat and Shopping chapters later.)

Johnston St is the centre of Melbourne's small but lively Spanish-speaking community, with its tapas bars, the Spanish Club, and several Spanish delicatessens. It also hosts the annual Hispanic Festival every November.

Melbourne's Rock 'n' Roll High School
Back in 1978, Joey Ramone of the Ramones sang:

'I don't care about history,
'cause that's not where I wanna be.
I just wanna have some kicks,
I just wanna get some chicks.
Fun, fun, rock 'n' roll high school...'

In 1990 Melbourne's rock 'n' roll chicks got their own rock 'n' roll high school when Stephanie Bourke decided to start a summer-school for aspiring young female rock stars. From humble beginnings the school has grown to become an icon in Melbourne's music scene and something of a mecca for female musos. Over the years numerous touring international bands have visited the school, including Sonic Youth, who donated guitars and money.

The school itself is an old, red-brick house in the inner-city suburb of Collingwood. The front walls are painted with brightly-coloured murals, and inside there's a cluttered and somewhat chaotic assortment of offices, rehearsal rooms and classrooms. There are more than 250 students 'enrolled' here – mostly female, and mostly studying their various instruments on a casual or part-time basis. The school has been the birthplace of numerous bands, with names like Gritty Kitty, Hecate, Cherry Bombs and Tuff Muff.

On a practical level the school offers music lessons, studio and mixing courses, and band-management, but in a broader sense it also provides young female musicians with a support structure, role models, and a chance to challenge some of the stereotypes that exist about women in the music industry.

The Rock 'n' Roll High School (☎ 9416 1663) is at 186 Easy St in Collingwood – a couple of houses along from where Easy St intersects with Hoddle St. The school offers individual lessons in electric guitar, classical guitar, bass, drums, piano, flute, cello and voice. A 45-minute lesson costs around $15, and lessons are held at rostered times every day. Phone the school for more info. ∎

Smith St forms the border between Fitzroy and Collingwood, and this retail streetscape is reassuringly unpretentious and undeveloped. It's also the home of the Last Laugh Theatre Restaurant (Melbourne's comedy centre), as well as a great assortment of food stores, bookshops, discount stores and good pubs and restaurants.

Head up Brunswick St across Alexandra Pde into **North Fitzroy**, where there are quite a few interesting and quirky shops to explore, more historic buildings, the Edinburgh Gardens and one or two good pubs in which to enjoy an ale. The **Fitzroy Baths** swimming pool, on Alexandra Pde between Brunswick and Smith Sts, is open from November until the end of April.

RICHMOND

As Carlton is to Italy so Richmond (Map 7) is to Greece. This suburb, just to the east of the city centre, is the Greek centre of Melbourne. After Athens and Thessaloniki, Melbourne is said to be the next largest city in terms of Greek population. Richmond is, of course, the best place for a souvlaki in Melbourne! More recently Richmond became the centre for Melbourne's growing Vietnamese community, and colourful **Victoria St** is known as 'Little Saigon'.

The suburb is another centre for Victorian architecture, much of it restored or in the process of restoration. With Richmond's working-class roots, many of the houses are small workers' cottages and terraces, although the Richmond Hill area (between Lennox, Church and Swan Sts and Bridge Rd) has some impressive old mansions.

The **Bridge Rd** and **Swan St** areas form something of a Melbourne fashion centre, with shops where many Australian fashion designers sell their seconds and rejects alongside the outlets of some of Melbourne's best young designers. **Dimmey's** department store at 140 Swan St is an old-fashioned and chaotic wonderland of junk and bargains, and one of the cheapest and most bizarre places to buy just about anything.

Turn the corner from Swan St into Church St to find a shopping experience at the opposite extreme to Dimmey's in terms of price. **Dutton** is half car dealer and half car museum; nothing costs much under $100,000, and price tags over $250,000 for particularly fine examples of Italian exotica are not at all unusual. It even sells racing cars from time to time, if you have an interest in acquiring a rare old Formula One car. Despite the rarefied prices, visitors are quite welcome to wander around and nobody is ever so indiscreet as to offer to give you a trade-in valuation on your old car outside. Just don't kick the tyres. Dutton even has its own cafe – the funky, chrome-clad Cafe Veloce, which serves great coffee, snacks and simple meals.

In the adjacent suburb of Burnley, alongside the Yarra River, you'll find the **Richmond Public Golf Course**, the Burnley Horticultural College and the **Burnley Gardens** off Yarra Blvd, with their lovely lawns, lily ponds and exotic trees.

MARK ARMSTRONG

Streetfront grocery shops in 'Little Saigon' – otherwise known as Victoria St, Richmond.

SOUTH YARRA & TOORAK

South Yarra and Toorak (Map 10) are on what's referred to as the 'right' side of the river – the high-society side of town. South Yarra is a bustling, trendy and very style-conscious suburb – the kind of place where avid readers of *Vogue Living* will feel very much at home. Farther west, Toorak is the poshest suburb in Melbourne and home to Melbourne's wealthiest (or at least the most ostentatious) home-owners. Toorak doesn't hold much interest for travellers, although it can be interesting to drive around the tree-lined streets looking at the palatial homes.

While in South Yarra, visit **Como** at 16 Como Ave, one of Australia's finest colonial mansions (see the boxed aside).

Toorak Rd

Toorak Rd (Map 10) forms the main artery through both suburbs, and is one of Australia's classiest shopping streets, frequented by those well-known Toorak matrons

Historic Houses

Como and Ripponlea, two of Melbourne's most magnificent early homesteads, are open to the public and are well worth a visit. If you're particularly interested in Victoria's heritage, the National Trust publishes a brochure that gives details of other historic properties throughout the state that open to the public.

Como Overlooking the Yarra River from Como Park in South Yarra, Como was built between 1840 and 1859. The home with its extensive grounds has been authentically restored and furnished and is operated by the National Trust. Aboriginal rites and feasts were still held on the banks of the Yarra when the house was first built, and an early occupant writes of seeing a cannibal rite from her bedroom window.

Como is open from 10 am to 5 pm every day and admission is $7 (students $4.50, children $3.50, family $16.50) and you can get there on tram No 8 from the city – get off at stop 30 on Toorak Rd and walk down Como Ave.

Ripponlea Ripponlea is at 192 Hotham St in Elsternwick, close to St Kilda. It's another fine old mansion with elegant gardens inhabited by peacocks. Ripponlea is open from 10 am to 5 pm daily and admission costs are $8 adults, $5 students, $4 children and $18.50 for families. The tearooms are open between 11 am and 4 pm on weekends only. The easiest way to get there is to take a Sandringham-line train to Ripponlea Station, from which you'll have a five-minute walk to the property.

Labassa Labassa (☎ 9527 3891), at 2 Manor Grove in Caulfield, is an elaborate French Renaissance-style, two-storey mansion noted for its richly detailed interior. It's well worth seeing, but is only open on the last Sunday of each month from 10.30 am to 4.30 pm – ring for details. ■

RICHARD NEBESKY

Como House

in their Porsches, Mercedes Benzes and Range Rovers (known as 'Toorak Tractors').

The main shopping area in South Yarra is along Toorak Rd between Punt Rd and Chapel St. Along here you'll find dozens of exclusive boutiques and specialist shops, cafes and restaurants, some great bookshops, such as Black Mask, Readings and Martin's, and the Longford Cinema.

The **Como Centre**, on the corner of Toorak Rd and Chapel St, is a sleek and stylish commercial development which houses upmarket boutiques and shops, offices, cafes, the Como Cinemas and the five-star Como Hotel.

At the St Kilda Rd end of Toorak Rd stands the copper-domed **Hebrew Synagogue**, built in 1930. On the south side of Toorak Rd between Punt Rd and St Kilda Rd is **Fawkner Park**, an attractive and spacious park with large expanses of grass, tree-lined paths, tennis courts and various sports ovals. It's a great spot for a stroll or a picnic or perhaps a kick of a football.

At the Toorak end of Toorak Rd is the smaller and more exclusive group of shops and arcades known as the **Village**, between Wallace Ave and Grange Rd. The Village is the local convenience shopping area for some of Melbourne's wealthiest citizens – don't expect any bargains, but this is a great spot for window-shopping and people-watching. If you want to see how and where Melbourne's moneyed classes live, go for a drive through streets like St Georges Rd and Grange Rd – you'll see some of the biggest mansions in the country.

Chapel St

Chapel St (Map 10) is one of Melbourne's major and most diverse retail centres. The South Yarra end, between Toorak Rd and Commercial Rd, is probably Melbourne's trendiest and most stylish centre for retail fashion, and is virtually wall-to-wall clothing boutiques (with a sprinkling of hip bars and cafes). If you want to see fashion, this is where you'll see it – in the shop windows, sitting outside the cafes and walking the street.

The **Jam Factory** at No 500 is a large shopping and entertainment complex that has recently been redeveloped in a glitzy, somewhat controversial 'Hollywood-meets-Disneyland' style. It's fairly over the top, but contains a wide range of speciality stores, an eight-screen cinema complex, and plenty of bars and restaurants.

PRAHRAN

Prahran (Maps 9 & 10), surrounded by its more affluent neighbouring suburbs of South Yarra, Toorak and Armadale, is a blend of small Victorian workers' cottages, narrow, leafy streets and high-rise, government-subsidised flats for low-income earners. This area is populated by people from a broad range of ethnic backgrounds and is enlivened by a variety of cultural influences.

It has some lively streets, the most notable being Chapel St. Prahran's sector of Chapel St stretches from Malvern Rd (the eastbound continuation of Commercial Rd and the border between Prahran and South Yarra) down to Dandenong Rd, and is more diverse and less fashion-conscious than the South Yarra sector. The delightful **Prahran Market** is just around the corner from Chapel St on Commercial Rd (see Markets in the Shopping chapter).

Commercial Rd (Map 9) is something of a focal centre for Melbourne's gay and lesbian community, and has a diverse collection of nightclubs, bars, pubs, bookshops and cafes.

Malvern Rd (Map 10) is another interesting shopping precinct, with a large number of antique shops and quite a few second-hand and bric-a-brac shops, clothes boutiques, nurseries and other hidden gems along its length. In Essex St (off Malvern Rd) is the **Prahran Pool**, and beside the pool is the popular **Skatebowl**, a council-run skateboarding centre with a large concrete bowl and metal ramp.

Running off Chapel St beside the Prahran Town Hall, **Greville St** (Map 9) has a quirky collection of offbeat retro/grunge clothing shops, galleries, bookstores, junk shops and some good bars and cafes – well worth checking out.

See the Shopping chapter later for more details on Prahran's shops and markets.

ST KILDA

St Kilda (Map 11) is one of Melbourne's liveliest and most cosmopolitan areas, a fact jointly attributable to its seaside location and its chequered history.

In Melbourne's early days, St Kilda was something of a seaside resort, the fashionable spot for those wanting to escape the increasingly grimy and crowded city. Horse trams, and later cable trams, ran along St Kilda Rd carrying day-trippers, and by 1857 the railway line to St Kilda was completed. During the gold-rush period, many of the wealthier citizens built mansions in St Kilda, and Fitzroy St became one of the city's most gracious boulevards. Hotels were built, dance halls opened, sea baths and fun parks catered for the crowds, and St Kilda was *the* place to go in search of fun and entertainment.

As things became more hectic, the wealthy folk moved on to the more exclusive areas like Toorak. With the economic collapse of the 1890s, St Kilda's status began to decline. Flats were built and the mansions were demolished or divided up, and by the 1960s and 1970s, St Kilda had a reputation as a seedy centre for drugs and prostitution. Its decadent image of faded glories (and cheap rents) attracted a diverse mixture of immigrants and refugees, bohemians and down-and-outers.

In recent years, St Kilda has undergone an image upgrade. It has returned to the forefront of Melbourne's fashionable suburbs, the place it occupied more than a century ago, but with a few characteristic differences. Its appeal is now a mix of the old and the rejuvenated, the ethnic and the artistic, the stylish and the casual. St Kilda is a place of extremes – backpackers' hostels and fine-dine restaurants, classy cafes and cheap takeaways, seaside strolls and Sunday traffic jams. Despite its improved image, however, some elements of its seedy past remain, and it can still be somewhat perilous to wander the streets late at night, particularly for women.

Of interest is an historic **Corroboree Tree**, a 350-year-old Aboriginal ceremonial tree located between the Junction Oval and the intersection of Queens Rd and St Kilda Rd. The **St Kilda Botanical Gardens** were first planted in 1859 and have recently been upgraded and improved, and feature a new garden conservatory and the Alister Clarke Memorial Garden (a bed of roses). The gardens are tucked away off Blessington St, not far from the bottom end of Acland St, and are well worth searching out.

The *St Kilda Heritage Walk* brochure, with 22 historic points of interest, is available from the town hall on the corner of St Kilda Rd and Carlisle St. The walk concentrates on the foreshore and Esplanade area, although another interesting walk is to explore the St Kilda Hill area where some of the oldest and grandest buildings remain.

The **National Theatre** (☎ 9534 0221), a great old theatre on the corner of Barkly and Carlisle Sts, houses a ballet and drama school and stages a wide variety of productions – ring to find out what's on.

If you follow **Carlisle St** across St Kilda Rd and into St Kilda East, you'll find some great Jewish food shops, bakeries and European delicatessens. Carlisle St is

RICHARD NEBESKY

KRZYSZTOF DYDYNSKI

The Big Dipper and entrance to Luna Park, St Kilda.

much less trendy than the bayside areas, and the shops generally less expensive.

The **Jewish Museum of Australia**, at 26 Alma Rd, houses displays relating to Jewish history and culture, as well as hosting regular exhibitions. It's open Tuesday, Wednesday and Thursday from 10 am to 4 pm and Sunday from 11 am to 5 pm; entry costs $5/3.

The **St Kilda Festival**, held on the second weekend in February, is a great showcase for local artists, musicians and writers, and features street parties, parades, concerts, readings and lots more. Acland St is closed to traffic and filled with food stalls and entertainment, and in Fitzroy St all the restaurants bring their tables out onto the footpath. The finale of the festival and the weekend is a music concert and fireworks display over the beach.

Fitzroy St

Originally a proud and stylish boulevard, Fitzroy St followed St Kilda's turn-of-the-century decline and became a seedy strip of ill repute. Today, however, Fitzroy St is at the leading edge of St Kilda's revival and has been given new life by the opening of a growing number of stylish new bars, restaurants and cafes. It's now one of Melbourne's hippest and most interesting eating and drinking precincts, and day and night the street is crowded with a fascinating blend of people.

Acland St

Farther south, the section of Acland St between Carlisle and Barkly Sts is famed for its continental cake shops, delicatessens, and central European cafes and restaurants such as Scheherezade. This part of Acland St became the focal centre for the wave of Jewish and European refugees who settled in this area during Hitler's rise to power and after WWII, and their influence and presence remain strong. The older places have been joined by a group of stylish bars and eateries, making Acland St another of Melbourne's favourite food strips. The street also has good book and music shops, fish shops, discount clothing boutiques and gift shops, and on weekends in particular, Acland St is bustling with people who come from everywhere to enjoy the atmosphere.

North of Carlisle St, Acland St is mostly residential all the way to Fitzroy St – with a few exceptions. The grand old two-storey mansion at 26 Acland St has been converted into the **Linden-St Kilda Arts Centre**. Registered by the National Trust, the building houses a contemporary art gallery, artists' studios, workshops and performance spaces. Linden is open daily and admission is free.

At 14 Acland St is the home of the excellent **Theatreworks**, a local fringe theatre group (see Theatre in the Entertainment chapter).

Seaside St Kilda

St Kilda's foreshore has undergone the same rejuvenation as the rest of the suburb. The beaches have been cleaned up, the foreshore parks landscaped and bike paths built. The sight of boats and yachts moored in the lee of the breakwater, the Canary Island palm trees planted along the foreshore and people promenading along the pier are all familiar sights. Two of St Kilda's most popular restaurants are superbly located in converted foreshore buildings: the stylish seafood restaurant The Pavilion was once a bathing pavilion, and The Stokehouse was originally an Edwardian teahouse.

The **St Kilda Pier** and breakwater are a favourite spot for strollers, who often reward themselves with a cappuccino or a snack at Kirby's Kiosk, a restored turn-of-the-century tearoom at the junction of the pier. On weekends and public holidays ferries run from the pier across the bay to Williamstown (see the Getting Around chapter). Bicycles can be hired at the end of the pier in summer. From the pier, you can also take a boat cruise with **Penguin Waters Cruises** (☎ 0412 311 922) to see a local penguin colony. One-hour cruises depart nine times daily, costing $15 by day and $25 at night.

On the foreshore south of the pier, the site of the former **St Kilda Baths** is currently undergoing a major and somewhat controversial redevelopment which will transform St Kilda's foreshore when it is completed – hopefully, for the better. The new complex will house a 25m saltwater swimming pool, treatment baths, spas, a high-tech gym and health centre, shops, cafes, bars and restaurants.

The famous laughing face and twin-towers entrance of **Luna Park** (Map 11), on the Lower Esplanade, has been a symbol of St Kilda since 1912. Luna Park, with its motto 'Just for Fun', is a somewhat dated and old-fashioned amusement park but has some great rides, including the roller coaster, disco swings, Dodgems, a Ferris wheel and ghost train. Admission is free if you want to wander in and look around. Each ride costs $3 for adults, $2 for kids, $1 for infants (three years or younger) and you can buy multiple-ticket booklets at discounted prices. The opening times vary; ring the

RICHARD NEBESKY

The Esplanade Hotel, St Kilda

recorded information number (☎ 1902 240 112) for details.

The **Palais Theatre** across the road was built in 1927. At the time it was one of the largest and best picture palaces in Australia, seating over 3000, and it's still a great venue for a wide variety of live performances.

Built in 1880, the marvellous **Esplanade Hotel** on the Upper Esplanade is the musical and artistic heart and soul of St Kilda, and perhaps the best-known pub in Melbourne. The actress Sarah Bernhardt stayed here back in 1891. Today the 'Espy' is much loved by St Kilda's locals, with its free live bands, comedy nights, great food and a uniquely grungy atmosphere, but due to its prime location and run-down state its future is constantly being threatened by developers who want to 'redevelop' it (ie, renovate it so it looks like every other renovated pub in town). See the Places to Eat and Entertainment chapters for more details on the Espy.

The **Esplanade Art & Craft Market**, every Sunday along the Upper Esplanade, features a huge range of open-air stalls selling a great variety of arts, crafts, gifts and souvenirs.

PORT MELBOURNE

Port Melbourne (Map 8), often simply called Port, has to some degree avoided the gentrification which has swept the inner suburbs, and retains more of its working-class roots than other areas close to the city. It still has a few factories and semi-industrial areas, but many of its small Victorian workers' cottages have been restored by the new breed of inner-city dwellers. The areas closest to the bay are currently undergoing a major transformation, with old factory sites being converted into hip new residential developments and a string of apartment buildings being built near Station Pier.

Port's main street is **Bay St**, which is the continuation of City Rd and runs down to the bay. Many of its historic verandah-fronted terrace buildings have been restored and revamped. Bay St is full of heritage character and has a 'village' feel about it – there's a good range of shops and some great pubs.

Station Pier is Melbourne's major passenger shipping terminal and the departure point for ferries to Tasmania. It also has good views of the city and a couple of old-fashioned kiosks.

SOUTH MELBOURNE

South Melbourne (Maps 8 & 9) had humble beginnings as a shanty town of canvas and bark huts on the swampy lands south of the Yarra. The area was originally called Emerald Hill, after the grassy knoll of high ground that stood above the muddy flatlands. Nowadays, South Melbourne is an interesting inner-city suburb with a rich architectural and cultural heritage and quite a few sights worth seeing.

Clarendon St is the main street. It runs through the heart of South Melbourne from Spencer St in the city to Albert Park Lake. In the central shopping section, many of the original Victorian shopfronts have been restored and refitted with their verandahs, and you'll find all sorts of shops and quite a few pubs (the survivors from the days when the area boasted a pub on every corner).

Emerald Hill, between Clarendon, Park, Cecil and Dorcas Sts, was the first area built on and is now a heritage conservation area, with some fine old mansions and terrace houses, and the impressive **South Melbourne Town Hall** on Bank St, which has been restored. The **South Melbourne Market**, which dates back to 1867, is on the corner of Cecil and Coventry Sts (see Markets in the Shopping chapter).

The **Victorian Tapestry Workshop** (Map 9; ☎ 9699 1494), at 260 Park St, produces large-scale tapestries which are the collaborative work of skilled weavers and contemporary artists. At the workshop you'll be able to see the creation of 'one of Western civilisation's oldest and richest art forms', and some pieces are available for sale. The workshop is open to the public on weekdays from 10 am to 4 pm ($3), and tours are given every

Wednesday and Thursday at 2 and 2.30 pm ($5). You need to ring and book a tour.

The **Chinese Joss House** (Map 9) (1856), 76 Raglan St, is said to be one of the finest Chinese temples outside China. It was built by the Sze Yup Society as a place of worship for the Chinese who came during the gold rush, and is open daily except Friday from 9 am to 4 pm.

At 399 Coventry St, a set of three **portable iron houses** (Map 8), which were prefabricated in England and erected here during the heady gold-rush days of 1853, have been preserved by the National Trust. Many early colonial dwellings were prefabs, and these are some of the few remaining examples. The houses are open to the public on Sunday from 1 to 4 pm (2 to 4 pm during daylight savings).

ALBERT PARK

Wedged between South Melbourne and the bay, Albert Park (Maps 8 & 9) is a small 'village' suburb which is populated by an interesting blend of migrants, young families and upwardly mobile types. A large percentage of its Victorian terrace houses and cottages have been renovated and the suburb is a popular spot with beach-goers in summer and cafe-lovers at any time of the year.

On **Bridport St** (Map 8) between Montague and Merton Sts is a small but lively shopping area, with a high proportion of shops in the food or clothing categories. Here you'll find some excellent and stylish cafes and delicatessens, a few exclusive speciality shops and boutiques, and the Avenue Bookstore.

In summer, crowds of sun-lovers flock to Albert Park's beaches, especially those around the **Kerferd Rd Pier** – it's a great spot to observe Aussie beach 'kulcha' in action (Map 8).

The **St Vincent Place** (Map 8) area is worth exploring. The central St Vincent Gardens are beautifully land-scaped and maintained, and surrounded by some of Melbourne's finest Victorian architecture.

Albert Park Lake (Map 9) is a 2.5-km-long artificial lake surrounded by parkland, sports ovals, a golf-course and other recreation areas. The lake circuit is popular with strollers, runners and cyclists, and the sight of dozens of small yachts sailing across the lake on a sunny Saturday is one of Melbourne's trademark images. There are several restaurants and bars around the lake where you can sit and enjoy the views. The road around the lake was used as an international motor-racing circuit in the 1950s, and in March 1996 it became the new venue for the Australian Formula One Grand Prix race.

The staging of this major international event has accelerated the plans to redevelop and modify the park and its facilities. A new golf-driving range has opened in the north-west corner of the park (off Canterbury Rd), and the old golf course is being extended and upgraded. The new Melbourne Sports & Aquatic Centre, due to open in early to mid-1997, will include Olympic-length swimming and diving pools, and facilities for basketball, table tennis, squash and other sports. The Grand Prix pit buildings will also be used as an indoor sports complex when they are not required for race duties.

BEACHES

Melbourne has some fairly good beaches close to the city, though there's no surf in the bay. The bay is reasonably clean and fine for swimming, although the water tends to look a little murky, especially after high winds and rain.

Starting from the city end, Albert Park, Middle Park and St Kilda are the most popular city beaches. Farther around the bay there's **Elwood**, **Brighton** and **Sandringham**, which are quite pleasant. Next comes **Half Moon Bay** which, for a city beach, is very good indeed, as is **Black Rock** nearby. Beyond here you have to get right around to the Mornington Peninsula before you find some really excellent bay beaches, especially around **Mt Eliza** and **Mt Martha**.

If you want to go surfing or see spectacular and remote ocean beaches, the Mornington Peninsula and Bellarine Peninsula, both a little over an hour's drive from the city, are the places to head for. (See the Excursions chapter.) A drive right around the bay is a good day trip – Portsea and Queenscliff, near the tip of each peninsula respectively, are joined by a ferry service.

WILLIAMSTOWN

Back in 1837, two new townships were laid out simultaneously at the top of Port Phillip Bay – Melbourne as the main settlement, and Williamstown as the seaport. With the advantage of the natural harbour of Hobson's Bay, Williamstown (Map 12) thrived, and government services such as customs and immigration were based here. Many of the early buildings were built from locally quarried bluestone, and the township quickly took on an air of solidity and permanence.

When the Yarra River was deepened and the Port of Melbourne developed in the 1880s, Williamstown became a secondary port. Tucked away in a corner of the bay, it was bypassed and forgotten for years.

In the last decade or so Williamstown, or Willy as it's often called, has been rediscovered and is experiencing a renaissance, especially on weekends when crowds of day-trippers take ferry rides across the bay and promenade along the foreshore soaking up the historic seaside atmosphere.

Nelson Place, which follows the foreshore and winds around the docklands and shipyards, was patriotically named after the British Navy's Admiral Horatio Nelson, famous for his victory in 1805 over the combined French and Spanish fleets in the Battle of Trafalgar. Nelson Place is lined with historic buildings, many of them registered by the National Trust, while the yacht clubs, marinas, boat builders and chandleries along the waterfront all add to the maritime flavour. Williamstown's other attractions include restaurants and cafes, some good pubs and bars, art and craft galleries and interesting speciality shops.

There's a small **Tourist Information Booth** on Nelson Place, which opens on Monday, Friday and Saturday from 11 am to 4 pm and Sunday from 10 am to 4 pm. Between Nelson Place and the waterfront is **Commonwealth Reserve**, a small park where a **craft market** is held on the first and third Sunday of each month. It's also the main site for the Williamstown Summer Festival, held over the Australia Day weekend in January.

Moored at Gem Pier is the **HMAS Castlemaine**, a WWII minesweeper that was built at Williamstown in 1941 and has been converted into a maritime museum. It is staffed by volunteers from the Maritime Trust of Australia and contains nautical exhibits and memorabilia, and is open on weekends from noon to 5 pm. Admission is $4 for adults, $2 for children or $10 for a family.

The **Historical Society Museum**, housed in the old Mechanics Institute building (1860) at 5 Electra St, has displays of maritime history, model ships, antique furniture and some strange relics including a spring-loaded fly-disturber. It opens on Sunday from 2 to 5 pm and admission is $2 (children free).

The Australian Railway Historical Society's **Williamstown Railway Museum** is open on weekends and public holidays from noon to 5 pm (also on Wednesday from noon to 4 pm during school holidays). It's a good spot for kids and rail enthusiasts, with a fine collection of old steam locomotives, wagons, carriages and old photos, and mini-steam-train rides for kids. It's part of the Newport Railway Workshops on Champion

Rd in North Williamstown, and admission is $4 for adults, $2 for children.

On the corner of Nelson Place and Syme St, the **Customs Wharf Market & Gallery** houses an interesting collection of arts and crafts and speciality shops: it's open daily from 11 am to 6 pm and entry costs $1. On the corner of Osborne and Giffard Sts, the small but lovely **Williamstown Botanic Gardens** are also worth a visit.

North along the Strand at **Parson's Marina**, Williamstown Boat Hire (☎ 9397 7312) hires out boats for fishing and cruising, costing around $25 an hour (with a two-hour minimum). It also hires tackle and sells bait. You can also hire in-line skates from Apache Junction (☎ 9397 6555) at 20 Ferguson St.

The excellent Scienceworks Museum is just north of Williamstown in Spotswood (see Other Museums later).

Getting There & Away

From the city, Williamstown is about a 10-minute drive across the West Gate Bridge, or a short train ride (take either a Williamstown line train or a Werribee line train and change at Newport). You can also get there on the double-decker City Wanderer tour bus (see Organised Tours in the Getting Around chapter), and ferries link Williamstown with St Kilda and the city centre (see the Getting Around chapter).

A good bicycle path follows the foreshore reserve from the Timeball Tower and runs all the way to the West Cate Bridge, passing the Scienceworks Museum. An interesting option for cyclists wanting to get from the city side across to Scienceworks and Williamstown is The Punt (☎ 015 304 470), which ferries cyclists and pedestrians across the Yarra River from under the West Gate Bridge. The Punt operates from Friday to Monday (daily during school holidays) between 10 am and 5 pm and costs $3/5 one way/return.

OTHER ART GALLERIES

Apart from the marvellous collection at the National Gallery, Melbourne has a number of other art galleries open to the public.

At 7 Templestowe Rd in the suburb of Bulleen, the **Museum of Modern Art at Heide** (☎ 9850 1500) is on the site of the former home of John and Sunday Reed, under whose patronage the likes of Sir Sidney Nolan, John Perceval, Albert Tucker and Arthur Boyd created a new movement in the Australian art world. The gallery has an impressive collection of 20th-century Australian art. The sprawling park is an informal combination of native and deciduous trees, with a carefully tended kitchen garden and scattered sculpture gardens running right down to the banks of the Yarra. Known as 'Heide', the museum is open from Tuesday to Friday between 10 am and 5 pm and on weekends between noon and 5 pm. Admission costs $5, children under 12 are free. Heide is signposted off the Eastern Freeway. Otherwise, bus No 203 goes to Bulleen, and the Yarra bike path goes close by.

Montsalvat (☎ 9439 8771) is in Hillcrest Ave in Eltham (26 km north-east of the city), the mud-brick and alternative lifestylers' suburb. This artists' colony was established by Justus Jorgensen in the 1930s when the suburb was all hills and bush. Montsalvat features and sells the works of a variety of artists and craftspeople, and there's an eclectic collection of rustic stone and mud-brick buildings to explore. As well as hosting the Montsalvat Jazz Festival each January and the National Poetry Festival each December, Montsalvat is open daily to visitors from 9 am to 5 pm. Admission costs $5 for adults, $2.50 for children, and it's about a two-km walk from Eltham railway station.

The **Australian Centre for Contemporary Art** (Map 9; ☎ 9654 6422), on Dallas Brooks Drive across the road from the main entrance to the Royal Botanic Gardens, is well worth a visit, with regular exhibitions of cutting-edge contemporary art. It also hosts lectures, screenings and other events, and welcomes visitors. The centre opens Tuesday to Friday from 11 am to 5 pm and weekends from 2 to 5 pm: entry is free.

Other free public galleries include the **Linden-St Kilda Art Gallery** at 26 Acland St in St Kilda, the **Westpac Gallery** at the Victorian Arts Centre, the **RMIT Gallery** in the city, and the **Sir Ian Potter Gallery** and **Griffin Gallery**, both at Melbourne University.

See also the section on Commercial Art Galleries in the Shopping chapter.

OTHER MUSEUMS

The science and technology section of the Museum of Victoria, **Scienceworks**, is at 2 Booker St in Spotswood, under the shadows of the West Gate Bridge (Map 13). It was built on the site of the Spotswood pumping station, Melbourne's first sewage works, and incorporates the historic old buildings. This place has a huge and fascinating array of tactile displays. You can spend hours wandering around inspecting old machines, poking buttons and pulling levers and learning all sorts of weird facts and figures. There's also a separate 'sportsworks' section devoted to the science of sport. Scienceworks is open daily from 10 am to 4.30 pm – it's very popular with school groups and can get pretty crowded. The quietest times are weekday afternoons during school terms and Saturday mornings – Sunday is hectic. Admission costs are $8 adults, $4 kids and concessions, and $20 families. The museum is a 15-minute walk from Spotswood railway station down Hudsons Rd. It's signposted.

The **Jewish Holocaust Museum** (☎ 9528 1985), at 13 Selwyn St in Elsternwick (close to Elsternwick railway station and Ripponlea), is a small but detailed museum with pictorial displays, documents and various items from the Nazi death camps of WWII. It tells a grim story, but one that must be told – the museum guides are survivors from the camps. School groups visit the museum daily, and it's open to the public Monday to

---

Free Melbourne

Experiencing some of the things that Melbourne has to offer needn't cost you anything.

Most of Melbourne's parks and gardens are free to visit, including the Royal Botanic Gardens, St Kilda Botanic Gardens and the System Garden at Melbourne University.

You can take a tour of Parliament House of Victoria, or if you're interested in seeing how the legal system operates you can sit in on a court case (the Law Courts are in William St between Lonsdale and Little Bourke Sts).

There are lots of free art galleries, including the Australian Centre for Contemporary Art and, on Monday, the ground and 1st floors of the National Gallery of Victoria. See the section on Art Galleries in this chapter for details of others.

In the State Library, the municipal libraries or the universities you can go book-browsing and reading; a walk along High St or Malvern Rd in Prahran will give you the chance to do some antique-browsing; or you could try taking a tour of Melbourne's major cathedrals such as St Patrick's or St Paul's.

If you want to do something energetic, you can crew a racing yacht on the weekend (see the Sailing section); or if you want to sample an Australian Rules game, the gates are opened at three-quarter time (around 4 pm) and you can see the last quarter for free.

The Shrine of Remembrance is free and offers good views of the city; a wander through the Melbourne General Cemetery in Carlton provides some interesting genealogical insights; and any of Melbourne's markets are worth a visit, to see what's on offer or just to people-watch. ■

Thursday from 10 am to 2 pm and Sunday from 11 am to 3 pm. There is no entry fee (but donations are accepted).

Schwerkolt's Cottage is on Deep Creek Rd, about 500m from the corner of Maroondah Highway and Deep Creek Rd, Mitcham (about 30 km east of the city). Built in the 1860s and turned into a museum in the late 1960s, the museum has several period-style buildings containing plenty of articles from Melbourne's past. It's open on weekends and public holidays, and admission is $2 ($1.50 for children).

At 174-180 Smith St in Collingwood, the **Australian Toy Museum** opens daily from 10 am. Out at Moorabbin airport in Cheltenham, the **Moorabbin Air Museum** has a collection of old aircraft, including a number from WWII. It's open daily from 10 am to 5 pm.

The **Victoria Racing Museum** at Caulfield Racecourse has a collection of horse-racing memorabilia, and opens Tuesday and Thursday from 10 am to 4 pm and race days from 11 am to 4.30 pm.

The **Living Museum of the West**, set in the wetlands and parkland of **Pipemakers Park** in Maribyrnong, is a unique 'eco-museum' with display boards and photos documenting the heritage of the western suburbs. You can cruise up the Maribyrnong River to the museum – see the River Cruises section in the Getting Around chapter.

ACTIVITIES

In-Line Skating

In-line skating (also known as Rollerblading, although Rollerblade is a brand name) is booming in Melbourne, and the best tracks are those around Port Phillip Bay from Port Melbourne to Brighton. You can hire gear for around $8 an hour or $20 a day from places like Rock 'n' Roll 'n' Skate Hire (☎ 9525 3434) at 11 Fitzroy St in St Kilda, Apache Junction Skate Hire (☎ 9534 4006) at 16 Marine Pde, also in St Kilda, and Albert Park In-Line Skates (☎ 9645 9099) at 185 Victoria Ave in Albert Park.

Canoeing

The Yarra River offers canoeists a variety of water from tranquil, flat stretches to rapids of about grade three (classified difficult and requiring some paddling technique). The best sections of river are in the upper reaches from Warburton to the lower reaches of Fitzsimons Lane,

Templestowe. The lower reaches are still scenic, offering respite from the city, but consist mostly of flat water.

Popular sections for those in kayaks and Canadians (open canoes) are Homestead to Wittons Reserve, Pound Bend including the tunnel (medium-water level and experienced paddlers only) and Fitzsimons Lane to Finns Reserve in Templestowe. In the lower reaches there's a canoe recreation area around Dights Falls.

The pamphlet *Canoeing the Upper Yarra*, provided free by the Upper Yarra Valley & Dandenong Ranges Authority (☎ 5967 5222), gives all the do's and don'ts, locations and information on essential safety equipment. You should observe warning signs and water-level gauges. The YHA also organises canoeing trips.

For more sedate canoeing in the city, see the section earlier on Yarra Bend Park.

Cycling

See the Bicycle heading in the Getting Around chapter for details on cycling in Melbourne.

Fishing & Boating

You can fish in the Yarra and Maribyrnong rivers, but you're better off heading down to the bay and hooking a few snappers or flatties. Try the Port Melbourne, Albert Park and St Kilda piers. Tackle shops like the Compleat Angler, at 19 McKillop St in the city, are good places for advice.

Boats can be hired for fishing on the bay, but the conditions can be deceptively treacherous – don't go out unless you're sure of the weather. Try Williamstown Boat Hire (☎ 9397 7312) at Parson's Marina in Williamstown – the same people operate Southgate Boat Hire, with motor boats for cruising along the Yarra River. Another good boatshed is the long-established Keefers Boat Hire (☎ 9589 3917) in Beaumaris, about a half-hour's drive south-east from the city.

Canoes and boats can be hired along the Yarra River – see the Yarra Bend Park section earlier for details.

Golf

Melbourne's sandbelt courses such as Royal Melbourne, Victoria, Huntingdale and Kingston Heath are world famous. It is tough to get a round at these members' courses, but there are also plenty of public courses where anyone can play. You will need to book on weekends. Green fees cost around $15 for 18 holes, and most courses have clubs and buggies for hire. Some good public courses close to town include Royal Park (☎ 9387 1326) in Parkville near the zoo, Yarra Bend (☎ 9482 2344) in Fairfield, Albert Park (☎ 9510 5588) next to Albert Park Lake and Elsternwick Park (☎ 9531 3200) in Elwood. Yarra Bend is the best of these.

Ice Skating

Every year from April until October, the Sidney Myer Music Bowl in Kings Domain next to the Royal Botanic Gardens has an ice-skating rink. Skating costs around $8 an hour. Call ☎ 9281 8360 for details.

Billiards/Pool/Snooker

There are lots of dim, smoky pool venues around town, and some popular places include the following: in the city, King's Pool at 256 King St and Charlton's at 139 Little Bourke St; in Fitzroy, the Cue at 277 Brunswick St and the Red Triangle at 110a Argyle St (off Brunswick St and up *lots* of stairs); in Carlton, Johnny's Green Room at 194 Faraday St and Matt's Blue Room at 769 Nicholson St; in Prahran, the Golden Triangle upstairs at 2 Walker St; in St Kilda, Masters at 150 Barkly St; and in Richmond, the Green Cloth at 110 Swan St.

Running

Melbourne has some great routes for runners. One of the favourites is the Tan track around the Royal Botanic Gardens. The bicycle tracks beside the Yarra and around the bay are also good runs, but watch out for cyclists. Albert Park Lake is another favourite, especially on Saturday when the sailboats are racing.

Melbourne's premier annual running event, the Melbourne Marathon, is held each October. Other major runs include the five-km and 10-km women-only Sussan Classic each March/April, and the eight-km Run to the MCG in April/May. For details of fun runs, check the calendar in the *Australian Runner* magazine or ring them on ☎ 9819 9225.

Sailing

With some 18 yacht clubs around the shores of Port Phillip Bay, yachting is one of Melbourne's most popular passions. Races and regattas are held most weekends, and the bay is a memorable sight when it's sprinkled with hundreds of colourful sails and spinnakers. Conditions can change radically and without warning, making

sailing on the bay a challenging and sometimes dangerous pursuit.

Many of the yacht clubs welcome and encourage
visitors to volunteer to crew on racing boats. Phone the
race secretary at one of the major clubs if you're keen.
The big four are: Royal Melbourne Yacht Squadron (Map
11; ☎ 9534 0227); Royal Brighton Yacht Club (☎ 9592
9589); Sandringham Yacht Club (☎ 9598 7444); and
Hobson's Bay Yacht Club (☎ 9397 6393) in Williamstown. For more leisurely sailing, boats can be hired from
the Jolly Roger School of Sailing (☎ 9690 5862) at Albert
Park Lake.

If you'd rather be a spectator, head down to the Royal
Melbourne (at the end of Fitzroy St in St Kilda) on the
weekends, where you can watch the boats preparing for
races and see them start and finish from out on the
breakwater. Williamstown is also a good spot for spectators.

Melbourne's two main ocean races are the Melbourne
to Devonport and Melbourne to Hobart races, held
annually between Christmas and New Year.

Surfing

The closest surf beaches to Melbourne are on the
Mornington Peninsula and the Bellarine Peninsula (both
about an hour's drive from the city). Bells Beach on the
Great Ocean Road near Torquay is recognised as a
world-class surfing beach.

Swimming

The Melbourne City Baths, on the corner of Swanston
and Victoria Sts, has a 25m indoor pool plus a gym, spas,
saunas and squash courts. The facilities are open from 6
am to 10 pm on weekdays and 8 am to 6 pm on weekends. A swim, spa and sauna costs $6.50.

For serious swimmers, the State Swimming Centre, in
Batman Ave, opens weekdays from 5.30 am to 7 pm and
weekends from 9 am to 3 pm. Other pools close to the
city include the Carlton Baths (outdoor) in Rathdowne
St, the Fitzroy Baths (outdoor) in Alexandra Pde, the
Prahran Pool (outdoor) in Essex St, the Richmond Baths
(indoor) in Gleadell St and the St Kilda Swimming
Centre (indoor) in Alma Rd. The outdoor pools are
generally open from late October until April.

One exception is the Harold Holt Swimming Centre
in High St, Glen Iris, which must be the only pool in the
world named after a prime minister who drowned. It's

RICHARD NEBESKY

Fancy a swim? Head for Melbourne City Baths in
Swanston St.

a great facility and open year round, with indoor and
outdoor pools, spas, saunas and aerobics. Lastly, don't
forget the bay – you can choose from many beaches and
the water is tolerable from mid-November to late March.

Tennis & Squash

Tennis-court hire is generally between $14 to $20 an
hour. On weekends rates are often higher, and for floodlit or indoor courts you can pay between $20 and $30 an
hour.

Except in January during the Australian Open, the public can hire one of the 23 outdoor and five indoor courts of the Melbourne Park National Tennis Centre (☎ 9286 1244) on Batman Ave. Other tennis centres near town include the Collingwood Indoor Tennis Centre (☎ 9419 8911) at 100 Wellington St; the Albert Reserve Tennis Centre (☎ 9510 3311) on the corner of St Kilda Rd and Hanna St in South Melbourne; the South Yarra Tennis Centre (☎ 9820 0611) in Fawkner Park on Toorak Rd; and the East Melbourne Tennis Centre (☎ 9417 6511) on the corner of Simpson and Albert Sts.

Squash courts cost around $12 to $18 an hour. There are courts in the city at the Melbourne City Baths (☎ 9663 5888): for courts in other areas, check the *Yellow Pages* phone book.

Windsurfing/Sailboarding

Close to the city, both Elwood and Middle Park beaches are designated sailboarding areas. A company called Repeat Performance Sailboards (☎ 9525 6475) at 87 Ormond Rd in Elwood hires out good boards from around $35 a day or $55 for a weekend.

LANGUAGE COURSES

The Council of Adult Education (CAE) (☎ 9652 0611), at 256 Flinders St in the city, runs good English as a Foreign Language (EFL) courses geared towards travellers. Their 12-week courses (two three-hour classes weekly) cost $555; short-term visitors can pay on a per-class basis.

RMIT University's Centre for English Language Learning (☎ 9639 0225), at 480 Elizabeth St in the city, also offers five different English courses. Fees are $250 a week for full-time study.

Other private language schools worth trying include Holmes College (☎ 9662 2055) and the Lyceum Language Centre (☎ 9428 4178).

The Foreign Language Bookshop (☎ 9654 2883), at 259 Collins St in the city, has an excellent range of language books and courses. Their notice board advertises tutors and courses.

Places to Stay

In Melbourne you have a choice between caravan parks and backpackers' hostels, pubs and motels, B&Bs and guesthouses, serviced apartments and deluxe hotels. Once you've decided what you're looking for, the tricky part is deciding which area to stay in. The city centre is convenient and close to things like theatres, museums and the train and bus terminals, although it can be a little lifeless at night. The alternative is to stay in one of the inner suburbs that ring the city.

The accommodation listed here is divided into the following categories and price brackets: caravan and camping parks; backpackers' hostels, where dorm beds cost $10 to $16 and singles/doubles around $25/35; colleges; pubs, most of which have simple rooms with shared bathroom for around $30 to $50; budget hotels and guesthouses, which vary enormously in quality and range from around $30 to $100 for a double room; motels, which range from $50 to $100 for a double room; B&Bs, most of which charge $100 or more for a double room; boutique hotels, where you'll pay between $100 and $200 a night; apartment hotels and serviced apartments, which are generally upmarket self-contained places costing anywhere from $80 to more than $200 a night; mid-range hotels which, like boutique hotels, charge between $100 and $200 a night; and top-end hotels, where you can pay anywhere from $200 a night for a room to $2000 or more for a luxury suite.

Rooms can be booked directly, or you can make reservations through the RACV's Victorian Tourist Information Centre (☎ 9650 1522), in the Melbourne Town Hall on the corner of Swanston Walk and Little Collins St in Melbourne.

Note that during major festivals and events accommodation in Melbourne is often very scarce, and you need to make reservations well in advance. This is especially the case during the Formula One Grand Prix, at which time you can also expect prices to rise substantially, even at the backpackers' hostels.

If you decide to stay longer, look in the *Age* classifieds on Wednesday and Saturday under 'Share Accommodation'. You could also try the notice boards in the hostels, or places like the universities, Readings bookshop in Carlton, Cosmos Books & Music and the Galleon restaurant in St Kilda, or the Black Cat Cafe in Fitzroy.

CAMPING & CARAVAN PARKS

Melbourne has a few caravan/camping parks in the metropolitan area, although none of them are very close to the centre. The most convenient place is probably the comprehensive Melbourne Caravan & Tourist Park in Coburg East (from the city, take tram No 19 or 20 from Elizabeth St then bus No 526; the bus doesn't run on Sunday). The sites include:

Bluegum Northside Caravan Park (☎ 9305 3614), 14 km north of the city on the corner of the Hume Highway and Cooper St, Campbellfield; camping $15, on-site units from $50.

Crystal Brook Holiday Centre (☎ 9844 3637), 21 km north-east of the city near the corner of Warrandyte and Andersons Creek Rds, Doncaster East; camping $17, on-site vans from $30, on-site cabins from $60.

Footscray Caravan Park (☎ 9314 6646), eight km west of the city at 163 Somerville Rd, West Footscray; no camping, on-site vans from $40.

Hobsons Bay Caravan Park (☎ 9397 2395), 17 km south-west of the city at 158 Kororoit Creek Rd, Williamstown; camping $14, cabins $30/35.

Melbourne Caravan & Tourist Park (☎ 9354 3533), 10 km north of the city at 265 Elizabeth St, Coburg East; camping $16, on-site vans $37, cabins from $43 to $55.

HOSTELS

There are backpackers' hostels in the city centre, Fitzroy, North Melbourne, Richmond and South Yarra, although the seaside suburb of St Kilda has the biggest collection of budget accommodation. The hostel scene is fairly competitive, and it can be hard to find a bed in one of the better places over summer. Several of the larger hostels have courtesy buses that do pick-ups from the bus and train terminals.

City Centre

The city has some good hostels, which have the advantage of being central and close to the railway station and bus depots. The best of these is *Toad Hall* (Map 1; ☎ 9600 9010) at 441 Elizabeth St, within easy walking distance of the bus terminals. It's a quiet, stylish and well-equipped place with a pleasant courtyard and off-street parking ($5). A bed in a four or six-bed dorm costs from $16; single/double rooms cost from $27.50/45, twins $50.

At 199 Russell St, *Exford Hotel Backpackers* (Map 1; ☎ 9663 2697) is a cheerful and well set-up hostel in the upper section of an old pub. Costs range from $13 in a 10-bed dorm to $17 in a four-bed dorm; twins/doubles are $42 a night.

At 22 Little Collins St, the *City Centre Private Hotel* (Map 1; ☎ 9654 5401) is clean and quiet, if somewhat prim. All rooms have shared bathroom and there's a TV lounge and kitchen on each floor. Backpackers pay $17 in a three or four-bed room and doubles are $35; serviced singles/doubles are $35/50.

Near the Franklin St bus terminal at 167 Franklin St is the very large *Downtown Backpackers Hostel* (Map 1; ☎ 9329 7525). A former student accommodation block, it feels a bit institutional but has pretty good facilities including a bar and a sunny rooftop with great views. It also offers free airport pick-ups and helps out travellers who are looking for work. Dorms (four to 16-bed) range from $13 to $16 and doubles from $35 to $40.

The *Backpackers City Inn* (Map 1; ☎ 9650 2734), upstairs in the Carlton Hotel at 197 Bourke St, has dorm beds at $14 and singles/doubles for $28/35, although both the pub and the accommodation are a bit rough around the edges.

Fitzroy

Well located on the fringe of the city at 116 Nicholson St is the *Nunnery* (Map 6; ☎ 9419 8637), one of the best budget accommodation options in Melbourne. It's a converted Victorian building with comfortable lounges, good facilities and a friendly atmosphere. The rooms are small but clean and centrally heated. Costs range from $17 in a 12-bed dorm to $18 in a three-bed dorm; singles are $35, twins/doubles are $54. Take tram No 96 heading east along Bourke St, and get off at stop No 13.

North Melbourne

Melbourne's YHA hostels are both in North Melbourne, north-west of the city centre. Both offer discounts for a four-day or longer stay. From the airport you can ask the Skybus to drop you at the North Melbourne hostels.

The YHA showpiece is the *Queensberry Hill Hostel* (Map 5; ☎ 9329 8599) at 78 Howard St. This huge, 348-bed place was only completed in mid-1991 and has excellent facilities, including modern bathrooms, a state-of-the-art kitchen, a rooftop patio with barbecues and 360° views of the city, and a security car park. Four or eight-bed dorms cost $17 for YHA members ($3 more for nonmembers); singles/doubles are $42/52, or $52/62 with private bathroom. There's a breakfast and dinner service available, and office hours are 7.30 am to 10.30 pm, although there is 24-hour access once you have checked in. Catch tram No 55 from William St and get off at stop No 14, or take any tram north up Elizabeth St to stop No 13.

The *Chapman Gardens YHA Hostel* (Map 2; ☎ 9328 3595), at 76 Chapman St, is smaller and older but can be a bit more intimate than Queensberry Hill. Dorms here cost $15, twin rooms $34 and doubles $38 ($2 more for nonmembers). From Elizabeth St in the city, take tram No 50 or 57 along Flemington Rd and get off at stop No 19, then walk down Abbotsford St. Chapman St is the first on the left.

Both hostels have good notice boards if you're looking for people to travel or share lifts with, cheap airline tickets or just general information. There are a number of very good tours which operate out of the hostels.

Opposite the Queen Victoria Market at 238 Victoria St, the *Global Backpackers' Hostel* (Map 5; ☎ 9328 3728) is in the top section of an old pub and has dorms ranging from $11 to $14, and singles/doubles at $25/36. Note that the pub downstairs (the Public Bar) has bands most nights and tariffs include free entry and discounted drinks – great if you're into live music, not so great if you're an early sleeper.

St Kilda

St Kilda is one of Melbourne's most interesting and cosmopolitan suburbs, and has a good range of budget accommodation as well as plenty of restaurants and entertainment possibilities. From Swanston St in the city, tram No 16 will take you down St Kilda Rd to Fitzroy St, or there's the faster light-rail service (No 96 from Spencer St and Bourke St) to the old St Kilda railway station and along Fitzroy and Acland Sts.

Enfield House Backpackers (Map 11; ☎ 9534 8159), at 2 Enfield St, is the original and probably the most popular of St Kilda's hostels. It's a huge and rambling Victorian-era building with over 100 beds, good facilities and staff who can help organise tours, nights out and activities. Three to eight-bunk dorms are $16, singles $25 and twins $38. The hostel's courtesy bus picks up travellers from the bus terminals, and from Station Pier for the Tasmanian ferries.

The excellent *Olembia Guesthouse* (Map 11; ☎ 9537 1412) at 96 Barkly St is more like a boutique hotel than a hostel. The facilities are very good and include a cosy guest lounge, dining room, courtyard and off-street parking. The rooms are quite small but comfortable and clean, and all have hand-basins and central heating. Dorm beds cost $14 to $15, singles are $35, and twins and doubles are $50. Book ahead.

At 169 Fitzroy St, the *Ritz for Backpackers* (Map 11; ☎ 9525 3501) is upstairs from a restaurant/bar and is quite stylish, with comfortable lounges and sitting rooms and a modern and well-equipped kitchen. Four to eight-bunk dorms cost $14, twins and doubles $34. There's also a good self-contained flat that sleeps eight people at $14 per person.

The *St Kilda Coffee Palace* (Map 11; ☎ 9534 5283), at 24 Grey St, is another long-running hostel that has recently been renovated and upgraded by its new owners. It's a big, spacious place with its own cafe and a modern kitchen. Dorms range from $12 to $14, twins and doubles are $32. Around the corner at 56 Jackson St is *Kookaburra Cottage* (Map 11; ☎ 9534 5457), a small and laid-back hostel. It's quite comfortable and has all the usual facilities; dorm beds are $13 and there are a couple of good twin rooms at $34.

On the corner of Grey and Jackson Sts is *Leopard House* (Map 11; ☎ 9534 1200), an old and roomy two-storey Edwardian house with four-bed dorms at $13.

South Yarra

Lord's Lodge Backpackers (Map 9; ☎ 9510 5658) is at 204 Punt Rd, which is a fairly hectic main road. This is a large, rambling, old two-storey mansion with a range of accommodation, including six to eight-bed dorms with their own kitchens at $14 and twins/doubles from $34 to $40.

Richmond

Packers Palace (Map 7; ☎ 9428 59 32), on the east side of the city at 153 Hoddle St (and beside West Richmond train station), is a cosy, straightforward and friendly two-storey hostel. Accommodation is in small four-bunk rooms and is good value at just $10 a night. The owners also run the Hard Wok Cafe in St Kilda, and tariffs include a $2 discount meal voucher.

The *Richmond Hill Guesthouse* (Map 7; ☎ 9428 6501), well located at 353 Church St, is another big Victorian-era building with spacious living areas and clean rooms. Dorm beds range from $15 to $18 a night, singles/twins are $35/44, and there's a B&B section with good single/double rooms at $55/66 and doubles with en-suites at $83.

Also in Richmond, although not as well located, is *Central House* (Map 7; ☎ 9427 9826) at 337 Highett St, with mostly four-bed dorms at $14 a night.

Preston

The *Terrace Travellers Hostel* (☎ 9470 1006) is at 418 Murray Rd, Preston – it's not a bad hostel, but unless you've got relatives in Preston it's hard to think of a reason for staying all the way out here.

COLLEGES

Melbourne's long-established University of Melbourne is just to the north of the city centre in Parkville. The following colleges have accommodation in the vacation period from late November to mid-February; B&B ranges from $25 to $45 per night, and there's a minimum stay of three nights:

International House (☎ 9347 6655)
Medley Hall (☎ 9663 5847)
Ormond College (☎ 9348 1688)
Queen's College (☎ 9349 0500)
Ridley College (☎ 9387 7555)
Trinity College (☎ 9347 1044)
University College (☎ 9347 3533)
Whitley College (☎ 9347 8388)

PUBS

There are still quite a few old pubs offering a varying range of accommodation in inner Melbourne.

City Centre

The *Stork Hotel* (Map 6; ☎ 9663 6237), close to the Franklin St bus terminal on the corner of Elizabeth and Therry Sts, is an old pub with simple upstairs rooms and a small guest kitchen. The owners organise various theme nights for backpackers. Twin rooms cost $17.50 per person, singles/doubles are $25/30.

Another good budget option in the city is the *Duke of Wellington Hotel* (Map 1; ☎ 9650 4984), on the corner of Flinders and Russell Sts. Built back in 1850, it's one of Melbourne's oldest pubs but has been recently renovated and has comfortable upstairs rooms with shared bathroom at $45/80 for singles/doubles, including breakfast.

East Melbourne

At 2 Hotham St (and on the corner with very busy Hoddle St), the *East Melbourne Hotel* (Map 6; ☎ 9419 2040) has very pleasant pub-style rooms upstairs for $40/50. There's a free car park, guest lounge and kitchen – there's also a stylish restaurant and bar downstairs.

Albert Park

The *Hotel Victoria* (Map 8; ☎ 9690 3666) has a great position overlooking the bay from 123 Beaconsfield Pde. It's an impressively restored and elegant hotel that dates back to 1888. Downstairs, it has a front bar, bistro and a rather grand formal dining room. Upstairs are 20 comfortable rooms with shared bathroom ranging from $60, and 10 double rooms with ensuite ranging from $90 to $150. Ask for one of the corner suites – the views alone are worth the $135 to $150.

Middle Park

Well located between Albert Park Lake and the bay, the *Middle Park Hotel* (Map 9; ☎ 9690 1958) on the corner of Canterbury Rd and Armstrong St is a trendy and popular inner-suburban pub. The upstairs rooms have been renovated and cost from $40 for singles/doubles with shared bathroom.

GAY & LESBIAN ACCOMMODATION

The Melbourne Guesthouse (Map 11; ☎ 9510 4707), in a leafy and quiet suburban street at 26 Crimea St, St Kilda, is a modern guesthouse for gay men with six rooms, one with its own ensuite, as well as a kitchen, lounge, and laundry. Tariffs for singles/doubles are $69/79.

The Laird (☎ 9417 2832), at 149 Gipps St, Collingwood (one block east of Hoddle St), is an old pub that has been converted into a gay men's bar and nightclub. Upstairs there are pub-style rooms (shared bathroom) and a self-contained flat, or across the road the quieter *Norwood Guesthouse* also has three rooms. The nightly cost is $55 per room, including breakfast.

More upmarket is *163 Drummond St* (☎ 9663 3081), 163 Drummond St, Carlton, a stylishly restored B&B with small single rooms from $40, doubles with shared bathroom from $65 and ensuite doubles from $95 to $105. The owner has another place nearby.

Palm Court B&B (☎ 9427 7365), 283 Punt Rd, Richmond, is another restored two-storey Victorian terrace house with four double rooms, two bathrooms, a guest lounge and a pleasant barbecue courtyard. Tariffs are $40/60 for singles/doubles including breakfast.

The *Exchange Hotel* (Map 9; ☎ 9867 5144), 119 Commercial Rd, Prahran, has oldish pub-style rooms upstairs costing $45/60 per night.

Other places that advertise themselves as being gay-friendly include the *Hotel Saville* (Map 9) in Prahran and the *Adelphi Hotel* (Map 1) in the city centre (see the Motels and Hotels – Top End sections respectively for details). If you're looking to stay longer, you'll find accommodation notices in *MSO* and *Brother Sister*, as well as on notice boards in many cafes and bookshops.

DISABLED TRAVELLERS

Accessible accommodation in Melbourne is at best limited, and expensive, being provided primarily by four and five star hotels. Canberra-based National Information Communication Awareness Network (NICAN; ☎ freecall 008 806 769) has a database of accessible accommodation and you can try Queensberry Hill YHA (☎ 9329 8599) which has an accessible bathroom on each of its four floors. The Victorian Disabled Motorists Association (☎ 9386 0413) has two accessible motel units at Coburg, north of the city. The Novotel Bayside Hotel (☎ 9525 5522) in St Kilda is a good but not cheap option with five accessible rooms.

BUDGET HOTELS & GUESTHOUSES

Moving up a level from the backpackers' hostels, there are some good budget options in and around the city centre, including small hotels, guesthouses, units and apartments. The places in this section generally have double rooms for under $100 a night.

City Centre

The hotels along Spencer St are convenient for the bus and train terminals, although this ain't exactly the most salubrious end of town. The *Terrace Pacific Inn* (Map 1; ☎ 9621 3333) at 16 Spencer St is a modern budget hotel with smallish rooms with ensuites from $99. The tariff includes a light breakfast. At 44 Spencer St, the *Hotel Enterprise* (Map 1; ☎ 9629 6991) is another refurbished hotel with budget singles/doubles from $40/50, or from $95 with ensuites. And at No 66, the *Batman's Hill Hotel* (Map 1; ☎ 9614 6344) has doubles from $125, including breakfast.

At 131 King St, the *Kingsgate Budget Hotel* (Map 1; ☎ 9629 4171) is a private hotel that has been renovated. It's a big old place, with budget rooms with shared bathroom from $29/45 or ensuite rooms from $60/80.

The *Hotel Y* (Map 6; ☎ 9329 5188), run by the YWCA, is close to the Franklin St bus terminal at 489 Elizabeth St. It has simple four-bed bunkrooms which cost $25, singles/doubles at $65/75/85 and deluxe rooms from $75/90/100. Recently refurbished, the 'Y' has good facilities including a budget cafe, communal kitchen and laundry, gym and heated pool.

The *Victoria Hotel* (Map 1; ☎ 9653 0441) at 215 Little Collins St is a notch up from the cheapest city hotels, and a bit of a Melbourne institution. There are 520 rooms in three categories: budget rooms with shared facilities at $42/55, standard rooms with ensuite and TV at $75/93, and executive rooms from $109 to $120. The Victoria is one of the best-located hotels in the city centre.

South Yarra

Tram No 8 from Swanston St in the city takes you along Toorak Rd into the heart of the chic suburb of South Yarra.

The *West End Private Hotel* (Map 9; ☎ 9866 5375), at 76 Toorak Rd, has B&B with singles/doubles at $35/50 – it's pretty old-fashioned, but has a certain shabby charm.

Farther east at 189 Toorak Rd, the vast *Claremont Accommodation* (Map 10; ☎ 9826 8000) has recently been converted into a guesthouse. The rooms are bright and freshly painted, with polished-timber floors, heating and modern communal facilities. Singles/ doubles with shared bathroom start from $39/52, including breakfast.

St Kilda

St Kilda has quite a few old boarding houses and private hotels, which mainly house longer-term residents and probably wouldn't suit most travellers. (I once stayed in one for a month, which was a bit like being trapped in a Henry Miller novel.)

Opposite St Kilda beach at 363 Beaconsfield Pde, *Warwick Beachside* (Map 11; ☎ 9525 4800) is a large complex of 1950s-style holiday flats. They're not glamorous, but they're quite well equipped, and there's a laundry and off-street parking. Costs range from $59 to

$69 for a studio (up to three people) and from $89 to $95 for two bedrooms (up to five people).

MOTELS

City Centre

There are several motels in or near the city. The *City Square Motel* (Map 1; ☎ 9654 7011), at 67 Swanston St, has fairly basic rooms but is right in the centre of town, with singles/doubles from $65/85, including a continental breakfast.

At the top end of town at 20-22 Little Bourke St, the *City Limits Motel* (Map 1; ☎ 9662 2544) has rooms with kitchenettes costing from $75/79.

At 288 Spencer St, the *Astoria Motel* (Map 1; ☎ 9670 6801) is close to the railway station and has its own restaurant and renovated rooms from $76/78. Nearby, the *Flagstaff City Motor Inn* (☎ 9329 5788) at 45 Dudley St costs $78/85.

The *Miami Motel* (☎ 9329 8499), at 13 Hawke St in the semi-industrial area of West Melbourne, is a cross between a motel and a backpackers' hostel. It's clean and simple, with rooms with shared bathroom at $36/53 and rooms with ensuites at $62/78, and the tariffs include breakfast.

East Melbourne

There are two choices here for motel buffs – neither inspiring but both convenient. The *George Powlett Lodge* (Map 6; ☎ 9419 9488) on the corner of George and Powlett Sts has 45 older motel-style rooms with kitchenettes from $75/80. The *Treasury Motor Lodge* (Map 6; ☎ 9417 5281) at 179 Powlett St costs $85/90.

Carlton

The *Downtowner on Lygon* (Map 6; ☎ 9663 5555), on the corner of Lygon and Queensberry Sts, has four-star motel-style units starting from $119 a night. Farther up Lygon St in the heart of the action is *Lygon Lodge Motel* (Map 6; ☎ 9663 6633) at No 220, with twins/ doubles/ triples all costing $99.

Parkville

There is a string of motels along Royal Pde. Trams trundle up this tree-lined avenue past Melbourne University and Princes and Royal parks.

The *Elizabeth Tower Motel* (Map 2; ☎ 9347 9211) is on the corner of Royal Pde and Grattan St, opposite the university. This multilevel motel has its own restaurant and bar, and rooms start from $115. Farther north at 441 Royal Pde is the *Royal Parade Irico Hotel* (Map 3; ☎ 9380 9221), which has a swimming pool, restaurant and convention centre, with units and apartments from $105. One tram stop farther north again is the budget *Ramada Inn* (Map 3; ☎ 9380 8131) at 539 Royal Pde, with singles/doubles for $79/84. The *Princes Park Motel* (Map 3; ☎ 9388 1000) is on the corner of Royal Pde and Park St, with singles/ doubles at $80/85.

North Melbourne

The *Marco Polo Inn* (Map 2; ☎ 9329 1788), near the corner of busy Flemington Rd and Harker St, is a big 1970s-style motel with 68 rooms plus a swimming pool, sauna and spa. Singles/doubles start at $88/98.

South Yarra

The *Hotel Saville* (Map 9; ☎ 9867 2755), 5 Commercial Rd, is a seven-storey octagonal building with refurbished motel-style rooms from $84/88, plus its own bar and restaurant.

The *St James Motel* (Map 9; ☎ 9866 4455) at 35 Darling St is an older motel with singles/ doubles costing $60/65, and up the road at 52 Darling St the *Domain Motel* (Map 10; ☎ 9866 3701) backs onto a park (but also the railway line) and has singles/doubles from $58/65.

The *Albany Motel* (Map 9; ☎ 9866 4485) on the corner of Toorak Rd and Millswyn St is a busy tourist motel opposite Fawkner Park and close to the Royal Botanic Gardens, with rooms from $60/65.

St Kilda

St Kilda has plenty of motels, but some of them are fairly dodgy. A couple of more respectable places are the *Cabana Court Motel* (Map 11; ☎ 9534 0771) at 46 Park St, with self-contained units from $80 to $85, and the *Cosmopolitan Motor Inn* (Map 11; ☎ 9534 0781) at 6 Carlisle St, with rooms from $73 and family units with kitchenettes from $107.

Another reasonably good option is the *Crest International Hotel/Motel* (Map 11; ☎ 9537 1788) at 47 Barkly St, a larger motel that incorporates a conference centre, restaurant and bar, with rooms starting from $89.

RICHARD NEBESKY

The city skyline viewed from St Kilda Pier.

The *Charnwood Motor Inn* (Map 11; ☎ 9525 4199), on the inland side of St Kilda Rd at 3 Charnwood Rd, is a good motel in a quiet suburban street with singles/doubles at $55/65.

South Melbourne

The *City Park Motel* (Map 9; ☎ 9699 9811), at 308 Kings Way in South Melbourne, is a 1970s-style motel on a busy road – singles/doubles start from $115.

BED & BREAKFAST

East Melbourne

On the fringe of the city, East Melbourne has a pleasant residential feel with its tree-lined streets and grand old Victorian terrace houses. The *Georgian Court Guesthouse* (Map 6; ☎ 9419 6353), at 21 George St, is an elegant and cosy B&B with singles/doubles at $55/65, or $75/85 with an ensuite; prices include a buffet breakfast.

South Yarra

Close to both Chapel St and Toorak Rd at 10 Motherwell St, *Ildemere B&B* (☎ 9826 2921) is a charming period home with one guest unit with its own private bathroom and sitting room. B&B costs $120 a double.

St Kilda

There are also a couple of good B&Bs in St Kilda. Opposite the beach at 335 Beaconsfield Pde, *Robinsons by the Sea* (Map 11; ☎ 9534 2683) is an elegant and impressive Victorian-era terrace house with five double ensuite rooms ranging from $110 to $150.

Victoria House B&B (Map 11; ☎ 9525 4512), at 57 Mary St, is a very comfortable and well set-up Victorian home with three double rooms, one of which has its own kitchen. It's a friendly place with pleasant gardens and an attractive courtyard, and is good value with singles/doubles at $75/95.

Williamstown

Williamstown is mainly thought of as a day-trip destination, but if you want to stay overnight in this very pleasant bayside suburb then the *Grange B&B* (Map 12; ☎ 9397 6288) at 219 Osborne St is a good option. It's a beautifully restored Victorian-era home with one double bedroom with its own ensuite and sitting room; nightly tariffs are $80/110 for singles/doubles.

Caulfield

If you're a horse-racing aficionado, you might be interested in *Lord Lodge B&B* (☎ 9572 3969), at 20 Booran Rd in Caulfield – it's adjacent to the Caulfield Racecourse (about 15 km south-east of the city centre) and attached to Colin Little's famous racing stables. An impressive historic home, it has three guest rooms, each named after famous racehorses that have come out of the stables. Doubles range from $95 to $120 a night.

BOUTIQUE HOTELS

East Melbourne

The *Magnolia Court Boutique Hotel* (Map 6; ☎ 9419 4222), at 101 Powlett St, is a bright and friendly small hotel in two halves. The older wing, formerly a ladies' finishing college, dates back to 1862, and spacious doubles in these Victorian-style rooms cost $130. The rooms in the new wing are a good standard but don't quite have the same charm, and cost $105/110. The best option is the cute and tiny two-room Victorian cottage with its own kitchen at $150. The hotel has a breakfast room, heated outdoor spa and garden courtyard.

South Yarra

The *Tilba* (Map 9; ☎ 9867 8844), on the corner of Toorak Rd and Domain St, is a small and elegant hotel that has been lovingly restored in gracious Victorian style. Stepping inside is like taking a trip back in time – the 15 suites all feature old iron bedheads, leadlights, decorative plasterwork and period-style bathrooms. Tariffs range from $130 to $185 a double, depending on the size of the room – highly recommended.

Toorak

At 220 Williams Rd, *Toorak Manor* (☎ 1800 062 689) is another excellent boutique hotel. Set in lovely gardens, it's an historic mansion that has been impressively converted, with 12 comfortable period-style rooms with ensuites, cosy lounges and sitting rooms. Tariffs range from $145 to $185 a night. Toorak Manor is a short walk from Hawksburn railway station.

APARTMENT-HOTELS & SERVICED APARTMENTS

Melbourne has plenty of apartment-style hotels and serviced apartments. These places are usually a bit more spacious than regular hotels, and, as they have their own kitchen and laundry facilities, they can work out to be better value than an equivalently priced hotel, especially for people travelling in a group.

City Centre

The modern apartment-hotel *Holiday Inn Park Suites* (Map 1; ☎ 9663 3333), at 333 Exhibition St, is a good place to stay if hotels make you claustrophobic. All rooms have a private balcony, separate lounge, full kitchen and laundry, and there's a heated pool and sauna on the roof. One-bedroom suites start from $195 a night, two-bedroom suites from $225 a night, and the penthouses are $600 a night.

Another very good self-contained option in the city is *Oakford Gordon Place* (Map 1; ☎ 1800 818 236) at 24 Little Bourke St. In an historic setting and built around a garden courtyard, the 59 stylish, self-contained apartments are very popular. Singles/doubles in studios cost $145, one-bedroom apartments are $171, two-bedroom apartments are $215 and split-level suites are $319 a night.

The *Stamford Plaza Melbourne* (Map 1; ☎ 9659 1000) at 111 Little Collins St has 283 rooms, mostly one-bedroom luxury suites with a separate lounge room and kitchenette, starting from $320 a night.

East Melbourne

There are quite a few serviced apartments in this area. The *East Melbourne Studio Apartments* (Map 6; ☎ 9412 2555), at 25 Hotham St, is a fairly stylish block of 1940s flats converted into 38 studio apartments, all recently renovated with good facilities and kitchenettes, ranging from $90 to $130 a night.

At 101 George St, the *George Street Apartments* (Map 6; ☎ 9419 1333) is a secure and friendly place. These apartments, with a bathroom, fridge and cooking facilities, cost from $75 a double.

The *Eastern Townhouses* (Map 6; ☎ 9418 6666), at 90 Albert St, is a refurbished complex with good studio units costing $88/98 for singles/doubles. Nearby at No 83, the *Albert Heights Serviced Apartments* (Map 6; ☎ 9419 0955) are a bit bigger and more motel-style, and cost $120 per night. *Birches Serviced Apartments* (Map 6; ☎ 9417 2344), at 160 Simpson St, is an unattractive corner block of flats with reasonable one-bedroom apartments from $120.

Carlton

Lygon Crest Lodgings (Map 3; ☎ 9345 3888) is at 700 Lygon St, opposite the Melbourne General Cemetery. These former flats have been refurbished to a good standard, and the one and two-bedroom apartments range from $125 to $150.

North Melbourne

The *City Gardens Apartments* (Map 2; ☎ 9320 6600), at 335 Abbotsford St, has 128 comfortable self-contained units on a busy street in a pleasant courtyard setting. The one, two and three-bedroom units range from $130 to $225 a night.

Fitzroy

Fitzroy is fairly light on for accommodation, but the *Royal Gardens Apartments* (Map 6; ☎ 9419 9888) in Royal Lane are well located in a quiet street, a block back from the Exhibition Buildings and close to Brunswick St. These 76 spacious and stylish apartments are built around a landscaped courtyard with a swimming pool, and they come in one, two or three-bedroom configurations, costing $165, $195 and $235 respectively.

South Yarra

South Yarra is the serviced-apartment capital of Melbourne. Most of them are blocks of flats that were built in the 1950s and 1960s and have been refurbished, some better than others. Note that quite a few companies manage multiple blocks of apartments.

One of the best options is *South Yarra Hill Suites* (Map 9; ☎ 9868 8222) at 14 Murphy St, an elegant apartment-style hotel in a quiet, leafy street close to Toorak Rd. The hotel has 24-hour reception, a heated pool, spa and sauna, with one-bedroom apartments from $195 and two-bedrooms from $240.

A couple of more affordable options are *Darling Towers* (Map 9; ☎ 9867 5200) at 32 Darling St, with good one-bedroom flats from $85 a night, and the *Manor House Apartments* (Map 9; ☎ 9867 1266) at 23 Avoca St, with well-equipped studios from $75 a night.

Oakford Apartments (☎ 1800 818 224) has apartments at six different addresses in South Yarra. These are all well furnished and equipped, and very popular with business executives. Some have tennis courts, others have pools and spas, and they range from studios at $100 to three-bedroom townhouses at $270.

St Kilda

Barkly Quest Lodgings (Map 11; ☎ 9525 5000), at 180 Barkly St, has 26 one-bedroom apartments costing $105 per night for two people or $135 for four people (two of them on a fold-up couch). They're on a busy street, but the apartments are well renovated and fully equipped. The same company has *Redan Quest Inn Apartments* (Map 11; ☎ 9529 7595) in a quieter and more suburban part of St Kilda at 25 Redan St, with studio apartments with kitchenettes from $75 per night.

St Kilda Rd/Queens Rd Area

A good option in this area is the *Oakford Fairways* (Map 9; ☎ 9820 8544) at 32 Queens Rd, an Art Deco-style apartment block opposite Albert Park's golf course and lake. These executive apartments have a tennis court, a pool and leafy landscaped grounds. One-bedroom apartments start from $150, two-bedroom ones from $175.

Port Melbourne

Near the top of the bay at 15 Beach St, the *Station Pier Condominiums* (Map 8; ☎ 9647 9666) has 54 modern and spacious apartments separated by landscaped gardens and boardwalks, with a pool and sauna, tennis court, conference facilities, and a stylish bar and restaurant with live jazz sessions on Sunday afternoons. Steffi Graf has stayed here a few times while in Melbourne for the Australian Open. The one-bedroom apartments start from $220 a night ($240 with bay views), two-bedroom ones from $240 ($285 with bay views).

HOTELS – MIDDLE

Melbourne has a dozen or so four-star hotels, most of which cater for corporate clients. On weekends they usually find themselves with lots of empty beds, so you'll find most of them offering great weekend deals that either discount the tariffs or include incentives like champagne, breakfasts, theatre tickets and dinners.

City Centre

The *Adelphi Hotel* (Map 1; ☎ 9650 2709), at 187 Flinders Lane, is one of the groovier inner-city small hotels with a good range of facilities including a pool, a hip basement restaurant and a great rooftop bar with views of the city. Standard rooms are $210, deluxe rooms $230 and executive suites $420.

The *Savoy Park Plaza* (Map 1; ☎ 9622 8888) at 630 Little Collins St was built in the 1920s and later became a police academy. It has recently been refurbished in period style. Its rooms start from $200 and its suites range from $286 to $600.

The *Welcome Hotel* (Map 1; ☎ 9639 0555), right in the heart of Melbourne's shopping district at 265 Little Bourke St, is a well-run three-star tourist hotel with modern rooms with kitchenettes from $120.

The *Centra Melbourne on the Yarra* (Map 1; ☎ 9629 5111), in the World Trade Centre complex on Spencer St, between Flinders St and the Yarra River, is a modern four-star hotel with rooms from $180 to $260. Farther up Spencer St on the corner of Flinders Lane is *Rydges on Flinders* (Map 1; ☎ 9629 4111), a new four-star with a trendy foyer, friendly staff and 204 modern rooms from $205. At 51 Little Bourke St, the *Crossley Hotel* (Map 1; ☎ 9639 1639) is a small four-star hotel in the heart of Chinatown with rooms from $130 and suites from $270. The *Novatel Melbourne on Collins* (Map 1; ☎ 9650 5800), at

270 Collins St, is a four-star tourist hotel with rooms from $170.

The *Sheraton Hotel* (Map 1; ☎ 9650 5000) at 13 Spring St dates back to the 1960s but has been refurbished to a reasonable standard. Rooms start from $165. Note that this hotel is not part of the Sheraton chain – the hotel took the name before the 'real' Sheraton thought of registering the name in Melbourne.

Carlton

At 701 Swanston St, the *Townhouse Hotel* (Map 6; ☎ 9347 7811) is a five-storey hotel built in 1970. It's comfortable and well run, and the facilities include restaurant, bar and a rooftop spa and sauna. Rooms start from $135.

Richmond

Rydge's Riverwalk Hotel (Map 7; ☎ 9246 1200), on the corner of Bridge Rd and River St, is an impressive four-star hotel beside the Yarra River. This place is better value and more spacious than city hotels in the equivalent price bracket, with tastefully decorated rooms starting from $210 for a courtyard room, $240 for a studio or river-view room (with a kitchenette), $295 for a two-bedroom apartment or $390 for a penthouse. The hotel has two restaurants.

St Kilda Rd/Queens Rd Area

The hotels along this stretch mostly cater for corporate travellers. While it's largely a commercial area it can still be a good part of town to stay in.

The *St Kilda Rd Travelodge* (Map 9; ☎ 9209 9888), on the corner of Park St and St Kilda Rd, is an older hotel which has been fully refurbished. The front rooms have great views of the Shrine of Remembrance and parklands opposite, and tariffs start from $200.

The modern and stylish *Eden on the Park* (Map 9; ☎ 9820 2222), at 6 Queens Rd, has 132 well-appointed and comfortable rooms. Standard rooms start from $160 and the suites, with great views over the lake and parklands, range from $215 to $255.

The *Carlton Crest Hotel* (Map 9; ☎ 9529 4300), at 65 Queens Rd, is a large tourist hotel with 385 rooms. A room in the older part of the hotel costs from $159, while the better deluxe rooms with views cost from $189. Tariffs include breakfast.

Around the corner at 562 St Kilda Rd is the *Parkroyal on St Kilda Road* (Map 9; ☎ 9529 8888), a flashy four-star with rooms from $235.

St Kilda

The modern high-rise *Novatel Bayside Hotel* (Map 11; ☎ 9525 5522) overlooks the bay from 14-16 The Esplanade. It's no architectural masterpiece, but the position is excellent and the front rooms have great views of the bay. There are 225 rooms ranging from $120 to $470 a night, as well as a heated pool, secure parking and all four-star facilities.

North Melbourne

The *Old Melbourne Hotel* (Map 5; ☎ 9329 9344) at 5 Flemington Rd is a large bluestone and brick hotel built around a cobbled garden courtyard. Its 226 rooms have recently been refurbished, along with its restaurant, bar, conference facilities and pool, and this is a good mid-range option. Rooms and suites range from $130 to $250.

HOTELS – TOP END

Most of Melbourne's five-star hotels are in the city centre. These hotels generally quote prices of more than $250 a night for a room, but in practice you'll find their prices are fairly negotiable. As with mid-range hotels, most of the five-stars have very good weekend deals and package deals on offer. These vary from time to time – ring around to see who's offering what.

City Centre

They call the *Windsor Hotel* (Map 1; ☎ 9653 0653), at 103 Spring St, Melbourne's 'Grand Lady', and she is indisputably the matriarch of Melbourne's hotels. There are other hotels more opulent, more luxurious and with better facilities, but there are some things you can't manufacture and a grand sense of history is one of them. Built in 1883 and restored during the 1980s, the Windsor is the epitome of old-world elegance. Beyond the top-hatted doorman, the foyer is all marble and mahogany, shaded lamps and potted palms. Rooms cost from $225 to $350, and the suites, which have housed everyone from the Duke of Windsor to Rudolf Nureyev, range from $400 to $1000.

The *Grand Hyatt Melbourne* (Map 1; ☎ 9657 1234), on the corner of Collins and Russell Sts, is the largest and most lavish of the modern hotels, with 580 luxuriously appointed rooms. It features a cavernous foyer chiselled out of Italian marble, as well as a pool, spa, sauna, gymnasium and rooftop tennis court. Rooms start from $275 and the suites range from $700 up to the Presidential Suite – a steal at $2500.

The *Hotel Sofitel* (Map 1; ☎ 9653 0000; formerly the Regent) is another excellent five-star hotel at the top end of Collins St, at No 25. The hotel's 365 rooms occupy the 30th to 49th floors of one of the twin towers of Collins Place, and the uninterrupted views are sensational. Rooms range from $385 to $460 and suites from $585 to $1600.

Le Meridien at Rialto Melbourne (Map 1; ☎ 9620 9111), at 495 Collins St, was formerly known as the Menzies at Rialto. The hotel is fronted by the historic and elaborate Gothic Revival facades of two buildings which date back to 1891. Inside, the individually styled rooms overlook an enclosed central atrium which covers the original cobbled laneway between the two buildings. This laneway now houses bars, cafes and restaurants. Rooms cost from $245 to $325.

Rockman's Regency Hotel (Map 1; ☎ 9662 3900), on the corner of Exhibition and Lonsdale Sts, prides itself on providing the level of personal service that only a small hotel can, and is particularly popular with visiting celebrities, including the Duchess of York. The rooms are spacious and tastefully decorated, and the hotel is close to the main theatres and Chinatown. Rooms cost from $195 to $295, suites from $395 to $1000.

At 321 Flinders Lane, the *Sebel of Melbourne* (Map 1; ☎ 9629 4088) is an intimate hotel (59 rooms) with an impressive style and personality. The staff are friendly, the rooms are spacious and the windows even open! Rooms range from $225 to $450.

The *Grand Southern Cross* (Map 1; ☎ 9653 0221), at 131 Exhibition St, is currently undergoing major renovations and will re-open as a five-star in mid-1997.

The *Crown Towers Hotel* (Map 1; ☎ 9685 4300), part of the massive Crown Casino development on the southern bank of the Yarra, was due to open in mid-1997. Rooms will start from $475, suites from $750.

East Melbourne

The *Melbourne Hilton on the Park* (Map 6; ☎ 9419 3311), at 192 Wellington Pde, is a very pleasant 10-minute stroll from the city through the Treasury and Fitzroy gardens. Close to the MCG, the Hilton has been extensively refurbished and has rooms from $240 and suites from $550 to $1100.

Southgate

Overlooking the Yarra from opposite Flinders St station
is the *Sheraton Towers Southgate* (Map 1; ☎ 9696 3100), at
1 Brown St, South Melbourne. This elaborately decorated and impressive hotel is part of the worldwide
Sheraton chain. It's well located, being close to the restaurants and cafes of Southgate, the Victorian Arts
Centre, the National Gallery and the gardens, not to
mention the spanking new Casino. Rooms start from
$280 and suites range from $650 up to $2000 for the Royal
Suite.

South Yarra

The *Hotel Como* (Map 10; ☎ 9824 0400), on the corner of
Chapel St and Toorak Rd, is an all-suite hotel which
prides itself on providing 'exclusivity, security, impec-
cable service...' The brochure may be over the top, but
so is the hotel. The design is subtle and distinctive, and
the 107 suites are very stylish. Then there's the pool, spa,
sauna and gym, and room-service meals from the adjacent Maxim's, a renowned local restaurant. Suites range
from $275 to $950.

Places to Eat

Melbourne is a marvellous place to have an appetite – and a terrible place to start a diet. Everywhere you go, there are restaurants, cafes, delicatessens, markets, bistros, brasseries and takeaways.

Melbourne's multiculturalism is reflected in the inexhaustible variety of its cuisines and restaurants. Food is something of a local obsession, and Melbourne is considered to be the country's eating capital. Sydney food and travel writer David Dale wrote, 'Melbourne has sensational food...I like to think of my trips to Melbourne as the equivalent of a Londoner saving up to spend one precious weekend a year in Paris, living on crusts and gruel for months afterwards.'

You don't have to go to that extreme – there are plenty of great eating places that don't cost a fortune. Compared with many other parts of the world, you'll find that food and wine in Melbourne are great value for money and of the highest standard.

Most of Melbourne's restaurants are either licensed to sell alcohol on the premises or BYO, meaning you can 'Bring Your Own' booze, but some are a bit of both. It's a grey area; the law says that licensed premises can also allow customers to BYO, although it's at the discretion of management. Some licensed restaurants will allow customers to bring their own beer or soft drinks but not wine or spirits. If you're not sure, check when you book. Most restaurants charge a small fee for 'corkage'.

Gay-friendly cafes and restaurants abound in Melbourne. Some of the more popular eateries include the *Aquarium Bar & Cafe*, *Angel Cafe* and *Cafe Rumours* in Brunswick St in Fitzroy, the *Blue Elephant Cafe* and *Menage á Trois* in Commercial Rd in Prahran, and the *Globe Cafe* in Chapel St in Prahran.

CITY CENTRE

Chinatown Area

The area in and around Chinatown (Map 1), which follows Little Bourke St from Spring St to Swanston St, is the city's best and most diverse food precinct. Here you will find acclaimed Chinese restaurants rubbing shoulders with cheap Chinese cafes, as well as Italian, French, Malaysian, Thai, and many other types of restaurants. Part of the fun is wandering around exploring

REIMUND ZUNDE

Roofline detail in Chinatown.

the narrow cobbled lanes that run off Little Bourke St, seeking out the city's hidden gems.

Starting from the top end of Little Bourke St, *Jan Bo* at No 40 has reasonably priced Chinese food, and serves great yum cha daily from 11 am to 3 pm. If you want authentic food, ask for the Chinese menu, not the Aussie version. At No 50, the *Shark Fin Inn* is also very popular, and stays open until 1.30 am. *Cafe K* (Map 1; ☎ 9639 0414), at No 35, is an elegant European-style bistro with very good and reasonably priced dishes in the $9 to $17 range. Cafe K is highly recommended – you may need to book.

Little Malaysia, round the corner at 26 Liverpool St, has excellent Malaysian food and generous banquet menus (for a minimum of four people) from $14.50 a head for lunch or $25 a head for dinner. Also just off Little Bourke St is the highly acclaimed *Flower Drum* (☎ 9662 3655) at 17 Market Lane, one of Melbourne's best (and most expensive) restaurants serving up the best Cantonese food this side of Hong Kong. The low-key *Yamato*, at 28 Corrs Lane, turns out excellent Japanese dishes from $6 to $13 and has banquets from $23.

King of Kings, at 209 Russell St, is another cheap Chinese place that stays open until 2.30 am. The understated *Supper Inn*, hidden away at 15-17 Celestial Ave, is definitely worth searching out for its excellent, authentic and reasonably-priced Chinese food. The *Ong Asian Food Court*, in the basement at 265 Little Bourke St, has a good range of Thai, Chinese and Malaysian stalls to choose from. The dishes are fresh, quick and priced from $5 to $8, and you can order by pointing at a photo (so you know exactly what your meal will look like!).

Bourke St Area

Next to the Metro nightclub at the top end of Bourke St, *Fast Eddy's* (Map 1) is a fast no-frills burger joint that stays open 24 hours a day. Across the road, down a narrow laneway and hidden away up a flight of stairs at 20 Myers Place, *The Italian Waiter's Restaurant* serves good, cheap Italian food in unglamorous but cosy surrounds. Back on Bourke St at No 66 is another Melbourne institution – *Pellegrini's*. This long-running bohemian Italian cafe/bar is a popular haunt and meeting place for struggling actors, writers, musicians and other sub-cultural types. The narrow (and usually crowded) front bar serves up excellent coffee and great apple strudel, pastas and risottos. The upmarket *Florentino Cellar Bar*, nearby at No 80, looks expensive but is actually very reasonable. Pastas are $8, and they also serve soup, focaccia and antipasto.

Collins St Area

One block across, Collins St (Map 1) has some of its own institutions. One of these is *Cafe Alcaston* at 2 Collins St, housed in one of the street's few remaining historical buildings. This place caters for breakfasts and lunches in rather noble surrounds, and attracts an upmarket clientele. Across the road, under the shadows of the twin towers of Collins Place, the Great Space has some good eateries. Take the glass lift up to *Babalu*, a quirky and whimsical cafe dominated by the totem-like sculptures of Giuseppe Romero. Most main dishes are $8 to $12. Come on a Friday or Saturday night when they have live Latin American bands – if you plan to eat you'll need to book, or you can just come for a drink and a dance.

Kenzan (☎ 9654 8933), in the lower ground floor of Collins Place (behind the glass lift), is a stylish, popular, licensed Japanese restaurant highly regarded for its sushi and sashimi. Main courses cost around $18 and the fixed-price lunch menu is good value at $13.50.

Farther down at 113 Collins St (actually tucked down a laneway called Georges Parade), *Il Solito Posto* is a wonderfully-Italian bar and restaurant with a warm, stylish and cosy ambience. It's a great place for breakfast, lunch, dinner, or just to meet someone for a drink. Nearby, the *Grand Hyatt Hotel* complex houses several eateries including the highly impressive *Max's*, and the *Hyatt Food Court*, with a good range of reasonably priced food stalls in spacious and stylish surrounds.

Other Areas

Cafee Baloo's (Map 1), at 260 Russell St, is perhaps the best budget eatery in the city centre. It's an atmospheric little place with Indian/Italian food – great antipasto plates ($4.40) and a range of pastas, curries and stir-fries ($5.40 to $6.40). It's open weekdays for lunch and nightly for dinner. Farther south at 122 Russell St, the classy *Pizza Napoli* has some of the best pizzas in town at $11.20.

The Lounge, upstairs at 243 Swanston St, is a groovy cafe/club with pool tables, a balcony overlooking Swanston Walk, and sausages, stir-fries, satays and salads from $7 to $10.

The cheapest place in town is *Gopal's* at 139 Swanston St, a vegetarian cafe run by the Hare Krishna sect. It's open for lunch and dinner and has dishes from $1 to $3, three courses for $5.50 or all you can eat for $8.50. The Hares also run nearby *Crossways*, although it's mainly for poor and homeless people.

At the other end of the price spectrum, *Marchetti's Latin* (☎ 9662 1985) at 55 Lonsdale St tops lots of people's list of Melbourne's best restaurants. The Italian food is superb, the service always just right, and the ambience uniquely chic, sophisticated and at the same time welcoming. Marchetti's is very expensive, and very popular – you'll need to book well ahead.

The block of Lonsdale St between Russell and Swanston Sts is Melbourne's small Greek enclave. *Stalactites*, on the corner of Lonsdale and Russell Sts, is a Greek restaurant best known for its bizarre stalactite decor and the fact that it's open 24 hours. Farther along Lonsdale St at No 195, *Electra Greek Tavern* serves hearty portions of traditional Greek food. Next door, *Tsindos the Greek's* is also good and good value, and has live bouzouki music on Thursday, Friday and Saturday nights.

As well as being the home of Melbourne's outdoor adventure shops, Hardware St is lined with cafes with outdoor tables. At No 25 *Campari Bistro* is a busy Italian bistro with pastas around $10 and other mains from $16 to $19. It's an old favourite for lots of Melburnians. Nearby, *Schwob's* is a great place for a sandwich or a roll, eat in or takeaway. The stylish *Panini* at No 54 has cooked breakfasts for $3.60 and a great selection of sandwiches, salads and hot foods; *Cafe Max* next door also has a huge salad bar as well as things like soups, roasts and sandwiches.

For a cheap pub lunch in town, try the old *Fox & Hounds Hotel* on the corner of Flinders and Queen Sts. For $5, you get a choice of three roasts, plus a beer or a wine.

The city's three major department stores – Myer, David Jones and Daimaru – each have wonderful food

Value-for-Money Eating
Eating to a budget? *The Age Cheap Eats in Melbourne*
($14.95) is the best local guidebook to Melbourne's cheap-
est and best-value eateries, and if you're staying a while
it will quickly repay your investment. It's available from all
bookshops and newsagents.

One of the best-value eateries in the city is *Cafee
Baloo's*, with tasty Indian/Italian dishes. Run by the Hare
Krishnas, *Gopals* has three-course vegetarian meals for
$5.50, while for pasta try the Italian Waiter's Restaurant.

In St Kilda, the burgers in the bar at *Tolarno's* are a
bargain, while *Chichio's* (Map 11) offers $7 backpacker
specials. *The Galleon* is wonderful and great value, *Bala's*
does cheap Asian dishes, and the *Felafel Kitchen* has
all-you-can-eat deals for $4.50.

There are plenty of bargains along Brunswick St. *Cafe
Cappadocia* does good Turkish tucker for not much dosh,
the *Vegie Bar* is vegie heaven with nothing over $8, and at
lunch time (or if you order before 7 pm) you can have the $12
set menu at the stylish Japanese restaurant *Akari 177*.

Much loved by Melbourne Uni students, *La Porchetta*
(Map 9) in Carlton is one of the cheapest pizza/pasta
joints, and now has branches in South Yarra, Williamstown
and North Melbourne. Head to 'Little Saigon' – Victoria St
in Richmond – for a huge range of outstanding Vietnamese eating bargains. Also in Richmond, Swan St is the
place to go for Greek food.

Good, cheap bar meals are always the sign of a good
pub. Most pubs have bistro meals and bar meals – bar
meals are often the same food at cheaper prices. Bar
meals are served in the public bar – the service and decor
are usually down-to-earth, but you can get a good feed for
around $4 to $7 and rub shoulders with the locals while
you eat, sometimes literally. Don't miss the *All Nations
Hotel* in Richmond – it's hard to find, and hard to forget
once you've found it. ∎

emporiums with a selection of goodies that should
satisfy even the most obscure craving. Particularly
worth searching out is the *Daimaru Sushi Bar*, at level one
in the Melbourne Central complex – the omelettes, sushi
boxes and udon soups are sensational value.

SOUTHGATE

Since opening in the early 1990s, the Southgate development at Southbank (Map 1), on the south side of the
Yarra River, has quickly become one of Melbourne's best
and most popular eating venues. It enjoys a great setting
overlooking the river and the city skyline, is close to the
galleries and theatres of the Arts Precinct and the

Colonial Tramcar Restaurant

Melbourne's most popular attractions include its trams and restaurants, but when some oddball came up with the idea of combining the two, most people thought it was a weird gimmick that would never last. Well, several years down the track (sorry) the *Colonial Tramcar Restaurant* (☎ 9696 4000) is still a huge success with both visitors and locals – a great novelty idea backed up with good food and service. You can dine in comfort while taking a scenic evening tram cruise around Melbourne's streets.

There are two sittings – early dinner costs $55 a head which includes three courses and all drinks, and late dinner is $80 ($90 on Friday and Saturday) which includes five courses and all drinks. The converted 1920s tram even has specially built stabilisers so you don't have to worry about sharp corners. The tram leaves from Southbank Boulevard beside the National Gallery and heads down St Kilda Rd, along the Esplanade to Acland St and back. ■

gardens of the Kings Domain, and has a broad range of bars, cafes and restaurants, most of which have outdoor terraces and balconies where you can dine alfresco in the warmer weather.

On the upper level is *Walter's Wine Bar* (☎ 9690 9211), a classy establishment with fine views across the river. The wine list is extensive, and there's a large selection of wines by the glass. The food is simple, 'globally-influenced' cuisine with main meals in the $18 to $21 range. There's also a selection of less expensive snacks, or you can just drop in for a glass of wine – it stays open until 1 am (3 am on Friday and Saturday nights). Right next door is *Simply French*, a smart bar and brasserie with 'business lunches' for $17.50, light meals from $8 to $10 and main courses from $16 to $22.

On the mid-level is the impressive Italian bistro *Scusa Mi* (☎ 9699 4111), serving up classical Italian cuisine in a sophisticated setting. It's popular but fairly pricey, with mains in the $20 to $24 range. Much more affordable, and even more popular, is the funky and casual *Blue Train Cafe*, which serves breakfasts, pastas and risottos, wood-fired oven pizzas, salads and more. There's a bar, tables inside and out, and a cruisey lounge area with armchairs and couches. Also on the mid-level, *Bon Bons* specialises in coffee and cakes but also has good breakfasts and sandwiches.

On ground level, the outstanding *Blakes* (☎ 9699 4100) serves modern and innovative food with mains in the $15 to $23 range, and the menu adds an interesting touch by recommending a wine to complement each meal – all wines are also sold by the glass (around $5). *Bistro Vite* is a casual and simple French bistro, where dishes like crisply roasted duckling or a chicken casserole range from $13 to $16. Next door, *E Gusto* is a stylish and traditional Italian bistro with pastas and risottos from $10 to $14 and other mains in the $16 to $19 range. *Akvavit* is a Swedish smorgasbord restaurant, where you can tuck into a little of everything or choose from the à la carte menu. The smorgasbord costs $20 a head at lunch time and between 6 and 7.30 pm, or $28 after 7.30 pm.

The centre of the ground floor is taken up by the *Wharf Food Market*, with scattered clusters of tables and chairs interspersed with a selection of excellent international food stalls. These places are all reasonably priced, the service is fast and if you're in a group there's no need for compromise – everyone can have something different. Choices include *Charmaine's* gourmet ice-cream parlour, *Rive Gauche* French patisserie, *Shoji* with Japanese and Korean cuisine, *Choise China Bar* serving Chinese, Malaysian and Thai foods, *Rhumba's* fine-food bar and delicatessen, *Lettuce & Lovage* with salads and fresh juices, and even a gourmet fish & chip shop called *Ritzy Fish*.

ARTS PRECINCT

There are two licensed restaurants within the Victorian Arts Centre (Map 1). The casual *Treble Clef* (☎ 9281 8264) is in the Concert Hall overlooking the river and city skyline; it opens from 11 am until around midnight, serving snacks, light meals or more substantial main courses from $11 to $18. *The Vic/Roberto's* (☎ 9281 8180) in the Theatres Building is a bit more formal – it's part coffee shop and part restaurant, with snacks and sandwiches around the $5 mark and main courses ranging from $15 to $18. There are pre and post-performance sittings, and bookings are usually necessary.

In the National Gallery (Map 6) is the terrific *Garden Restaurant & Cafe*, which opens daily from 11 am to 4 pm and serves lunches and morning and afternoon teas. This is a very civilised place to take a break from your gallery tour, with main courses in the $9 to $18 range and a good buffet with tasty salads and desserts ($6.90/11 for small/large plates).

The Malthouse Cafe, in the Malthouse Theatre (Map 6) at 113 Sturt St, is a great little cafe with all sorts of tasty snacks and meals. It's a popular spot for a quick bite before or after a show, but it's also open during the day and attracts an interesting blend of actors, writers, directors and other arty types.

ST KILDA

St Kilda has been transformed almost beyond recognition in the past decade or so, and in many ways its eateries are a reflection of both the past and the future. The past is a noisy hamburger joint, a fast-felafel bar, or even a well-worn Italian bistro. The future is an ultra-hip cafe with fabulous European styling and a clientele to match. This is the suburb with something for everybody, where the past and the future sit comfortably side by side.

St Kilda's two main eating precincts are along Fitzroy and Acland Sts, but there are also some good places down by the sea.

Fitzroy St

This street (Map 11) is at the forefront of St Kilda's metamorphosis, and lately it seems that not a week goes by without a new bar, cafe or restaurant opening along here.

The beach end of Fitzroy St is now crowded with groovy eateries, most of which are open-fronted with tables spilling out onto the footpath. *Mr Munchy*, at No 7, is one of the more affordable places with pizzas and pastas, good salads and other continental dishes in the $8 to $13 range. Next door, the very chic *Madame Joe Joe* (☎ 9534 0000) is one of the best of the new breed of St Kilda restaurants. It serves up fabulous Mediterranean-style food and is fairly pricey, but great for a splurge.

Farther along at No 23, *The Street Cafe* is a big and bustling cafe, bar and restaurant with something for everyone – sit out the front and play the see-and-be-seen game. Next door at No 25, *Cafe Barcelona* is a smooth, atmospheric Spanish eatery offering a selection of tapas-style dishes (mostly $6 to $8) and a great range of paellas ($11 to $16 per person).

In the next block at No 31, the slick and sophisticated *Cafe Di Stasio* (☎ 9525 3999) has a reputation for outstanding Italian food, although if you don't have *the* look (ie, very hip or just plain rich) you might feel a little out of place here. If so, head for the tiny and cheerful *Hard Wok Cafe* (Map 11) at No 49, with Asian stir-fries, laksas and curries from $6 to $10. At 55 Fitzroy St, *Leo's Spaghetti Bar* is something of a St Kilda institution, with a coffee bar, bistro and restaurant, while farther along at No 73 *Patee Thai* is a tiny Thai-food cafe with tasty tucker and mains from $12 to $15.

On the corner of Fitzroy and Park Sts, *Bortolotto's* is dominated by a large and colourful St Kilda beach mural. The excellent food is Italian provincial, with main meals from $16 to $22. Next door, *Cafe Menis* is a laid-back bar and bistro with mains from $8 to $14.

A couple of blocks farther up at No 42, the wonderful *Tolarno Bar & Bistro* (☎ 9525 5477) features the quirky wall murals of local artist Mirka Mora. The restaurant specialises in Mediterranean-styled cuisine, and you can order à la carte or there's a $35-a-head menu which gives you a sample of six different dishes. Next door, the small bar/eatery offers snacks and meals in the $5 to $10 range, including the best burgers in Melbourne ($7.50 with fries).

Back on the busy side of the street, the bustling *Topolino's* at No 87 is the place to go for a pizza or big bowl of pasta (try the spaghetti marinara for $11.20 – you won't go home hungry!), especially late at night when it's usually packed. It stays open until around sunrise. *Bar Ninety Seven*, at 97 Fitzroy St, is a very fashionable bar/eatery with good food – wear sunnies by day, something black if you're coming at night. *Chichio's*, at No 109, is a popular budget eatery that offers meals for two people for $7 each – you get pizza or pasta, salad, bread and a drink. Most of their other dishes are under $10.

On the corner of Fitzroy and Grey Sts is the *George Hotel*. A hundred years ago, the George was one of St Kilda's grandest hotels, but as the years passed the old pub slid into disrepair and punkish ill-repute. But since being taken under the wing of local restaurant guru Donlevy Fitzpatrick, the George has made a welcome return to the forefront of St Kilda style. The corner bar/cafe is known as the *Melbourne Wine Room*, and features fine food, great snacks, an outstanding selection of Victorian wines and live music.

Acland St Area

At the northern end of Acland St (Map 11) at No 6, *Chinta Blues* is a hip Malaysian restaurant with a New York kind of ambience and delicious main courses ranging from $7.50 to $12.

Farther down Acland St on the corner of Fawkner St, you'll find a trio of European-style places with something for everybody. *Spuntino* is a laid-back Italian street cafe serving focaccias, pastas, antipasto, etc, while next door the *Harley Court Cafe* is a great place for coffee and cake, and has tasty snacks like filled croissants and mini pizzas. And at No 54, the *Dog's Bar* is the place where the truly hip people hang out, and they usually come in droves. If you can get in, this popular and hectic bar also serves good food at reasonable prices.

Down south at 71 Acland St, the unassuming *Vineyard Restaurant* is the place to head for if you're craving a big juicy steak – the grills are huge and range from $11 to $26 (add another $4.30 for salad!). Just off Acland St at 9 Carlisle St, *The Galleon* is a local favourite with a quirky 1950s concrete-and-laminex decor, good music and everything from toasted sandwiches and apple crumble to chicken and leek pie – all at very reasonable prices. There's also a shared accommodation notice board here.

Back on Acland St at No 94, *Chinta Ria* (☎ 9525 4664) combines terrific Malaysian food with jazz and soul images and sounds – main meals are $7 to $12, and you'll need to book. Next door the quirky and opinionated *Cafe Goa* serves spicy Portuguese, Indian and vegetarian dishes, most of which are between $6 and $8.50.

On the next corner, *Amber* is a popular Indian place with excellent food at reasonable prices, while a little farther up Shakespeare Grove, *Bala's* does quick, cheap and tasty Thai, Malaysian, Indian and Japanese dishes. Most dishes are $6 to $10, and takeaways are even cheaper.

Scheherezade, at No 99, serves up central-European food in generous proportions. This old-fashioned, low-key cafe is a good place to come when you're really hungry, with hearty dishes like Russian borscht, Hungarian goulash, cabbage rolls and gefilte fish.

Down at No 130, *The Felafel Kitchen* does felafels, souvlakis, chicken and salads, and offers an all-you-can-eat deal for $4.50. Across the road at No 130, *Cicciolina* is a very hip, very popular little Italian bistro with lunches from $4.50 to $9 and dinners from $10 to $16.

Acland St is also renowned for its fine delis and cake shops – the window displays emanate so many calories you're in danger of putting on kg just walking past.

Around the corner at 211 Barkly St, *Wild Rice* is a very good organic/vegan cafe with stir-fries, casseroles, burgers, salads and more from $5 to $9, as well as a pleasant courtyard out back. It's open daily from noon to 10 pm. Around the next corner is the popular *Rasa's Vegie Bar* at 5 Blessington St, a tiny vegetarian bar with tofu or lentil burgers at $5.40 and vegetarian stir-fries, curries and pastas from $8 to $11.

Seaside

The Stokehouse (Map 11; ☎ 9525 5555), down on the fore-shore at 30 Jacka Boulevard, has one of the best settings in town and is just about a 'must-see' for visitors to Melbourne. The restaurant section upstairs is fairly pricey but has wonderful views and outstanding food in the 'modern Mediterranean/Asian' style, while downstairs is a big, bustling bar/bistro with an outdoor terrace and tasty tucker like antipasto, burgers, fish & chips, and gourmet pizzas, all from $9 to $14. But nobody comes here just to eat – they come to see (sunsets over the Bay, the passing parade of strollers, in-line skaters, joggers and cyclists, and all the beautiful people) and be seen. So enjoy already.

The Pavilion (☎ 9534 8221), nearby at 40 Jacka Boulevard, has an equally good position. It's a classy licensed restaurant with an elegant Art Deco-influenced dining room, a great outlook over the Bay, and some of the best seafood in Melbourne with mains in the $18 to $22 range. For those of us without gold Amex cards there's also a takeaway section with great fish & chips and outdoor tables.

Last but by no means least is the wonderful *Espy Kitchen* way up the back of the Esplanade Hotel. It's always busy, the food is great (mains from $9 to $15), and after you've eaten you can play pool or check out one of the (usually free) live bands.

FITZROY

Brunswick St

You haven't really eaten out in Melbourne until you've been to Brunswick St (Maps 3 & 6). It's the funkiest and most fascinating street in town, and for a couple of blocks north and south of Johnston St it's lined with dozens of great cafes, bars and restaurants. It's also the street that best reflects Melbourne's multiculturalism and its obsession with food. You'll find Thai, Indian, Turkish, Greek, Italian, French, Malaysian, even Ethiopian and Afghan restaurants – you can virtually travel the culinary world in three blocks.

MARK ARMSTRONG

Brunchin' at The Fitz, Brunswick Street, Fitzroy.

With so many places to choose from, perhaps the thing to do is promenade along the street and consider your options. Have a beer here, a glass of wine there, and study the menus and the crowds. Like trucks outside a good roadhouse, you can usually tell which restaurants are good by how crowded they are. There are far too many eateries along here to list in this book – the following are just a few of the places worth checking out.

Try to avoid driving here – on most nights you haven't got a snowball's chance in hell of getting a park within coo-ee of Brunswick St. Jump on a tram instead.

Most of the action is up around Johnston St, but there are quite a few interesting places down the city end near Gertrude St. *Nyala* (Map 6), at 113 Brunswick St, serves exotic Ethiopian and Sudanese food in a casual bluestone and cane setting, with most main courses from $10 to $13 and banquet menus at $22 and $25. The combination plate has a good variety of dishes, which you scoop up with spongy bread known as 'injera'. At No 177, *Akari 177* (Map 6) is a stylish but low-key licensed Japanese restaurant which is very popular. They have set lunches and early dinner deals (order before 7 pm) which are both great value at $12, and they also offer a choice of set menus from $18 to $40. Next door, *De Los Santos* (Map 6) is a groovy bar/cafe with a Spanish-influenced menu offering good tapas, paella and other dishes from $6 to $12.

Brasserie Gregoire (Map 6), farther north at No 201, is a small cafe-grill which serves French/Mediterranean/Moroccan dishes in the $10 to $15 range – good value, and good fun. Next door at No 199, *Cafe Rumours* (Map 6) is a popular cafe, particularly with members of the gay and lesbian community.

A little farther north is the hip *Black Cat Cafe* (Map 3) at No 252, where the decor is very 1950s – lots of vinyl and laminex. The Cat has a good snack menu with most dishes under $6, and (to my eternal happiness) it's one of the last remaining refuges of the endangered spearmint milkshake. It also has a shared accommodation notice board.

This part of the street is well endowed with the flavours of the Orient. *Sala Thai* (Map 3), at No 266, has good Thai food in the $9 to $13 range , and particularly good vegetarian dishes. Choose between a traditional table or cushions on the floor. *Thai Thani* (Map 6), at No 293, is another good option for spicy Thai food.

On the corner of Johnston St, *Cafe Provincial* (Map 3; ☎ 9417 2228) is unrecognisable as the old pub it once was. It's now sparse, spacious and stylish, with a front bar, a great Italian bistro where you can watch the chefs at work and a burger grill next door. *Mario's* (Map 3), at

303 Brunswick St, is highly favoured by the locals. It's a fairly hip cafe with an arty, devout clientele and wonderful Italian-based food for any time of day or night.

If you're finding Brunswick St too trendy, try *Cafe Cappadocia* (Map 3) at No 324 – it's an unpretentious, down-to-earth Turkish restaurant with honest (and cheap!) food.

Another good option is *The Fitz* (Map 3) at No 347, which has a delicious range of breakfasts ($3 to $7), good cakes ($4.90) and lunches and dinners from $7 to $14, plus tables out on the footpath.

Rhumbarella's (Map 3), across at No 342, is an arty, barn-sized place which is everything from a coffee bar to a restaurant. There's an art gallery upstairs. *Babka Bakery-Cafe* (Map 3) at No 358 is famous for its breads and pastries – it's also a great place for breakfast, with interesting dishes like corn fritters, bacon and tomato from $4.50 to $5.50. For lunch try their delicious pies and sandwiches.

At No 366, *Joe's Garage* (Map 3) has a central bar, with benches and stools on one side and a dining area on the other. It's a friendly place with a great atmosphere. Breakfasts, focaccias and salads are $5 to $8, pastas, risottos and other mains are $10 to $14. Next door, *Charmaine's* (Map 3) has simply sensational ice cream, cakes and other indulgent delights.

On the corner of Rose St, the *Vegie Bar* (Map 3) exudes delicious aromas and has a great range of vegetarian meals under $8 – it's so popular that it has recently taken over the shop next door. Another Brunnie St favourite is *Bakers Cafe* (Map 3) at No 384 – it has plenty to choose from and reasonable prices.

A couple of blocks north on the Westgarth St corner, the very laid-back *Cafe Retro* (Map 3) is a spacious 1950s-style cafe.

Johnston St

The stretch of Johnston St between Brunswick and Nicholson Sts (Map 3) is known as Melbourne's Spanish quarter. There's a small collection of tapas bars and restaurants in the vicinity of the Spanish Club *(Hogar Español)* at 59 Johnston St, which has a simple bar and restaurant of its own which is open to the public.

At 74 Johnston St, the *Carmen Bar* (☎ 9417 4794), is a hectic and down-to-earth restaurant with authentic Spanish food (main courses mostly $8 to $13) and live flamenco and Spanish guitar from Thursday to Saturday nights. Their outdoor barbecue is popular in summer – buy your meat or fish at the counter and cook it yourself. Or you could try the rather old-fashioned *Colmao Flamenco*, nearby at No 60.

Farther west there's a cluster of tapas bars serving tasty Spanish snacks and dishes, which you can wash down with a glass of sangria or vino. Most of these places play lively and loud Latin music, and some also feature flamenco shows. Bars include *La Sangria* at No 46 and *Kahlo's* at No 36, while *Bar Salona* at No 48 is more of a dance club. Up near Brunswick St at No 95 is the huge *Bull Ring*, which is part Spanish restaurant, part tapas bar and part nightclub.

Johnston St isn't all Spanish food – *Chishti's*, at No 15 near the corner of Nicholson St, has excellent Indian and vegetarian food with mains from $10 to $13.

Gertrude St

Farther south, Gertrude St (Map 6) has an interesting collection of galleries, art suppliers, costume designers and antique shops, as well as a few good eateries. At No 193, *Arcadia* is a groovy little cafe, while at No 199 the very straightforward *Macedonia* does char-grilled meats, goulash and other Balkan specialties – it's BYO, with meals in the $10 to $16 range. On the corner of Gertrude and Gore Sts, the arty and cosy *Builders Arms Hotel* serves dinners from Wednesday to Sunday nights, with interesting, quirky dishes from $6 to $10.

Smith St

Forming the border between Fitzroy and Collingwood, Smith St (Map 6) also has some good eateries. It's an interesting multicultural streetscape, a lot less fashionable than Brunswick St but still well worth exploring.

Down at 14 Smith St, the *Smith St Bar & Bistro* is a very pleasant and stylish bar/restaurant. There's a front bar with snacks ($3 to $7), a spacious lounge area with couches and an open fire, and an elegant dining rooms with French/Italian mains in the $13 to $15 range.

North at No 117, *Vegetarian Orgasm* is a bright and friendly vegie cafe with an interesting range of dishes from $8 to $10. *Cafe Birko* at No 123 is a rustic bar/restaurant with burgers, stir-fries, risottos and pastas around $7.50, while on the corner of Peel St, the *Grace Darling Hotel* is a great pub with live jazz, rock and blues on weekends, cheap bar snacks, and an excellent restaurant.

At 275 Smith St, the *Soul Food Vegetarian Cafe* is a popular vegan cafe with salads and hot foods from $6.50 to $9 and an organic grocer next door. Next door again at No 279, *Blonds* is a fun and friendly Swedish bar-eatery with hearty Scandinavian-style food including a good range of vegetarian dishes.

Farther north across Johnston St at 354 Smith St, *Cafe Bohemio* (Map 3) is a quirky, laid-back Latin-American cafe with mains from $8 to $11. A popular meeting place for the Spanish-speaking community, it has live jazz some Thursdays and Fridays, a second-hand bookshop and an upstairs gallery that hosts Latin dance classes, films and workshops.

CARLTON

Lygon St

This street (Maps 3 & 6) was once affectionately thought of as the multicultural centre of Melbourne. That was back in the days when Melbourne was a dull city devoid of alternative culture, and Lygon St, with its fascinating blend of cosmopolitan immigrants and bohemian university students, was thought of as a glimpse of Europe. But, progress being progress, eventually the old Italian

RICHARD NEBESKY

Sampling the tucker at Lygon Street, Carlton.

tailors and small shopkeepers moved out and the developers and entrepreneurs moved in.

Nowadays Lygon St is all bright lights, big restaurants and flashy boutiques – a local writer calls it an 'Antipodean Via Veneto'. No longer considered a trend-setter in Melbourne's restaurant scene, it now caters mainly to tourists and out-of-towners, although some of the long-running places are still worth searching out.

Tram Nos 1 or 21, which run along Swanston St, will take you there from the city centre, or if you feel like walking, it's a very pleasant stroll up Russell St.

Down the city end at No 125 is the elegant *Cerabona's* (Map 6). It has a street-front cafe section with a good range of meals and snacks under $10, and a restaurant that serves up delicious and unusual pastas and risottos from $12 to $16 and other mains from $14 to $18. *Casa Malaya* (Map 6), across the road at No 118, is an excellent Malaysian restaurant with superb and reasonably-priced food.

Farther up at No 177, the long-running *Notturno* (Map 6) serves breakfasts, suppers and everything in between. It stays open until 2 or 3 am midweek, and all night long on weekends. Also good is *Nyonya* (Map 6) up at No 191. Nyonya food, a blend of Malay spices and ingredients and Chinese cooking styles, originates from Singapore, and they do it well here. The setting is bright and cheerful and the prices are very good, with most mains in the $7 to $12 range.

Also worth a visit is *Borsari Ristorante* (Map 6), on the corner of Grattan and Lygon Sts. It's a busy bistro with tables out on the footpath and traditional Italian cuisine. Pastas are $13 to $15, other mains $18 to $27 – the seafood is particularly good.

Papa Gino's (Map 3), at No 221, is a straightforward and long-running pizza-and-pasta joint with a good reputation.

A block farther north at No 303, *Tiamo* (Map 3) is another old Lygon St campaigner. It's an old-fashioned Italian bistro that's popular with Melbourne Uni students, and has tasty pastas around $7 and great breakfasts just like mama used to cook for $7.50.

At No 333, *Jimmy Watson's* (Map 3; ☎ 9347 3985) is one of Melbourne's most famed institutions. Wine and talk are the order of the day at this long-running winebar/restaurant – the annual Jimmy Watson trophy is Australia's best known red wine award, so you can count on the wines being drinkable. This has always been a great spot for long, leisurely lunches, and nowadays it's also open at night. With one of Melbourne's top chefs at the helm, the small upstairs dining rooms are now used for fine-dining.

Across the road, *Trotters* (Map 3) at No 400 is another popular little bistro, serving good breakfasts and hearty Italian fare in the $7 to $12 range. Lygon St also has plenty of dark little coffee houses, tempting, calorie-stuffed cake shops and great gelati bars.

Recently relocated from Lygon St to bright new premises around the corner at 201 Faraday St, *Shakahari* (Map 3; ☎ 9347 3848) is one of Melbourne's oldest, and still one of the most innovative, vegetarian restaurants. Open the door and you'll be drawn in by those wonderful wafting aromas. The ingredients are fresh and seasonal, the main dishes are all $10 to $12, and you should save room for the wonderful desserts at $5.50.

Elgin St

In the next block up, at 118 Elgin St (Map 3), *Chinta Ria R&B* serves up great Malaysian food in a smooth, sophisticated setting. Main courses range from $10 to $16. Right across the road at No 109, *Abla's* is Melbourne's best Lebanese restaurant by a mile. OK, it hasn't got too much competition, but the food is great and it's almost always crowded. Their banquet menus are good value at $25 and $30 a head.

Rathdowne St

Rathdowne St (Map 3), which runs parallel with Lygon St, has some good alternatives to its more crowded commercial cousin.

At No 166 is *Wine Bar II*, a classy and intimate bar/bistro run by the owners of the exceptionally successful *Walter's Wine Bar* at Southbank. Main courses are in the $18 to $22 range. Nearby at 174 Rathdowne St, *Cafe Amritas*, is a casual and popular place serving up affordable Thai, Indian and Malaysian dishes.

Farther north is the *Paragon Cafe* at No 651. The food here is excellent, with pastas around $8, main dishes like calamari fritti around $15, and a great range of cakes and desserts. Another block north at 370 Rathdowne St is the *Kent Hotel*, a stylish bar/cafe specialising in wood-fired oven pizzas and calzone, with nothing over $10. Their outdoor tables are a great spot to be on a sunny day or warm night. Up the road at No 392 is *La Porchetta*, which has pastas and pizzas from $4 to $7. The cheap prices, plus the fact that the food's pretty good, accounts for its enormous popularity with students from the university. If you can't get in, try up the road at *La Trattoria*, which attracts an older crowd and is slightly more expensive but still good value.

NORTH MELBOURNE

North Melbourne (Map 5), home to the YHA hostels, doesn't have the glamour or the range of some other inner suburbs, but there are some great places to eat if you're prepared to hunt amongst the semi-industrial, dark streetscapes.

Victoria St has a good range of places. *Amiconi* (☎ 9328 3710), at 359 Victoria St, is one of the most popular eateries. This traditional little Italian bistro has been a local favourite for years, and you'll probably have to book. Across the road at No 488, the *Peppermint Lounge Cafe* is a top spot for breakfast or lunch, while nearby at No 480 the modern Deco-styled *Cafe Hotel* has interesting meals in the $7 to $10 range, as well as pool tables and live acoustic music on weekends.

Warung Agus, farther along at 305 Victoria St, is a cosy and simple two-room restaurant that serves great Balinese food with mains from $10 to $13.

For Vietnamese food, head down towards the Queen Victoria Market – across the road, *Viet Nam House* at 284 Victoria St and *Dalat's* at No 270 both have cheap Vietnamese food with lunches around $5 and mains from $7 to $12.

For good and inexpensive pasta, the locals head to *Maria Trattoria* at 122 Peel St. Nearby on the corner of Victoria and Peel Sts, the busy *La Porchetta* is a budget bistro with pizzas and pastas from $4 to $7 and other mains under $10.

The *Eldorado Hotel*, at 46 Leveson St, is an old pub that has been revitalised into a fun, bustling 'cafe saloon'. The menu covers lots of territory – burgers, grills, chillis, pastas – and there's a pleasant covered courtyard. The open fires in winter make it a cosy place for a beer.

If you're looking for somewhere romantic and slightly old-fashioned with good French food, try *La Chaumière* (☎ 9328 1650) at 36 Abbotsford St (actually in West Melbourne). Nothing much has changed here since the 1970s, apart from the prices. The food is still great, it's BYO, and a three-course meal for two will cost about $80.

RICHMOND

Victoria St

Walk down Victoria St (Map 7) and you'll soon realise why this area has become known as 'Little Saigon'. Melbourne's growing Vietnamese community has transformed what was once a dull and colourless traffic route into a fascinating, bustling commercial centre. The stretch of Victoria St between Hoddle St and Church St is lined with Asian supermarkets and groceries, butchers and fishmongers, discount stores selling Asian goods, and dozens of bargain-priced Vietnamese restaurants.

If you're coming by car, note that parking spaces are at a premium. Otherwise, trams No 42 or 109 from Collins St in the city will get you there.

Don't expect vogue decor in the restaurants, but the food will be fresh, cheap and authentic, and the service lightning fast and friendly. You can have a huge, steaming bowl of soup that will be a meal in itself for around $4, and main courses generally cost between $4 and $8, so you can afford to be adventurous.

One of the original, and still one of the most popular places, is *Thy Thy 1*, hidden away up a narrow, uninviting set of stairs at 142 Victoria St. This no-frills place is dirt cheap, but the food is fresh and excellent. The same people have a slightly more upmarket place called *Thy Thy 2* down the road at No 116. Try the pork, chicken, prawn or vegetable spring rolls – 10 for $5, complete with mint and lettuce leaves for do-it-yourself construction.

Vao Doi at No 120 is another good place to try, as is *Victoria* across the road at No 311. The menu here also offers Thai and Chinese food, and no, you can't eat those big fish in the tank up the back – they bring the owners good luck! *Tran Tran* at No 76 is also popular.

Farther along at No 397, *Minh Tan III* is a bit more upmarket than most other places, and specialises in seafood. Banquets cost from $16 to $22, lunches from $5.

Back down at the city end of Victoria St at No 66, the ultra-modern *Tho Tho* is a surprisingly stylish bar/restaurant that would be more at home in South Yarra, or maybe New York, but despite the slick decor the food here is still dirt-cheap with mains ranging from $6 to $10.

Swan St

Richmond's Swan St (Map 7), in the block east of Church St, is something of an enclave for Greek cuisine. You'll find half a dozen or so Greek restaurants in this area, all reasonably priced and offering similar menus: an assortment of dips such as tzatziki and taramasalata with pitta bread, souvlaki and sausages, sardines and calamari, stuffed peppers and moussaka – all the old favourites! The pub on the corner sells retsina. To get here from the city, take tram No 70 from Batman Ave, by the river, to the corner of Swan and Church Sts.

Elatos Greek Tavern, at 213 Swan St, is one of the best places – lively, licensed and good value, and the seafood here is particularly good.

Across the road at No 262, *Agapi* has traditional Greek dishes, with mains from $7.50 to $16 and banquets for $18, $20 or $22 a head. It's also licensed or you can BYO. Next door the tiny *Salona* is also good, and has similarly priced food.

At No 256, *Kaliva* is fairly plain, although you can dine to live bouzouki music Thursday to Sunday nights.

Bridge Rd

Running parallel with and between Swan and Victoria Sts, Bridge Rd (Map 7) also has some great food options. Take tram Nos 48 or 75 from Flinders St in the city to these restaurants.

Starting at the city end, there's the *Downtown Bar & Bistro* at 14-16 Bridge Rd, a reasonably priced place serving pizzas, pastas, focaccias and other Italian tucker. Next door is *Chilli Padi* at 18 Bridge Rd, which serves authentic and excellent Malaysian food in an elegant setting. It has an $8.50 three-course lunch special, noodle and vegetable dishes from $8 and other mains from $13 to $18.

At 78 Bridge Rd the *Tofu Shop* is definitely popular with the vegetarian and health-kick crowds. It can be a squeeze finding a stool at the counter at lunch time but never mind, the salads, vegetables, filled filo pastries and 'soyalaki' (a great invention!) are tasty and filling.

Across the road at No 61 is the famed *Vlado's* (☎ 9428 5833). This place has a reputation for serving the best steaks in the country, and if you're into prime red meat and strawberry pancakes, you'll be more than happy to pay $55 a head for the four-course set menu.

A good place for Indian food is *Radjoot* at 142 Bridge Rd. If you've travelled in India you might remember that name as a popular Indian motorcycle brand! The restaurant is a small place with excellent Indian food including some great tandoori dishes. *Gold Bridge* at No 176 has good $5 lunches and Thai meals ranging from $9 to $13.

Across Church St at 270 Bridge Rd you'll find *Silvio's*, serving up some of the best pizzas in town. Nearby at No 288, *Spargo's* is a bustling open-fronted cafe-eatery with a designer-rustic decor and a fabulous cake counter – try the chocolate, date and almond torte. They also serve up breakfasts, pastas, risottos and wood-fired oven pizzas (all $10 to $12) as well as a selection of Asian-Mediterranean style mains ($12 to $16).

If you're looking for bargain eats, it's worth heading a few blocks farther east. *Thai Oriental*, down at No 430, has cheap and tasty Thai, Malay and Indian food with most main courses around $6 – great value. And right next door, *Pasta Pronto* does good pasta dishes for $6 to $8.

Lennox St

The *London Tavern*, at 238 Lennox St (Map 7; midway between Swan St and Bridge Rd), used to be Lonely Planet's local pub, until we moved office. It remains the archetypal Aussie corner pub, with a cast of local characters permanently inhabiting the front bar and a bistro serving up the old stagers like schnitzels, parmigianas, steaks and pastas (all $7 to $9). There's a bright and sunny courtyard where you can eat outside.

Also in Lennox St, but much farther north, is the great *All Nations Hotel* at No 64. It's hard to get to because of a series of one-way streets, but if you make the effort you'll be rewarded with some of the best pub food in town. It's an original, honest and friendly pub, the sort of place everyone wishes they had as a local. It's open Tuesday to Sunday for lunch and Wednesday to Friday for dinner, and meals range from $8 to $16.

SOUTH YARRA

Most of South Yarra's eateries are along Toorak Rd and Chapel St. The No 8 tram from the city will get you there.

If your favourite pastimes include shopping and eating, you'll be right at home wandering along these two streets. Foodwise, no particular cuisine dominates. Variety is the key, although being one of Melbourne's more affluent areas, there aren't too many cheapies. Still, you'll find some honest Italian bistros, some good places to take lunch and rest your weary shopping feet, and dozens of stylish cafes and restaurants ranging from the simple to the extravagant.

Toorak Rd

Starting from the Punt Rd end, *Ticino's Bistro* (Map 9) at 16 Toorak Rd is a tiny, rustic place with good pizzas and pastas from $6 to $9. Across the road at No 11, the bustling and stylish *France-Soir* (Map 9; ☎ 9866 8569) is one of the best French brasseries in town, with excellent food and mains in the $17 to $20 range. It's open for lunch and dinner, but you'll probably need to book.

Across at 58 Toorak Rd, *Winchell's Deli* (Map 9) offers breakfast specials from $4.50 and is a popular spot for lunch. If you're feeling indulgent, pop into *Frenchy's* (Map 9) at No 76 for a coffee and one of its sublime French pastries.

Fine Dining

The Age Good Food Guide ($16.95) is the local bible to Melbourne's best restaurants. If you're looking for somewhere special – and money is no object – the following places are consistently rated amongst Melbourne's best (prices indicate an approximate per person cost for a three-course meal, not including drinks).

Jacques Reymond's (Map 10; ☎ 9525 2178), set in a grand historic mansion at 78 Williams Rd in Windsor, is currently rated number one in Melbourne by the AGFG team for its exquisite blend of food, service and setting. The superb food is French-based, with Asian-Australian influences. (Fixed price lunches are from $25, dinner from $65.)

Marchetti's Latin (Map 1; ☎ 9662 1985), 25 Lonsdale St in the city, is Melbourne's favourite 'high society' restaurant – the Italian food is superb and the service slick ($55).

Head to the *Flower Drum* (Map 1; ☎ 9662 3655), at 17 Market Lane in Chinatown, for sensational regional Cantonese cuisine in stylish surroundings ($60). *Suntory* (☎ 9525 1231), at 74 Queens Rd in South Melbourne, is over the top in both setting and wonderful Japanese food ($50).

Vlado's (☎ 9428 5833), at 61 Bridge Rd in Richmond, is famous for its charcoal-grilled, aged beef steaks and strawberry pancakes. Its four-course set menu costs around $55. *Chinois* (☎ 9826 3388), at 176 Toorak Rd in South Yarra, serves innovative East-meets-West cuisine in ultra-hip and stylish surroundings. (Fixed price lunches from $25, or $35 on Sunday; dinner around $55.)

Many of Melbourne's finest restaurants specialise in French cuisine. Set up by the famous French chef himself, the *Paul Bocuse Restaurant* (☎ 9660 6600) in the Daimaru Department Store has some of the best, and most expensive, French food in town – dinner is around $85, lunch around $55. If that's a little steep, *France Soir* (Map 9) in South Yarra is also highly rated, and quite a bit cheaper.

These places are just the tip of Melbourne's culinary iceberg. Other places that stand out include *Max's* at the Grand Hyatt Hotel, *Le Restaurant* at the Sofitel (Map 1), the *Mask of China*, in Chinatown, *The Pavilion* in St Kilda (for seafood by the sea), *Blake's* and *Walter's Wine Bar* at Southgate, *Caffe e Cucina* in South Yarra and the *Isthmus of Kra* in South Melbourne. ■

Next door at No 74, the popular *Barolo's* (Map 9) is a narrow bistro with a pleasant rear courtyard. It has quick lunch specials for $6.50, good pastas for $12 to $17 and interesting Italian-style mains from $18 to $22. If that sounds a bit pricey for you, head down to *La Porchetta* (Map 9) at No 93 – it's one of the best-value pizza/pasta joints in town (from $4 to $7) with other mains under $10.

Tamani's (Map 9), at 156 Toorak Rd, and *Pinocchio's* (Map 9), nearby at No 152, are both popular Italian restaurants in the casual-rustic mode. Pinocchio's is essentially a pizzeria while Tamani's is more a general bistro. If you're watching your cash, Tamani's is the cheaper of the two.

Over the hill and across the railway line is *Pieroni* (Map 10) at 172 Toorak Rd, a cavernous and overtly glamorous bar/restaurant. Next door at No 176, *Chinois* (Map 10; ☎ 9826 3388) is equally glamorous and over-the-top, but it's also one of Melbourne's most acclaimed restaurants, specialising in innovative East-meets-West cuisine. Its lunch menus are excellent value, with a $25 'business lunch' for two courses and a glass of wine or a $35 'Sunday adventure' lunch for three courses. The à la carte menu is more expensive, with mains ranging from $22 to $33.

A block past the Chapel St intersection is the strange spectacle of four almost identical Italian bistros, side by side, each fronted by a sun terrace with umbrella-shaded tables. All four are popular, but for the record *Portofino* (Map 10) is the cheapest and *Vecchio Trastevere* (Map 10) the most expensive.

For something completely different try *Johnny Rocket*s (Map 10), a kitsch, 1950s-style hamburger joint at 257 Toorak Rd. It features waiters on rollerskates – I kid you not.

Chapel St

Don your designer sunnies and head down Chapel St (Map 10) – you'll find plenty of interesting cafes, bars and restaurants in amongst the fashion boutiques between Toorak Rd and Commercial Rd.

Caffe e Cucina (☎ 9827 6076), at 581 Chapel St, is one of the smallest, coolest and best cafe/restaurants in town, with great Italian meals in the $14 to $21 range. It's also one of *the* places in Melbourne to see and be seen, so ring ahead and book – or be prepared to queue. Down at No 571 is the friendly *Chapell's*, a bar/restaurant with quite good food – and, most importantly, it's open round the clock. Right next door at No 569 is *Kanpai*, a popular little Japanese restaurant with modestly priced dishes, and the menu even has a beginner's guide to Japanese phrases.

Across the road at No 560, *Cafe Greco* is a very slick bar and eatery with a Deco-inspired decor, sexy red-leather booth seating and a pretentious wish-we-were-truly-groovy clientele.

Thai 505 at 505 Chapel St is a small and intimate Thai restaurant with a reputation for very good food. At No

478, *La Lucciola* is a small, reasonably priced Italian bistro that is very popular with the locals. *La Camera*, at No 446, is another good Italian bistro. It's a stylish open-fronted place with interesting artwork and snacks and meals in the $6 to $12 range.

At 425 Chapel St is one of Melbourne's few African restaurants, *African Tukul* (☎ 9827 9448). It's a casual, quirky place decorated with interesting African artwork. It's BYO, with vegeterian dishes at $12 and meat dishes $13.

PRAHRAN

Commercial Rd & Chapel St

Commercial Rd is the border between South Yarra and Prahran. The Prahran Market (which is actually in South Yarra; Map 9) is a wonderful place to shop, with some of the best fresh vegetables, fruit and fish in Melbourne. All that fresh food must attract restaurateurs, because there are also plenty of eateries around here.

This stretch of Commercial Rd is something of a centre for Melbourne's gay and lesbian community, and around the market there's a string of popular cafes and restaurants.

Opposite the market at No 194, the *Blue Elephant Cafe* (Map 10) is a funky little cafe with great-value meals including breakfasts from $4.50, pastas and pizzas for $5.50 and other mains under $9. Nearby at No 176, *Chinta Ria* (Map 9) has good Malaysian meals ranging from $7 to $12, and you can dine to a background of good jazz and soul music.

At 153 Commercial Rd, the *Diva Bar* (Map 10) has good snacks and meals and a popular 'retro-80s' night on Saturday. Next door is a small cafe known as *Cafe 151*, and next to that at No 149 is *Menage à Trois*. Owned by two chefs, it's a simple shopfront restaurant with fine food – mains range from $13 to $18, or for $19.50 you can try a selection of three different dishes. At No 147 is the 'open-all-day' *Ramjet's Cafe*. Heading south back on Chapel St, *Ankara* at No 310 is a narrow and inexpensive Turkish restaurant which features a belly dancer on Friday and Saturday nights. The *Globe Cafe* (Map 10), at No 218, is definitely worth searching out. It has wonderful food – Thai, Cajun, Indian, Italian and lots of other influences, as well as a sensational cake counter. It's open for lunch and dinner and mains all range from $9 to $15.

At 190 Chapel St, the friendly *Gurkha's Brasserie* (Map 10) is an atmospheric Nepalese restaurant with a great selection of vegetarian dishes, char-grilled meats and curries, mostly around $10 or $11. Next door at No 188, *Wood Apple* specialises in Sri Lankan cuisine and is also very good value.

At No 135 *Patee Thai* (Map 10) is the best Thai restaurant in this area – it has an exotic, intimate feel and meals around $12 to $16. Farther down at 68 Chapel St in Windsor, *Marmara* (Map 11) is another cheap Turkish restaurant with great marinated kebabs and delicious thick Turkish bread. If you're looking for good food and good value down this end of Chapel St during the day, try the tiny, quirky and old-fashioned *Cafe Marie* (Map 11) at No 34.

Greville St

Greville St (Map 9), which runs off Chapel St beside the Prahran Town Hall, has an eclectic collection of grungy and groovy clothes boutiques, book and music shops, and a few good eateries. Beside the railway tracks at No 95 is the ever-popular *Cafe Feedwell*, an earthy vegetarian cafe serving interesting and wholesome food in the $5 to $10 range. The *Continental Cafe* at No 132 has wonderful food at affordable prices and a hip, sophisticated atmosphere – it's open from 7 am until midnight.

PORT MELBOURNE

Most of Port's eateries (Map 8) are along busy Bay St. *Molly Bloom's Hotel*, on the corner of Bay and Rouse Sts, is a popular Irish pub with a small courtyard and good bistro meals. At No 190 *The Flower* is an open-fronted bar/restaurant with cafe-style lunches and dinners priced in the $12 to $15 range. It's quite upmarket and popular with young corporate types, and has DJs and live music on weekends.

Farther up at 309 Bay St, the *Rose & Crown* is an old pub that has been converted into a slick bar and eatery. It serves an excellent range of breakfasts ($3.50 to $7.50), meals and snacks from $6 to $10. Its restaurant menu has mains from $14 to $19.

Port Melbourne also has some classic Aussie pubs in the back streets. These are the places where you will find true-blue characters tucking into a steak and chips and studying the horse-racing form guide at the same time.

The *Railway Club Hotel*, at 107 Raglan St, has a dining room that hasn't changed since the 1970s. Dishes like Camaroon curry and Asian pork stir-fry are $12 to $16, while in the public bar they serve good bar meals for $5 and $6. Another local with good old fashioned pub grub is the *Clare Castle Hotel* on the corner of Graham and Ross Sts.

ALBERT PARK

If you're in Albert Park and hungry, just follow the tram line (No 1) that runs down to the beach. Most of the area's eateries are along this route (Map 8). *Stavros Tavern*, down the beach end of Victoria Ave at No 183, is a loud and lively Greek taverna which has good food and live bouzouki music on Friday and Saturday nights. *Corey's Cafe* at No 173 is a quirky, friendly little place with great grills, salads and vegetarian meals at very reasonable prices – try the chicken breast burger with satay sauce ($6.90).

Vic Ave Pasta & Wine, at 135 Victoria Ave, is a bustling Italian bistro with a courtyard out back – pastas are around $12, other mains $16 to $19. Farther up at 7 Victoria Ave is my favourite local eatery, *Misuzu's*, a small and extremely popular 'village-style' Japanese cafe. It's open daily (except Monday) for breakfast, lunch and dinner, the food is great and the prices are very reasonable, with most dishes from $7 to $10.

Albert Park has a thriving and very trendy cafe scene, and there are some excellent daytime eateries around Bridport St and Victoria Ave. Popular places include the *Albert Park Deli*, the *Villagio Deli* and *Dundas Place Cafe*, all on Bridport St; *Morning Glory* at 59 Cardigan Place; and the *Avenue Foodstore* on the corner of Victoria Ave and Richardson St. All of these places serve great coffee, cooked breakfasts, gourmet sangers, focaccias, filled croissants, salads, pastas and home-made cakes. You can eat in, take away or sit out on the footpath and watch the trams roll by.

Ricardo's Trattoria (☎ 9699 5536), at 99 Dundas Place, is a chic and popular open-fronted Italian bistro, where you can eat pasta for around $12 or other main meals for $16 to $18.

SOUTH MELBOURNE

Kobe (Map 8; ☎ 6990 2692) at 179 Clarendon St is a simple Japanese restaurant with good main meals in the $14 to $18 range and three-course lunches from $10 to $16. At 225 Clarendon St, *Centro Cafe* (Map 8; ☎ 9699 5904) is a small and classical bistro specialising in food from the Bologna region of Italy (mains from $12 to $18) and wines from Victoria. It's open for weekday lunches and dinner nightly except Sunday – highly recommended.

Farther up Clarendon St at No 331, the *Chinese Noodle Shop* (Map 9) serves up noodle and other dishes that will fill you up for around $9 to $14. On the corner of Clarendon and Park St, the *Limerick Arms Hotel* (Map 9) is a groovy little pub with a pleasant courtyard restaurant with mains from $11 to $18 and bar meals and snacks from $5 to $8. Down the road at No 375, *Taco Bill's* (Map 9) is a licensed link in a chain of Mexican restaurants – good value and good fun, and much better than the American chain Taco Bell. Come on Tuesday nights when the meals are half-priced! Up near Albert Rd, the *Cricket Club Hotel* (Map 9), a cosy old pub run by friendly young people, has good pub meals.

If you transplanted a 1920s Aussie pub to provincial Italy, you'd end up with something like the *Locanda Veneta* (Map 9), at 273 Cecil St – a traditional bistro serving good food in a cosy atmosphere. Pastas are $10 to $17, main meals $15 to $18.

The Isthmus of Kra (Map 9; ☎ 9690 3688) at 50 Park St is one of Melbourne's best Asian restaurants. It's a classy and elegant place with fine service, specialising in southern Thai cuisine with Malaysian influences. Main courses are mostly $12 to $17, banquets (four or more people) are $30 to $45   you'll need to book.

WILLIAMSTOWN

Willy (Map 12) has a fine assortment of cafes and restaurants, most of them spread along Nelson Place, and catering to the hordes of day-trippers. *Hobson's Choice Foods*, at 213 Nelson Place, is an extremely popular street-front cafe with great food, all made on the premises – pies, brioches, breakfasts, sandwiches, vegetarian meals and lots more. Nearby at No 203 is the *Scuttlebutt*

MARK ARMSTRONG

Sam's Boatshed, Williamstown

Cafe, a groovy little 1950s-style place with interesting snacks and meals at reasonable prices. *Kohinoor*, farther up at No 223, looks pretty basic but serves good-value Indian food, with main meals from $7 to $10.

The next stretch of Nelson Place, beyond the Cole St roundabout, also contains its fair share of good pubs and eateries. The *Atomic Bar* has tasty pastas for $9 and a wide range of mains from $7 to $14, plus a billiards club upstairs. On the Syme St corner is the Customs House Market & Gallery, behind which you'll find the tiny *Flaming Burgers* doing great char-grilled burgers and *Sam's Boatshed*, a bar/eatery built around an old clinker boat. Their open-air courtyard is a very pleasant spot to tuck into one of their wood-fired oven pizzas. A couple of blocks farther along Nelson Place, the *Prince of Wales* hotel is an old pub renovated with a seafaring flavour. It has good bistro meals and a nightclub section.

On the south side of the peninsula overlooking the sandy Williamstown Beach is one of this area's newest and most inspiring eateries: *Siren's* (☎ 9397 7811), a stylishly converted bathing pavilion that incorporates a smart bar/bistro, an open-air timber decking area and an elegant restaurant. The food is modern Australian, with meals ranging from $8 to $15 in the bistro and $18 to $22 in the restaurant. Highly recommended.

Appropriately, Willy also has quite a few good seafood restaurants. The elegant *Sails* (☎ 9397 2377), upstairs at 231 Nelson Place, has seafood mains in the $20 to $22 range and live jazz on Sunday afternoons, while downstairs the more casual *Quarterdeck Cafe* has mains in the $9 to $12 range.

The Strand (☎ 9397 7474), on the corner of The Strand and Ferguson St, is stylish, simple and ultra-modern, with a small bar, an open-air courtyard and good views out over the Bay. The menu is predominantly seafood, with main courses in the $14 to $25 range, and there's an upmarket fish & chips takeaway joint next door.

Another good option is *The Anchorage* (☎ 9397 7799), half a km north along The Strand. This former boat shed sits over the water and has a cosy maritime feel, with timber decking, fishnets hanging from the roof, and a wonderful outlook across the Bay to the city skyline. Main courses are around $20.

Entertainment

When you're travelling, you feel obliged to do your fair share of sightseeing. As local author Helen Garner writes in *The Children's Bach*:

What do tourists do? They walk, they stand, they look, they buy. They fumble for money on buses, not knowing whether to pay the driver or conductor. They visit famous monuments, fountains, old houses full of stone and shutters and anachronistic lace...

But it doesn't have to be all famous monuments and fountains.

Melbourne has a thriving nightlife, a lively cultural scene and, due to the most flexible licensing laws in the country, some great bars and nightclubs. Melbourne has everything from a Latin dance club, a stand-up comedy night or a live band in a crowded pub to an opera at the Concert Hall or a play at one of its dozens of theatres.

The best source of 'what's on' information is the *Entertainment Guide (EG)* which comes out every Friday with *The Age* newspaper. *Beat* and *Inpress* are free music and entertainment magazines that have reviews, interviews and dates of gigs. They're available from pubs, cafes and venues.

Bass Victoria (☎ 11 500) is the main booking agency for theatre, concerts, sports and other events. For ticket enquiries ring ☎ 11 566, for credit card bookings ring ☎ 11 500 (or from outside the Melbourne metropolitan area ring ☎ 1800 338 998) and to book sporting events call ☎ 11 522. The telephone services operate Monday to Saturday from 9 am to 9 pm and Sunday from 10 am to 5 pm. Besides taking bookings by phone, Bass has about 15 outlets in places such as Myer stores, major theatres and shopping centres.

If you're looking for cheap tickets, visit the Half-Tix (☎ 9650 9420) booth in the Bourke St Mall, which sells half-price tickets to shows and concerts on the day of the performance. There are usually some great bargains going, but make sure you find out where you'll be sitting, as obviously they don't sell the best seats in the house at half price. Half-Tix opens Monday and Saturday from 10 am to 2 pm, and Tuesday to Friday from 11 am to 6 pm (to 6.30 pm on Friday). They don't accept credit cards – cash only.

THEATRE

The Victorian Arts Centre (Map 1; ☎ 9281 8000), in St Kilda Rd, is Melbourne's major venue for the performing arts. Flanked by the Yarra River on one side and the National Gallery on the other, the complex houses the *Melbourne Concert Hall* and three theatres – the *State Theatre*, the *Playhouse* and the *George Fairfax Studio*.

If you're in Melbourne during the summer months watch out for the excellent open-air theatre productions staged in the Royal Botanic Gardens. See the *EG* listings or ring Bass for details.

Theatre Companies

The Melbourne Theatre Company (MTC) is Melbourne's major theatrical company. Its headquarters is the *Russell St Theatre* (Map 1; ☎ 9686 4000) at 19 Russell St, although its larger performances are held at the Victorian Arts Centre. The MTC stages around 15 productions each year, ranging from contemporary and modern (including a large percentage of new Australian works) to Shakespearean and other classics.

Melbourne's other major theatre companies include the following:

Anthill (☎ 9699 3253)
Gasworks Theatre, 21 Graham St, Albert Park – stages four to six productions each year, many of them innovative interpretations of classic European works.
Handspan Theatre (☎ 9427 8611)
Performing at various theatres, this group is Australia's foremost puppet-theatre company. Their work has a strong visual element, using effects like shadow screens and animation, and their strength is children's theatre.
La Mama (Map 3; ☎ 9347 6142)
La Mama Theatre, 205 Faraday St, Carlton – a tiny and intimate forum for new Australian works and experimental theatre, with a reputation for developing emerging young writers.
Playbox (Map 6; ☎ 9685 5111)
Malthouse Theatre, 113 Sturt St, South Melbourne – this outstanding company stages predominantly Australian works by established and new playwrights.
Theatreworks (Map 11; ☎ 9534 4879)
Theatreworks Theatre, 14 Acland St, St Kilda – combines community theatre and storytelling with innovative productions.

In addition to those listed previously, Melbourne's major theatres include:

Athenaeum Theatre (Map 1; ☎ 9650 3504)
188 Collins St, Melbourne.
Comedy Theatre (Map 1; ☎ 9242 1000)
240 Exhibition St, Melbourne.
National Theatre (Map 11; ☎ 9534 0221)
Corner of Barkly and Carlisle Sts, St Kilda.
Princess Theatre (Map 1; ☎ 9663 3300)
163 Spring St, Melbourne – restored for the Australian
production of *Phantom of the Opera*, Melbourne's most
historic theatre was built in 1854 with gold-rush money.
Regent Theatre (Map 1; ☎ 9299 9500)
191 Collins St, Melbourne – reopened in 1996 following a
massive restoration project, this theatre became the Melbourne home of *Sunset Boulevard*.
Universal Theatre (Map 3; ☎ 9419 3777)
13 Victoria St, Fitzroy – offers a range of productions from
comedy to narrative.

Melbourne also has a huge amateur and fringe-theatre
circuit, so much so that the magazine *Stage Whispers* is
devoted solely to fringe and amateur news – see that
magazine or the *EG* for listings of current productions.

RICHARD NEBESKY

The historic Princess Theatre is now home to the latest
international musicals.

Theatre Restaurants

The *Last Laugh Theatre Restaurant* has some of the best floor shows – see the following Comedy section for details.

There are a number of other 'dinner-and-show' type places. *Dracula's Cabaret Restaurant* (☎ 9347 3344), on the corner of Victoria and Cardigan Sts in Carlton, is very popular with its 'ghost train' ride and a spooky, fun show. Tickets are $34 during the week, $42 on Friday and $47 on Saturday. Other theatre restaurants include *Witches in Britches* (☎ 9329 9850) at 78 Dudley St in West Melbourne; *Dirty Dick's Medieval Madness* (☎ 9329 3555) at 45 Dudley St in West Melbourne; the *Lido* (☎ 9818 1509) at 675 Glenferrie Rd in Hawthorn; and *Rio's Brazilian Churrascaria* (☎ 9428 9787) at 316 Church St in Richmond.

COMEDY

Melbourne prides itself on being the home of Australian comedy. Even the comedians who have used Melbourne as a launching pad to international stardom have fond memories of their home town and its influences. Looking forward to a return visit, Barry Humphries once said:

Visiting Melbourne today is like entering the hushed bed-chamber of a dying relative and telling him he looks great.

Among other things, Humphries' characters such as Dame Edna Everage, Sir Les Patterson and Sandy Stone taught Melburnians how to laugh at themselves – and maybe that's why nobody takes themselves too seriously in this town.

During the International Comedy Festival, held in April each year, the whole city is turned into a festival venue, and local comedians join international acts (including many from the famous Edinburgh Festival) to perform in pubs, clubs, theatres and city streets.

Melbourne has a few regular comedy venues and nightspots where stand-up comics show their wares. Look in the *EG* for weekly gigs.

The *Last Laugh Theatre Restaurant* (Map 6; ☎ 9419 8600), at 64 Smith St in Collingwood, is the grandaddy of Melbourne's comedy venues and a great night out. It's an old cinema/dole office, done up in a dazzling mishmash of styles with room for 200 people to have a good time. The food is reasonably good (vegetarians are catered for) and there's a bar. Dinner and show tickets cost from $35 to $45, and for the show only it's $16 to $18. *Le Joke*, a smaller stand-up comedy venue upstairs, has shows for around $15 and occasional dinner and show tickets at around $40.

The *Comedy Club* (Map 3; ☎ 9348 1622), at 380 Lygon St in Carlton, is another good cabaret-style comedy venue with regular shows.

The *Prince Patrick Hotel* (Map 6), at 135 Victoria Pde in Collingwood, is another old stager in the comedy scene. Other stand-up venues include the *Waiting Room*, held in the Esplanade Hotel's Gershwin Room (Map 11) at 11 the Upper Esplanade in St Kilda, the *Star & Garter Hotel* in Nelson Rd, South Melbourne, and *Nicholson's Hotel* at 551 Nicholson St, North Carlton.

For information on comedy around town, listen to *The Cheese Shop* show on radio 3RRR-FM (102.7) on Monday from 5 to 7 pm.

PUBS & LIVE MUSIC VENUES

For the bigger local and international acts, Melbourne's main live music venues are the National Tennis Centre, the Concert Hall at the Victorian Arts Centre, the Sports & Entertainment Centre with its bad acoustics, the old, barn-like Festival Hall, Palais Theatre and Dallas Brooks Hall. Some (mainly classical) concerts are held at the outdoor Sidney Myer Music Bowl in the Kings Domain.

As advertising guru John Singleton once said, 'It's un-Australian to drive past a pub'. Melbourne has always enjoyed a thriving pub-rock scene and is widely acknowledged as the country's rock capital. The sweaty grind around Melbourne's pubs has been the proving ground for many of Australia's best outfits. Internationally successful bands like AC/DC, INXS, Crowded House and Nick Cave & the Bad Seeds all had their roots deep in Melbourne's pub-rock scene.

To find out who's playing where, look in the *EG*, *Beat* or *Inpress*, or listen to the gig guides on FM radio stations like 3RRR (102.7) and 3PBS (106.7), both of which are excellent independent radio stations. Cover charges at the pubs vary widely – some gigs are free, but generally you'll pay $4 to $10.

In St Kilda, the famed *Esplanade Hotel* (Map 11), on the Esplanade of course, has free live bands every night and Sunday afternoons. It's also a great place just to sit with a beer and watch the sun set over the pier, or have a meal in the *Espy Kitchen* out the back. You can't leave Melbourne without visiting the Espy.

In the city, *The Lounge*, upstairs at 243 Swanston Walk, is a hip, semi-alternative club which features everything from Latin rhythms to techno and hip-hop.

In Fitzroy, the *Rainbow Hotel* (Map 6), an old back-street pub at 27 St James St, has (free) live bands nightly, ranging from jazz, Cajun and blues to funk and soul. On the corner of Brunswick and Kerr Sts, the *Evelyn Hotel* (Map 3), with its newly sandblasted exterior and funked-up interior, is still one of Fitzroy's major band venues, while across the road at 376 Brunswick St the grungy *Punters Club* (Map 3) has bands most nights. The *Builders Arms* (Map 6) at 211 Gertrude St is another good Fitzroy watering hole.

In Collingwood, *The Club* (Map 6) at 132 Smith St attracts good bands and stays open until dawn-ish, while the *Prince Patrick Hotel* (Map 6) at 135 Victoria Pde alternates between bands and comedy.

RICHARD NEBESKY

The Punters Club Hotel on Brunswick St, Fitzroy.

Richmond has always been something of an enclave for grungy rock pubs; they include the *Cherry Tree Hotel* (Map 10) at 53 Balmain St, the *Corner Hotel* (Map 7) at 57 Swan St and the *Central Club Hotel* (Map 7) at 293 Swan St. Then there's the slick and stylish *Black Match* (Map 10) at 545 Church St. The famed *Great Britain Hotel* (Map 10) at 447 Church St held the title of Melbourne's grungiest rock pub for many years; it's now more kitsch than grunge. Speaking of grunge, the *Public Bar*, opposite the Queen Vic Market at 238 Victoria St, has a nightly line-up of bands playing through until the early hours. Nearby, on the corner of Queensberry and Elizabeth Sts, *Arthouse* at the *Royal Artillery Hotel* (Map 5) is the place to head if you're into death metal.

The *Limerick Arms* (Map 9), on the corner of Park and Clarendon Sts in South Melbourne, is a friendly little pub with jazz bands on Thursday and DJs on Friday and Saturday.

Joey's Ministry of Sound (Map 9), at 138 Commercial Rd in South Yarra, is a recent addition to the live venue scene and features some great line-ups.

The *Sydney Liars Club* at 337 Racecourse Rd in Flemington is a fun pub to visit. As you enter, you are greeted by life-size statues of former PMs Malcolm Fraser and Gough Whitlam and the former Governor-General Sir John Kerr. The walls are covered with photos, bizarre stories, anecdotes and framed quotes – lies, all of it. The club also has live music every night.

Cabaret Clubs

The *Continental* (Map 9; ☎ 9510 2788), above the cafe of the same name at 134 Greville St, Prahran, is a sophisticated and popular cabaret-style venue where you have a choice of dinner-and-show deals from $35 to $55, or standing-room-only ($15 to $20).

Another good cabaret-style venue is the *Carousel* (Map 9; ☎ 9696 2777), an upmarket bar and restaurant overlooking Albert Park Lake from Aughtie Drive. There's live music during dinner, and then DJs go through until 5 am or so. The Sunday barbecues (noon to 9.30 pm) are popular, and the outdoor decking area has great views and is a pleasant spot to while away a Sunday arvo.

The *Odeon* (☎ 9826 6844), on the 1st floor at 445 Toorak Rd in Toorak, also does the dinner-and-show thing.

Folk & Acoustic Music

If you're into mellower music, the *EG* has an 'Acoustic & Folk' listing. One of the main venues is the *Dan*

O'Connell Hotel (Map 3), at 225 Canning St in Carlton. As a measure of its Irishness, it claims to sell more Irish whiskey than Scotch whisky. Another popular Irish pub is *Molly Bloom's Hotel* (Map 8) on the corner of Bay and Rouse Sts in Port Melbourne, which has traditional Irish folk music seven nights a week.

Brewery Pubs

Pubs which brew their own beer ('boutique beers') were all the rage a few years back. A few places have survived, and while the beer is certainly not cheap, it makes a nice change from the standard mass-produced stuff. For homesick Europeans, these are the places to look for some *real* bitters. Popular brewery pubs include the *Redback Brewery* (Map 2), at 75 Flemington Rd in North Melbourne, the *Geebung Polo Club*, at 85 Auburn Rd in Auburn, and *Bell's Hotel & Brewery*, at 157 Moray St in South Melbourne.

Jazz & Blues

There are some great jazz joints in Melbourne's city centre. Hidden down a narrow lane off Little Lonsdale St (between Exhibition and Russell Sts), *Bennett's Lane* (Map 1) is a quintessentially dim, smoke-filled, groovy jazz venue – well worth searching out. It's open every night (except Tuesday) until around 1 am, and until 3 or 4 am on weekends. *Ruby Red* (Map 1; ☎ 9662 1544), at 11 Drewery Lane (near the corner of Swanston and Lonsdale Sts), is an old warehouse with a dimly lit bar, a restaurant and a small stage. It has live jazz, soul, R&B and blues from Tuesday to Saturday nights – you'll need to book if you're coming for dinner. A recent addition to the scene is *Jazz Lane* (Map 1; ☎ 9670 5550), a bar/bistro at 390 Lonsdale St which opens from Wednesday to Saturday.

Quite a few pubs also have good jazz and blues sessions on certain nights – check the gig guide in the *EG*. They include the *Limerick Arms* (Map 9) in South Melbourne; the *George Hotel*, on the corner of Fitzroy and Grey Sts in St Kilda; the cosy *Commercial Hotel*, at 238 Whitehall St in Yarraville; the *Rainbow Hotel* (Map 6) in Fitzroy; the *Grace Darling Hotel* (Map 6) on the corner of Smith and Peel Sts in Collingwood; the *Fountain Inn Hotel* in Bay St in Port Melbourne; the *Emerald Hotel* at 414 Clarendon St in South Melbourne; and *McCoppin's Hotel* (Map 3) at 166 Johnston St in Fitzroy.

During January and February, the Royal Melbourne Zoo in Parkville has an extremely popular 'Zoo

Twilights' season of open-air sessions with jazz or big bands performing from 7 to 9.30 pm on Thursday, Friday, Saturday and Sunday nights. Call the zoo's recorded Twilight Line (☎ 0055 33 653) for details. You can also order a picnic hamper or book for the restaurant on this number.

NIGHTCLUBS

Melbourne has a huge collection of nightclubs. The club scene is diverse and ever-changing, and what's hot today isn't necessarily hot tomorrow. Clubs range from the exclusive 'members-only' variety (where if you haven't got the right 'look' or know the right people you don't get in) to barn-sized discos (where anyone who wants to spend money is welcomed with open arms). Cover charges range from $5 to $10, although some places don't charge at all.

Most places have certain dress standards, but it is generally at the discretion of the people on the door – if they don't like the look of you, they might not let you in.

Mainstream Clubs

The city centre is home to most of Melbourne's mainstream clubs, and *The Metro* (Map 1) at 20 Bourke St is a good place to start any exploration of club land. It's the biggest nightclub in the southern hemisphere, and with eight bars on three levels it's very impressive, especially on the busier nights.

King St in the city is a busy but somewhat sleazy and seedy nightclub strip, with a cluster of places that include *Inflation* (Map 1) at No 60, the *Grainstore Tavern* (Map 1) next door, *Heaven* at No 189 and the *Sports Bar* (Map 1) at No 14. Another popular city club is the *Tunnel* at 590 Little Bourke St.

Outside the city centre, the *Chevron* (Map 9) at 519 St Kilda Rd in South Melbourne has been around for ever. It's a huge place with a mixture of DJs and live bands, a cocktail bar and cheap drink deals. Also popular is the *Redhead* (Map 9), beside Albert Park Lake on Aughtie Drive, with an outdoor marquee section, pool tables and several DJ rooms. A little farther around the lake is the very slick *Carousel*.

Down in St Kilda there's *The Ritz* at 169 Fitzroy St, which is part band venue, part nightclub, or you could try *Joey's*, upstairs at 61 Fitzroy St – it's a seedy dive, but if you're desperate it stays open until sunrise.

The more 'upmarket' nightclubs attract an older, more sophisticated (and more affluent) crowd, and generally have stricter dress codes, flashier decor and higher prices. If you're more into cocktails and high heels than slammers and peaked caps, try places in the city like *Lazar* (Map 1) at 240 King St, the *Ivy* (Map 1) at 145 Flinders Lane and *Monsoon's* at the Grand Hyatt Hotel (Map 1) in Collins St, or head to *Silvers* at 445 Toorak Rd in South Yarra.

Alternative Clubs

Melbourne has a vibrant alternative and 'Indie' club scene. Most venues host different club nights on different nights and names change as quickly as Melbourne's weather, so the only way to keep up is to check the alternative club pages in the entertainment papers.

Dream (Map 6), at 229 Queensberry St in Carlton, is one of the best alternative venues – it goes Gothic on Friday, Indie/alternative on Saturday and has gay/S&M nights on Sunday. The long-running *Chasers* (Map 10) at 386 Chapel St in Prahran is still one of the hottest dance-music clubs. Other good alternative venues include *The Lounge* (Map 1) at 243 Swanston St, the *Venue* at 168 Russell St, *Club 383* at 383 Lonsdale St (all in the city) and *The Mansion* at 83 Queens Rd in South Melbourne (hosts the *Hellfire Club* on Sunday).

In Fitzroy, the extremely hip *Night Cat* (Map 3) at 141 Johnston St is well worth a visit, with great 1950s decor and jazz and soul bands from Thursday to Sunday. Farther down Johnston St at No 48, *Bar Salona* (Map 3) is a small and funky Latin-style dance club that opens every night - until 3 am on Saturday and Sunday. In South Melbourne, *Saratoga* (Map 9) at 46 Albert Rd is another small, dim nightclub - if you can get in, you might find yourself drinking and dancing with some of Melbourne's semi-famous muses, actors and comedians.

BARS

Due to its unique licensing laws, Melbourne has a great collection of stylish, ultra-fashionable bars, most of which stay open until 1 am early in the week, and around 3 am on Thursday, Friday and Saturday nights. They are all individual, but generally have a few things in common such as stylised design, booze, good food and music, and very groovy clientele – if you want to rub shoulders with Melbourne's dedicated funksters, the following places are all worth checking out.

In the city, there's the *Six Degrees Bar* (Map 1) in Meyers Place (off the top end of Bourke St), *Sadie's Bar*

(Map 1) at 1 Coverlid Place (off Little Bourke St near Russell St) and *Le Monde* (Map 1) at 18 Bourke St next to the huge Metro nightclub.

In Fitzroy, the *Gypsy Bar* (Map 3) is in the thick of things at 334 Brunswick St. Johnston St is home to the local Spanish scene and has some good tapas bars which often feature live music, including the huge *Bull Ring* (Map 3) at No 95, *La Sangria* (Map 3) at No 46 and *Kahlo's* (Map 3) at No 36.

In Prahran, Chapel St has some of the grooviest bars, such as the *Kazbar* (Map 10) at No 481, the *Zum Pelican Cafe-Bar* (Map 10) at No 382 (next to Chaser's nightclub), and way down south near Dandenong Rd is *Cha Cha's* (Map 11) at No 20, a short walk from the Astor Cinema. Also worth checking out in Prahran is the *Candy Bar* (Map 9), at 162 Greville St.

In St Kilda, the *Dog's Bar* (Map 11) at 54 Acland St is the original and still one of the most popular hangouts for social barflies. The front bar at the *George Hotel* (Map 11), on the corner of Fitzroy and Grey Sts, is another popular local, and the *Snakepit* is a narrow and super-groovy underground bar in the same complex. At the southern end of Acland St, the downstairs bar at *Veludo* (Map 11) is usually crowded with well-heeled hipsters.

GAY & LESBIAN VENUES

VM's Cocktail Bar (Virgin Mary's until the Catholics got their lawyers on to it), in Commercial Rd, Prahan, is the most popular gay and lesbian bar in Melbourne. Young, loud and brash, with a rooftop bar and unique and wild drag shows, it is open six days a week and is busiest on Friday and Sunday. *Three Faces Nightclub* (Map 9), also in Commercial Rd, has drag shows and a dance floor and attracts a young crowd. It's open nightly (except Monday) till late. The *Exchange Hotel* and *Diva* are two other popular bars in the 'gay strip' of Commercial Rd.

Collingwood has some good men's venues. *The Peel Dance Bar* (Map 6), on the corner of Peel and Wellington Sts, opens every night till dawn with Go Go dancers on podiums and DJs spinning trance, house and garage music. *The Laird*, 149 Gipps St, is a gay men's pub catering to an older crowd, with pool tables, a beer garden and theme nights that include bootscootin' on Sunday and Leather Men on Tuesday and Thursday.

Also in Collingwood, the *Glasshouse Hotel* (Map 6), on the corner of Gipps and Rokeby Sts, is a women's pub that has live bands (mostly female, mostly rock 'n' roll) from Thursday to Saturday night till 3 am. Another good women's venue is *Rascal's Hotel*, 194 Bridge Rd, Richmond, which also has live bands, pool comps etc.

Precinct 3182 is a huge, new gay men's complex in St Kilda (on the corner of Martin St and Brighton Rd), consisting of a pub, cinema, sauna, theme rooms and a sex club. *The Prince of Wales* front bar is Melbourne's oldest surviving gay bar, and attracts an eclectic and eccentric, if somewhat seedy, crowd.

CINEMA

Melbourne has plenty of mainstream cinemas playing latest releases, although if you've come from the US or Europe they might be last year's latest. The main chains are Village, Hoyts and Greater Union, and the main group of city cinemas can be found around the intersection of Bourke and Russell Sts. Tickets cost around $9.50 during the day, around $11.50 at night.

Melbourne also has an excellent collection of independent cinemas that feature arthouse, classic and alternative films. Tickets at these places range from $8 to $11. Some cinemas have discounted tickets on certain nights – usually Monday or Tuesday.

Independent cinemas include the not-to-be-missed Art Deco nostalgia of the *Astor* (Map 11; ☎ 9510 1414) on the corner of Chapel St and Dandenong Rd in St Kilda, with double features for $10 every night (and great ice creams!). Other good places to see independent and arthouse movies include the intimate old *Carlton Moviehouse* (Map 3; ☎ 9347 8909) at 235 Faraday St in Carlton; the mini-twin *Cinema Nova* (Map 3; ☎ 9347 5331), nearby at 380 Lygon St in Carlton; the modern twin-complex *Kino* (☎ 9650 2100) in Collins Place (Map 1) at 45 Collins St in the city; the *Longford* (Map 9; ☎ 9867 2700) at 59 Toorak Rd in South Yarra; the twin *George Cinemas* (Map 11; ☎ 9534 6922) at 133 Fitzroy St in St Kilda; the *Lumiere* (☎ 9639 1055) at 108 Lonsdale St in the city; the *Trak* (☎ 9827 9333) at 445 Toorak Rd in Toorak; and the *Westgarth Cinema* (☎ 9482 2001) at 89 High St in Northcote.

The *State Film Centre* (Map 1; ☎ 9651 1515), at 1 Macarthur St in East Melbourne, is a venue for film festivals, experimental and cultural works, and film-society screenings. The *Chinatown Cinemas* (☎ 9662 3465), at 200 Bourke St in the city centre, screens Chinese films.

If you have your own wheels, you can head for the Village Drive-In (☎ 9354 8633) on Newlands Rd in Coburg.

The cinemas at the universities also have interesting and inexpensive non-mainstream screenings. The

---

Open-Air Cinema
During the summer months, the wonderful open-air *Moonlight Cinema* (☎ 9427 1311) in the Royal Botanic Gardens screens classic, arthouse and cult films from Wednesday to Sunday at 8.45 pm. Tickets cost from $7.50 to $11, bookings are handled by Ticketek (☎ 13 2849) and you enter through Gate F on Birdwood Ave. BYO rug, picnic basket and wine! ■

---

closest are the *Union Theatre* (☎ 9344 6966) at Melbourne University and the *Union* (☎ 9660 3717) at RMIT.

Check the *EG* in Friday's *Age* or other newspapers for screenings and times.

GAMBLING

Gambling has swept through Melbourne like a plague during the 1990s, leaving in its wake a trail of financial devastation and cultural destruction. That might sound like a puritanical and hysterical over-reaction, but the architects of Melbourne's so-called 'casino-led recovery' have a lot to answer for.

First came the introduction of poker machines. Overnight, hundreds of pubs and clubs were converted into 'gaming rooms' – live music venues, restaurants and bars had to make way for the pokies, and instead of bands, bistros and conversations, pubs were suddenly filled with people sitting moronically feeding money into coin slots, watching lemons spin round and round...

Then in 1993 Melbourne got its own casino. Flooded on a daily basis with thousands of people wanting to get rid of their excess cash, the casino has quickly become an extremely effective tool for the redistribution of wealth – the rich get richer, while the poor pour money they don't have into the casino's coffers. And as the casino thrives, hundreds of other local businesses – restaurants, retailers, theatres etc – claim to be suffering as a direct result. Meanwhile, the churches and welfare groups are left to try to clean up the social destruction.

Anyway, now that I've got that off my chest, there are plenty of opportunities if you're interested in having a gamble in Melbourne. Apparently, Melbourne's massive *Crown Casino*, which dominates the south bank of the Yarra, will open 24 hours a day when it opens in mid-1997. Almost every second pub and club has poker machines, while the more traditional forms of gambling include horse racing, the trots (harness racing) and the dogs (greyhound racing).

RICHARD NEBESKY

Gambling at the local – poker machines can be found in many pubs, like the Rathdowne Tavern, Carlton.

POETRY READINGS

Some of Australia's best young poets (and some of the older ones) read their poetry at *La Mama* (Map 3) at 205 Faraday St, Carlton at 8 pm on the first Monday of most months.

Several pubs and other venues have performance poetry sessions on a regular basis, and newcomers are usually welcomed along to listen or even perform their own work. Venues include the *Dan O'Connell Hotel* (Map 3) at 225 Canning St in Carlton, the *Empress Hotel* (Map

3) at 714 Nicholson St in North Fitzroy, the *Evelyn Hotel* (Map 3) on the corner of Brunswick and Kerr Sts in Fitzroy, the *Lounge* (Map 1) in Swanston St in the city and *Corey's Cafe* (Map 8) at 173 Victoria Ave in Albert Park. Check the 'Readings' listing in the *EG* for more details.

CHILDREN'S ENTERTAINMENT

The *EG* has a section called 'Children's Activities' that details what's on for children over each weekend – things like pantomimes, animal nurseries, sanctuaries and museum programmes. Other good options include bowling alleys, ice-skating rinks, video arcades and go-kart racing – there are a number of go-kart centres within half an hour's drive of the city, listed under Go-Karts in the *Yellow Pages* phone book.

Some of the favourite places to take kids include the *Royal Melbourne Zoo*, *Luna Park* on the Lower Esplanade in St Kilda, the *Fun Factory* (Map 10) in South Yarra and *Puffing Billy*, a vintage steam-train that runs through the Dandenong Ranges (see Excursions).

The Melbourne City Council runs an excellent baby-sitting/child-minding centre at 104 A'Beckett St in the city (☎ 9329 9561) for children up to five years old. They will mind kids for up to four hours and costs are very reasonable at $2.80 an hour.

SPECTATOR SPORT

When it comes to watching sport, Melburnians are about as fanatical as they come. You've probably heard the old expression that Aussie punters would bet on two flies crawling up a wall – well, at times it seems like half of Melbourne would queue up to watch two snails race, and most of them wouldn't mind laying a bet on the outcome, either. The two biggest events on the calendar are a horse race and a game of Australian Rules football!

Melbourne Cup & Spring Racing Carnival

Horse racing takes place in Melbourne throughout the year – at Flemington, Caulfield, Moonee Valley or Sandown – but spring is when it's most colourful and frenetic.

The Melbourne Cup, one of the world's greatest horse races, is the feature event of Melbourne's Spring Racing Carnival, which runs through October and finishes with the Melbourne Cup early in November. The carnival's

major races are the Cox Plate Handicap, the Caulfield
Cup, the Dalgety, the Mackinnon Stakes and the holy
grail itself, the Melbourne Cup. Apart from these races,
Derby Day and Oaks Day feature heavily on the spring
racing calendar.

The two-mile (3.2 km) Melbourne Cup, which is
always run on the first Tuesday of November at
Flemington Racecourse, was first run in 1861. Mark
Twain, after seeing the race in 1895, wrote:

And so the grandstands make a brilliant and wonderful spectacle, a delirium of colour, a vision of beauty. The champagne
flows, everybody is vivacious, excited, happy; everybody
bets...

If he were to visit now he'd probably write much the
same.

The Cup brings the whole of Australia to a standstill
for the three or so minutes during which the race is run.
Cup day is a public holiday in the Melbourne metropolitan area, but people all over the country are affected by
Melbourne's spring racing fever.

Serious punters and fashion-conscious racegoers
pack the grandstand and lawns of the Victoria Racing
Club's beautiful Flemington Racecourse, once-a-year
betters make their choice or organise Cup syndicates
with friends, and the race is watched or listened to on
TVs and radios in pubs, clubs, TAB betting shops and
houses across the land.

The race has in recent years attracted horses and
owners from Europe, the US and the Middle East, but
New Zealand horses and trainers have had a strangle-
hold on the coveted gold cup for many years.

Many people say that to be in Melbourne in November and not go to the Cup is like going to Paris and
skipping the Louvre, or turning your back on the bulls
in Pamplona! Tickets for reserved seats in the Lawn
Stand can be booked through Bass and cost around $70,
or you can just front up on the day and buy a general
admission ticket for around $20.

The Footy

Without a doubt, Australian Rules football – otherwise
known as 'the footy' – is the major drawcard, with games
at the MCG regularly pulling crowds of 50,000 to 80,000.
If you're here between April and September you should
try to see a match, as much for the crowds as the game.
The sheer energy of the barracking at a big game is

exhilarating. Despite the fervour, crowd violence is almost unknown.

The Australian Football League (AFL) runs the nation-wide competition, and while there are teams based in Perth, Adelaide, Sydney and Brisbane, Melbourne is still considered the game's stronghold. It's also the place where Aussie Rules Football was created – on 7 August 1858, the first game was played between Melbourne Grammar and Scotch College on the very spot where the MCG and its car parks now stand. The playing field was a rough 1.5-km-long paddock, and each team had 40 players. There was no result after the first day, so the teams met on the following two Saturdays, at the end of which the game was declared a draw. Since then the footy rules have been (slightly) refined.

Being the shrine of Aussie Rules, the MCG is the best place to see a match. The ground is steeped in tradition, and with the completion of the Great Southern Stand it has the best spectator facilities. Waverley Park is the other main stadium, but it lacks the atmosphere and tradition of the MCG and is way out in Mulgrave, in the south-eastern suburbs. It can be quite an experience to see a game at one of the suburban grounds such as Victoria Park in Collingwood or the Whitten Oval in Footscray. Here's where you get to literally rub shoulders with the fanatical one-eyed supporters who live and breathe football. For them, it's not a sport, it's a religion.

Tickets can be bought at the ground for most games, and entry costs $12.50 for adults, $6.50 concession, $1.70 for kids under 15 and $25 for a family (and you'll need another few dollars for the obligatory pie and a beer).

Cricket

The MCG is one of the world's great sports stadiums. For any cricket fan or general sports fan, a visit to the MCG is not only compulsory, it's something of a pilgrimage. During the summer, international Test matches, one-day internationals, Sheffield Shield (the national cricket competition) and local district matches are all played here. General admission to international matches is around $20, reserved seats cost $25 to $40.

Motorsport

Despite great opposition from local residents and environmentalists, the Australian Formula One Grand Prix moved from Adelaide to Melbourne's Albert Park circuit in 1996. This annual event – the opening stage of the

RICHARD NEBESKY

RICHARD NEBESKY

Guineas Day at Caulfield Racecourse, part of
Melbourne's Spring Racing Carnival.

world drivers' championship – takes place over Labor Day weekend in March. Prices vary: general admission is from $72.50 and grandstand seating from $301.50. Tickets are available through Bass.

From October 1997, the Australian Motorcycle Grand Prix will be held annually at Phillip Island; tickets are available through Bass.

Tennis

For two weeks every January the National Tennis Centre, in Melbourne Park on Batman Ave (south-east of the city centre), hosts the Australian Open tennis championships. Top players from around the world come to compete in this, the year's first of the big four Grand Slam tournaments. Tickets are available through Bass and range from about $15 to $20 for early rounds to $70 for finals.

Basketball

Basketball is the fastest rising spectator sport in the country. National Basketball League games are of a high standard and draw large crowds, the two main venues being the Glasshouse (at the Sports & Entertainment Centre) and the National Tennis Centre. Tickets to a game cost about $15 to $20, and games are played Friday and Saturday nights and some Sundays.

Shopping

Melbourne claims to be the shopping capital of Australia. Hype or no hype, it's true that many people do come from other parts of Australia just to shop in Melbourne.

The major department stores are in the city centre. Myer has 12 floors of different departments in two buildings – the main entrance is in the Bourke St Mall at No 314. David Jones, with stores on both sides of the Mall, is slightly more upmarket and a good place to look for top quality goods. The Melbourne Central shopping complex houses dozens of speciality shops plus the Daimaru department store. In the centre of the complex, a massive cone-shaped glass dome encloses a National Trust-classified brick shot tower.

If you're after bargains, a couple of handy publications worth looking out for are the magazine *Bargain Shopper's Guide to Melbourne* ($7.95) and the book *Pam's Guide to Discount Melbourne* ($12.95), both of which are available from most newsagents.

If you're looking for a particular item, you'll save a lot of time if you use the *Yellow Pages* phone directory – as they say, 'let your fingers do the walking'.

Some of Melbourne's best shopping areas (and reasons to visit them) are:

Acland St, St Kilda – cheap clothing, good bookshops and gift shops, cafes, restaurants, cake shops, fish shops, delicatessens and the feel of Eastern Europe

Bridge Rd & Swan St, Richmond – for fabulous fashion bargains from factory outlets and small boutiques

Brunswick St, Fitzroy – for bric-a-brac, groovy and offbeat clothing, great cafes, restaurants and a deep look into Melbourne's alternative soul

Chapel St, South Yarra – the cutting-edge and ultra-hip strip of fashion boutiques and import shops, with lots of funky bars and cafes

City Centre – major department stores, clothing and fashion shops along Bourke St, exclusive boutiques in Collins St, the lively and colourful Chinatown, stylish and sophisticated arcades like the Block and theme arcades like The Walk

Lygon St, Carlton – for glamorous imported Italian fashions and good food

Toorak Rd, South Yarra – shop in style and rub shoulders with the rich and famous

Victoria St, Richmond – known as Little Saigon, for excellent
Asian groceries, supermarkets, discount stores, restau-
rants and the flavours and feel of Vietnam and South-East
Asia

ABORIGINAL ART

Top of the list for any real Australian purchase would
have to be Aboriginal art.

Aboriginal art is a traditional and symbolic art form.
In ancient times, the main forms were body painting,
cave painting and rock engraving, and it's only recently
that Aboriginal artists have begun painting in more
portable formats and using Western art materials like
canvas and acrylic paints.

Prices of the best paintings are way out of reach for
the average traveller, but among the cheaper art-and-
craft works on sale are prints, baskets, small carvings,
decorated boomerangs, didgeridoos, music sticks etc,
and some very beautiful screen-printed T-shirts produced by Aboriginal craft cooperatives – and a larger
number of commercial rip-offs. It's worth shopping
around and paying a few dollars more for the real
thing.

Although Melbourne's a long way from the outback,
there are several commercial galleries selling authentic
Aboriginal art.

In the city centre, the Aboriginal Gallery of Dreamings
at 73-77 Bourke St, the Aboriginal Desert Art Gallery at
31 Flinders Lane, Aboriginal Handcrafts on the 9th floor
at 125 Swanston St and the Alcaston House Gallery at 2
Collins St all sell a wide range of bark paintings,
didgeridoos and other handicrafts from all over the
country.

Out of the city there's the Emerald Hill Gallery at 193
Bank St in South Melbourne, the Australian Aspect at
266 Yarra St in Warrandyte and Tingarri Aboriginal Art
at 123 Drummond St in Carlton.

AUSTRALIANA

'Australiana', a euphemism for souvenirs, ranges from
stuffed toys, especially koalas and kangaroos, to egg
flippers shaped like Australia. The seeds of many Australian native plants are on sale all over the place. Try
growing kangaroo paws back home, if your own
country will allow them in. Australian wines are well
known overseas; but why not try honey (leatherwood

TONY WHEELER

Melbourne Central, home to dozens of speciality shops as well as the Daimaru department store.

honey is one of a number of powerful local varieties), macadamia nuts (native to Queensland) or Bundaberg rum with its unusual sweet flavour. You can also get exotic tinned witchetty grubs (definitely an acquired taste!), honey ants and other bush tucker.

Distinctly Australian souvenirs are available from dozens of places around town.

In the city, places worth checking out include the Australiana General Store at shop 32 in Collins Place, 45 Collins St; the Bodymap shop at 300 Lonsdale St; Just Aussie at 263 Bourke St; and Monds Gifts & Souvenirs at 133 Swanston St. Out of town there's Cooee Concepts at 568 Malvern Rd in Toorak; Hall & Co at 1019 High St in Armadale; and Antipodes at 22 Toorak Rd in South Yarra.

Other good places to look for souvenirs or gifts include the Meat Market Craft Centre on the corner of Courtney and Blackwood Sts in North Melbourne, the Queen Victoria Market in the city and the shop at the National Gallery.

AUSSIE CLOTHING

While you're here, why not fit yourself out in some local clothes? Consider Blundstone or Rossi boots, anything from the RM Williams line (boots, moleskin trousers, shirts), some Yakka or King Gee work wear, a shearer's top or bush shirt, a greasy-wool jumper, a Bluey (a coarse, woollen, worker's coat), a Driza-bone (an oilskin stockman's coat) and an Akubra hat.

Sam Bear at 225 Russell St is a great place to go for tough, durable clothing and footwear – just like the real shearers and jackaroos wear. It's also a good place for things like camping and walking gear, cheap beanies (woollen hats) and warm socks.

Some other good shops for Aussie gear are RM Williams, with a large shop in the shot tower at Melbourne Central (300 Lonsdale St); the Thomas Cook Boot & Clothing Co at 60 Hoddle St in Abbotsford; and Hall & Co at 1019 High St in Armadale.

Australia also produces some of the world's best surfing equipment and surf/street wear, including brands such as Mambo, Hot Tuna, Mooks and Funk Essentials. A couple of places to try are the Melbourne Surf Shop in the Tivoli Arcade at 249 Bourke St and Surf Dive 'N' Ski at 213 Bourke St – both have been around nearly as long as Nat Young (an Aussie surfing legend).

Akubra hats are incredibly popular with travellers and are sold just about everywhere. Good city hat shops include City Hatters, beside the main entrance to Flinders St railway station at 211 Flinders St, and Melbourne's Top Hatters at shop 19, 259 Collins St.

OUTDOOR GEAR

The best area for outdoor shops is around the intersection of Hardware St and Little Bourke St in the city. In Hardware St you'll find places like Auski at No 9, the Melbourne Ski Centre at No 17 and Wetsports at No 83. In Little Bourke St, Mountain Designs is at No 377, Kathmandu is at No 373, Bogong Equipment is at No 374 and Paddy Palin is at No 360. Snowgum (formerly the Scout Outdoor Centre) is around the corner at 366 Lonsdale St, and the previously mentioned Sam Bear, at 225 Russell St, is also worth checking out.

These places generally stock top-quality outdoor gear – cheaper gear is available from the many army disposal stores (listed in the *Yellow Pages* phone directory).

OPALS

The opal is Australia's national gemstone, and opals and opal jewellery are popular souvenirs. It is a beautiful stone, but buy wisely and shop around – quality and prices can vary widely from place to place.

Some gem and opal stores in town include Andrew Cody on the 1st floor at 119 Swanston St, Bentine Gems at 115-117 Collins St, Rochi's Opals at 210 Little Collins St, Altman & Cherny at 120 Exhibition St and John H Mules at 110 Exhibition St.

ANTIQUES

If you're on the lookout for antiques, head for High St in Armadale, Malvern Rd in Malvern, Gertrude St in Fitzroy, and Canterbury Rd in Surrey Hills. Kozminsky Galleries, at 421 Bourke St in the city, was established back in 1851 and specialises in antique jewellery and collectables.

Look for early Australian colonial furniture made from cedar or Huon pine; Australian silver jewellery; ceramics – either early factory pieces or studio pieces (especially anything by the Boyd family); glassware such as Carnival glass; and Australiana collectables and bric-a-brac such as old signs, tins, bottles etc. *Carter's Price Guide to Antiques in Australia* is an excellent price reference which is updated annually.

FASHION & CLOTHING

In the city centre, the major department stores all have good ranges of both local and imported fashion. The Sportsgirl Centre, in Collins St between Swanston and Elizabeth Sts, has a great range of shops for female fashions, and the Australia on Collins complex nearby is also good. You'll find plenty of fashion houses along Bourke St, particularly in and around the mall, while Collins St is the home of the more exclusive and expensive designer boutiques. Shopping adventurers will have fun exploring the network of alleys, laneways and arcades that run through the heart of the city.

Bridge Rd and Swan St in Richmond are full of fashion warehouses, factory outlets and seconds shops – great places to find fashion bargains.

Brunswick St in Fitzroy has lots of groovy, grungy and offbeat clothing shops in among all the cafes and restaurants. You'll find innovative young designers alongside 'retro' shops that specialise in recycled fashions. Greville St in Prahran is probably *the* most fashionable address for retro shops – check out Mondo Trasho, Route 66 and Crimes of Fashion along here.

Chapel St in South Yarra is the most fashionable of Melbourne's fashion zones. The section between Toorak Rd and Commercial Rd is lined with ultra-trendy and generally expensive boutiques, and it's a fascinating area to visit, whether you come to shop or just to check out all the beautiful people.

Toorak Rd in South Yarra is the ultimate in style. This street is home to the most exclusive designers, specialist shops and galleries – even if you can't afford to buy anything, it's a fascinating street to wander along. You never know who or what you might see.

Lygon St in Carlton has the latest in upmarket and imported Italian clothes and shoes. High St in Armadale is another fashion shopping mecca, with quite a few designers sprinkled between the antique dealers and Persian-rug stores.

COMMERCIAL ART GALLERIES

Melbourne has dozens of private and commercial art galleries – the magazine *Art Almanac*, a monthly guide to all city and regional galleries, is available from the shop at the National Gallery and other galleries.

The top end of Flinders Lane in the city is something of an enclave for art lovers – and there are plenty of interesting galleries here, including Gallery Gabrielle Pizzi at No 141, William Mora at No 31, the Tribal Art Gallery at No 103 and the Flinders Lane Gallery at No 137.

Fitzroy also has some good galleries, including Roar Studios at 115 Brunswick St, the Women's Gallery at 375 Brunswick St, the Tolarno Gallery at 121 Victoria St and 200 Gertrude St (at 200 Gertrude St).

Also worth checking out are the Karen Lovegrove Gallery at 321 Chapel St and the Lula Bilu Gallery at 142 Greville St, both in Prahran; and Christine Abrahams'

Gallery at 27 Gipps St, and Niagara Galleries at 245 Punt Rd, both in Richmond.

HANDICRAFTS

Melbourne has many shops, galleries and markets displaying crafts by local artists, as well as goods from almost every region of the world. The local craft scene is especially strong in ceramics, jewellery, stained glass and leather craft. Pick up a copy of Craft Victoria's *Craft Shops & Galleries in Victoria*, available from their office (☎ 9417 3111) at 114 Gertrude St, Fitzroy, Melbourne.

Melbourne's best craft gallery is the Meat Market Craft Centre, on the corner of Courtney and Blackwood Sts in North Melbourne, which houses the state craft collection and other exhibitions, craft workshops, a bookshop and coffee shop. It's open Tuesday to Sunday from 10 am to 5 pm. Another good craft gallery is Distelfink at 105 High St in Armadale.

There are a number of good craft shops around town selling local and imported crafts, including the long-running Ishka Handcrafts with shops in South Yarra, Carlton, South Melbourne and Kew.

In many suburbs there are weekend craft markets like the Sunday market on the Upper Esplanade in St Kilda, and farther out there are craft places in Warrandyte and in small towns in the Dandenongs.

RICHARD NEBESKY

The Sunday market on the Upper Esplanade,
St Kilda sells a variety of hand-made goods.

DUTY-FREE

Duty-free shops abound in the city centre. Remember that a duty-free item might not have had much duty on it in the first place and could be available cheaper in an ordinary store.

BOOKSHOPS

Melbourne's largest bookshop chains include Angus & Robertson Bookworld, at 35-37 Swanston St; Collins Booksellers, at 115 Elizabeth St; and Dymocks, on the corner of Bourke and Swanston Sts. They all have several other city stores and suburban branches, and carry a broad range of books. The Myer department store also has a comprehensive book section.

Melbourne is blessed with excellent independent booksellers who don't generally compete with the big players for range but offer more specialised services. Bowyangs Maps & Travel Guides at 372 Little Bourke St has the city's most extensive range of travel books and maps, as well as travel accessories.

McGills at 187 Elizabeth St (opposite the GPO) is good for interstate and overseas newspapers and magazines, as well as general and technical books.

Other good city bookshops include Hill of Content at 86 Bourke St; the Whole Earth Bookshop at 246 Swanston St (good for 'alternative' books); the Paperback at 60 Bourke St; the ABC Shop, in the Galleria on the corner of Elizabeth and Bourke Sts; the Technical Book Company at 295 Swanston St (good for technical and specialist books); Greens Environment Bookshop at 247 Flinders Lane (books and products on conservation, bushwalking and the environment); and Mary Martin (across the river in the Southgate complex).

The Foreign Language Bookshop, downstairs at 259 Collins St between Elizabeth and Swanston Sts, has a wide selection of dictionaries, grammar books and cassettes.

The National Gallery Bookshop has an excellent range of art and Australiana books.

Outside the city centre, other highly recommended bookshops include:

Albert Park
    The Avenue Bookstore, 127 Dundas Place
Carlton
    Readings, 338 Lygon St
Fitzroy
    Brunswick St Bookstore, 305 Brunswick St

Prahran
      Dr Syntax, 196 Commercial Rd
      Greville St Bookstore, 145 Greville St
      Kill City, 126 Greville St (crime fiction specialist)
Richmond
      The Bookshelf, 116 Bridge Rd
South Melbourne
      Emerald Hill Bookshop, 336 Clarendon St
South Yarra
      Black Mask, 78 Toorak Rd
      Martin Book Company, 36 Toorak Rd
      Readings, 153 Toorak Rd
St Kilda
      Chronicles Bookshop, 91 Fitzroy St
      Cosmos Books & Music, 112 Acland St
      Metropolis Bookshop, 160 Acland St

Hares & Hyenas is an excellent gay and lesbian bookshop with branches at 135 Commercial Rd, Prahran and 360 Brunswick St, Fitzroy. The Shrew Women's Bookshop, 37 Gertrude St, Fitzroy, specialises in lesbian and feminist books.

Melbourne also has some excellent second-hand bookshops. At Alice's Bookshop, 629 Rathdowne St in Carlton, you'll find a collection of early editions of *Alice in Wonderland* among others. The Grub St Bookshop at 317 Brunswick St in Fitzroy is also well worth a browse, as is Pig's Wings at 53 Barry St in South Yarra.

MUSIC

Large city stores selling recorded music include the enormous Blockbuster Music store at 152 Bourke St (also in the Jam Factory at 500 Chapel St in South Yarra) and Brash's at 108 Elizabeth St.

Interesting independent stores around town include Gaslight at 85 Bourke St (great alternative music, open nightly till late, and its annual calendar compels customers to do strange things like shop in the nude), Missing Link at 262 Flinders Lane and Au Go Go at 349 Little Bourke St. Discurio at 285 Little Collins St has the best range of classical, jazz, blues and folk music and literature.

Greville Records at 152 Greville St in Prahran, Polyester Records at 387 Brunswick St in Fitzroy and Readings (with shops at 366 Lygon St in Carlton and 153 Toorak Rd in South Yarra) are other good stores to try if you're looking for something other than top 40.

JB Hi-Fi sells discounted tapes and CDs, and their stores include one in the city at 289 Elizabeth St.

MARKETS

The Queen Victoria Market, on the corner of Victoria and Elizabeth Sts in the city, is one of the best places to shop, not just for the huge range of goods and souvenirs, but also for the bustling atmosphere and exotic cast of characters. It has over 1000 stalls that sell just about everything under the sun, including fruit and vegetables, meat and fish, jeans, furniture, budgies and sheepskin products. It opens Tuesday and Thursday from 6 am to 2 pm, Friday from 6 am to 6 pm, Saturday from 6 am to 3 pm and Sunday from 9 am to 4 pm. On Sunday the fruit, vegetable, meat and fish stalls are closed and there are dozens more stalls selling jewellery, clothes, souvenirs, antiques and bric-a-brac. (See the Organised Tours section in the Getting Around chapter for details of walking tours of the market.)

Melbourne's other major markets are the South Melbourne Market in Cecil St, which opens on Wednesday, Friday, Saturday and Sunday; the Prahran Market in Commercial Rd, which opens on Tuesday, Thursday, Friday and Saturday; and the Footscray Market on the corner of Hopkins and Leeds Sts, which opens Thursday, Friday and Saturday.

There are also lots of good weekend markets selling crafts, clothes, second-hand goods etc. In St Kilda, the Esplanade Art & Craft Market operates every Sunday on the Upper Esplanade and has a good range of stuff on offer. One of the most popular 'trash and treasure' markets is the Camberwell Sunday Market (from dawn to mid afternoon) in Station St, Camberwell, which has over 300 stalls piled with everything including the kitchen sink – you might even find that hot pink T-shirt you lost back in 1979. Other popular markets include the Sunday Market at the Victorian Arts Centre (Sunday from 10 am), with arts and crafts from around the state, and the small and slightly grungy Greville St Sunday Market.

Excursions

If you have time during your stay, leave the city behind for a while and explore the areas surrounding Melbourne. You have plenty to choose from: the beaches and coastal townships of the Mornington and Bellarine peninsulas; the forests, gardens and bushwalks of the Dandenong Ranges; the wilds of the Kinglake National Park; the wineries of the Macedon Ranges; the Healesville Sanctuary in the scenic Yarra Valley, plus more wineries; the stunning natural features of the Great Ocean Road; and of course the famous tourist attractions such as the Penguin Parade at Phillip Island and the historic gold-mining township of Sovereign Hill in Ballarat.

Note that many of these places are popular holiday destinations, so if you're planning to stay overnight you should try to book accommodation in advance, especially during the Christmas holiday season, Easter and other school holidays.

This chapter recommends some of the best day or overnight trips from Melbourne, but it gives only an introductory coverage to the areas mentioned. For more details on these places and the rest of the state, see Lonely Planet's *Victoria* guide.

For long-distance calls (eg from Melbourne to the places in this chapter), dial the area code ☎ 03 before the local number.

SOUTH-WEST TO GEELONG

Geelong is Victoria's second largest city. It's a quick trip down the Princes Highway – and it's freeway all the way. You can leave Melbourne quickly over the soaring West Gate Bridge and enjoy the fine views of the city, and there are a few interesting detours and places to stop along the way.

Werribee Park Mansion & Zoo

Signposted off the freeway about 30 minutes from Melbourne is Werribee Park, with its free-range zoological park and the huge Italianate Werribee Park Mansion, built between 1874 and 1877. The flamboyant building is surrounded by formal gardens including picnic and barbecue areas and the **State Rose Garden,** with 3000 plants in the shape of a giant Tudor rose. Entry to the garden is free, but admission to the mansion costs $8 for adults and $4 for children.

The adjacent Werribee Zoo is a free-range park with African herbivores – zebras, giraffes, hippos, rhinoceroses, etc – in an Australian bush setting. Bus tours of the zoo cost $8 for adults and $4 for kids.

Werribee Park opens daily from 10 am to 5 pm (10 am to 4 pm between May and September). Met trains run to Werribee Station, and an infrequent bus service runs the five km between the station and the park – ring the Met for details (☎ 13 1638).

RAAF National Aviation Museum

Near Werribee is the National Aviation Museum at the RAAF base at Point Cook. Displays include one on the WWI German ace Baron von Richtofen. Its collection of 35 aircraft ranges from a 1916 Morris Farman Shorthorn to a 1970 F4 Phantom. Seven of the vintage planes still fly, and the resident aces use them for air shows. It's open Sunday to Friday from 10 am to 4 pm; admission is by donation of $4 for adults and $2 for children.

You Yangs Forest Reserve

Another worthwhile detour off the Princes Highway is to the You Yangs, a picturesque range of volcanic hills just off the freeway. Walks in the You Yangs include the climb up **Flinders Peak**, the highest point in the park, with a plaque commemorating Matthew Flinders' scramble to the top in 1802. There are fine views from the top down to Geelong and the coast.

GEELONG

Geelong (population 125,000), Victoria's largest provincial city, sits on the shores of Corio Bay. While it's the gateway to the Great Ocean Road and the south-west of Victoria, the city itself is known more as an industrial and manufacturing centre than a tourism hot spot. Driving through Geelong, there's little incentive to do other than keep driving – the routes of the main highways manage to pass through many of the least attractive areas. But beyond the highways, factories and railyards, Geelong is, in places, an historic and attractive bayside city, with fine parks and gardens, some impressive museums and galleries, good restaurants and modern shopping and recreational facilities.

Information

The Corio Tourist Information Centre (☎ 5275 5797) is on the corner of the Princes Highway and St Georges Rd, about seven km north of the centre. In the centre of town there's Geelong Otway Tourism (☎ 5222 2900) in the National Wool Centre on Moorabool St. Both open daily from 9 am to 5 pm, and both have lots of information and are very useful if you're going down along the Great Ocean Road, or to the Otways, or any other area around Geelong.

Things to See & Do

The city has more than 100 National Trust-classified buildings. **The Heights**, 140 Aphrasia St, opens Wednesday to Sunday between 1 and 5 pm; entry costs $5.50 adults, $3 children. **Barwon Grange** in Fernleigh St, Newtown, is another classified old homestead and is open on Wednesday and weekends from 2 to 5 pm; entry costs $4 for adults, $2.50 for children. **Corio Villa**, overlooking Eastern Beach, is another interesting old home, but it's not open to the public.

The impressive **National Wool Centre**, on the corner of Brougham and Moorabool Sts, is housed in an historic bluestone wool store and has a museum, a number of wool craft and clothing shops and a restaurant. It is open every day from 10 am to 5 pm and admission costs $7 adults, $5.80 students and $3.50 children.

The **Geelong Naval & Maritime Museum** in Swinburne St, North Geelong, is open daily (except Tuesday and Thursday) from 10 am to 4 pm; entry is free. The **Geelong Art Gallery** on Little Malop St has a good collection of early Australian and contemporary art; it opens weekdays from 10 am to 5 pm, weekends from 1 to 5 pm, and entry is $3.

Also worth a visit are **Eastern Beach**, the **Geelong Botanic Gardens** and **Eastern Park**.

Places to Stay

There are several caravan and camping parks opposite the Barwon River in Barrabool Rd, Belmont, with camping sites from $10 and on-site vans and cabins from $30. A bed at the basic *Geelong YHA Hostel* (☎ 5221 6583), 1 Lonsdale St, costs $12 ($14 nonmembers). Another budget option is *St Albans Backpackers* (☎ 5248 1229), set in an historic horse-stud property on Geelong's outskirts (bunks $15, doubles $40).

The old *Carlton Hotel* (☎ 5229 1954), 21 Malop St, has singles/doubles for $30/40, while the central *Kangaroo Motel* (☎ 5221 4022), 16 The Esplanade South, has rooms from $40/48.

Getting There & Away

V/Line (☎ 13 2232) runs frequent trains between Melbourne and Geelong; the trip takes about an hour and costs $8 economy, $11.20 1st class. Trains continue from Geelong to Warrnambool ($22.80/32) and Ballarat ($9.20).

Geelong is also well served by V/Line buses, with services along the Great Ocean Road to Torquay ($4.20), Lorne ($14.60) and Apollo Bay ($16.80) operating three times daily (twice on weekends).

McHarry's Bus Lines (☎ 5223 2111) operates the Bellarine Transit bus service with frequent buses from Geelong to Barwon Heads, Ocean Grove (both $3.40 one-way), Queenscliff and Point Lonsdale (both $5.25).

GEELONG REGION WINERIES

During the 19th century Geelong was one of Victoria's major wine growing districts, and the area is particularly known for its outstanding pinot noir and cabernet-sauvignon wines.

Today there are a dozen or so small wineries in the region. They include the **Idyll Vineyard & Winery** at 265 Ballan Rd in Moorabool and the tiny **Asher Vineyard** at 360 Goldsworthy Rd in Lovely Banks (both about eight km north of Geelong); the rustic **Mt Anakie Estate** and **Staughton Vale Vineyard** (both in Anakie, about 37 km north); **Tarcoola Estate** on Spillers Rd in Lethbridge (32 km north-west); the **Mt Duneed Winery** on Feehans Rd in Mt Duneed (10 km south); and the **Prince Albert Vineyard** on Leming Rd in Waurn Ponds (12 km south-west).

There are also several wineries on the Bellarine Peninsula: **Kilgour Estate** and **Scotchman's Hill Vineyard** are both off the road between Drysdale and Portarlington, and on weekends you can also visit the historic **Spray Farm Estate** near Portarlington – ring Scotchman's Hill (☎ 5251 3176) to check opening hours.

BELLARINE PENINSULA

Beyond Geelong the Bellarine Peninsula is a twin to the Mornington Peninsula, forming the western side of the entrance to Port Phillip Bay. This is a popular holiday

MARK ARMSTRONG

Corio Villa, one of the many National Trust-classified
buildings in Geelong.

region and boating venue. Queenscliff is a fashionable
seaside resort with upmarket guesthouses, historic
hotels and fine eateries (and a great golf course). Further
west, Ocean Grove and Barwon Heads have excellent
ocean beaches.

See the Geelong section for details of bus services to the
peninsula. A car and passenger ferry also operates daily
between Queenscliff and Sorrento – see the Mornington
Peninsula Getting There & Away section for details.

Queenscliff

Queenscliff was originally established as a settlement for
the sea pilots whose job it was to steer ships through the
treacherous Port Phillip Bay Heads. They weren't
always successful – the coast along here is littered with
the wrecks of ships that didn't make it.

During the gold rush, Queenscliff became one of the
favourite settlement areas for diggers who had struck it
rich. By the 1880s, Queenscliff was fashionably known
as the 'Queen of the South'. Some fine and extravagant
buildings were erected to accommodate the visiting
hordes, and many of these remain and give the town its
historic character.

In recent years Queenscliff has been 'rediscovered', with many of the grand old buildings now restored to their former glory.

Things to See & Do The most impressive buildings are along Gellibrand St, where you'll find the **Ozone Hotel**, the **Queenscliff Hotel**, **Lathamstowe** and a row of old **pilots' cottages** which date back to 1853. Hesse St, the main drag, also has some great buildings, in particular the **Vue Grand** with its ornate and opulent interiors.

Fort Queenscliff was built to protect Melbourne from the perceived threat of Russian invasion during the Crimean War. There are guided tours of the military museum, magazine, cells and Black Lighthouse, on weekends at 1 and 3 pm ($4 adults, $2 children) and weekdays at 1.30 pm ($5/2).

The **Bellarine Peninsula Railway** (☎ 5258 2069) is run by local rail enthusiasts, and a steam train does the Queenscliff-Drysdale run (1¾ hours return, $10 adults, $5 kids) at 11 am and 2.30 pm every Sunday (also on Tuesday, Thursday and Saturday during school holidays).

The peninsula is something of a mecca for scuba divers and snorkellers. The Queenscliff Dive Centre (☎ 5258 1188) and Dive Experience (☎ 5258 4058) run diving courses and hire out equipment. Bikes can be hired from 'Mr Queenscliff' (☎ 5258 3403) near the pier. One recommended excursion is to take the steam train to Drysdale and cycle back – it's downhill all the way.

There are quite a few interesting galleries and craft and antique shops in Hesse and Hobson Sts. The

MARK ARMSTRONG

The opulent Vue Grand, Queenscliff

Round the Bay in a Day
One of the best ways to appreciate Melbourne's bayside location is to circumnavigate Port Phillip Bay, making use of the ferry services between Queenscliff and Sorrento. It's an easy day trip by car (about 200 km driving), but you could make it a two-day trip, staying overnight on either the Bellarine Peninsula or the Mornington Peninsula. You could also do it by public transport or bicycle.

Going anticlockwise from Melbourne, the first highlight is the view from the West Gate Bridge, with the city skyscrapers behind you, the industrial areas to the west and the bay stretching south to the horizon. It's a quick 70 km down the freeway to Geelong, a small city built on the wealth of Western District wool – the National Wool Museum there is worth seeing. Look carefully for the road that takes you the 30 km to Queenscliff: although it's signposted it's easy to miss. There are two ferry services between Queenscliff and Sorrento (see the Mornington Peninsula Getting There & Away section of this chapter). Book your ticket then look around the town, particularly the old fort and the grand old hotels.

You can see Port Phillip Heads from the ferry, but it gives them a fairly wide berth to avoid the dangerous current known as the Rip. You might see dolphins frolicking round the bow of the boat, and lots of sea birds around Mud Island and the unfinished island fortress called Pope's Eye. The ferry runs parallel to the coast past Portsea, and you'll have a good view of the luxury cliff-top houses which overlook the bay. As you come in, the Sorrento beachfront is particularly attractive with its tall pine trees and old-style bandstand rotunda.

There's wonderful coastal scenery on the southern tip of the Mornington Peninsula, on both the Bass Strait side and the bay side, and especially in the Point Nepean National Park. You can't see the city from here during the day, but at night it's like a string of diamonds across the water. Heading back towards the bright lights, you can take the Nepean Highway which follows the coast, or the freeway which runs further inland. Take the more leisurely coastal route if you want to find out about urban sprawl – from Frankston to the city it's over 40 km of nonstop suburbia. ■

unattractive **Queenscliff Historical Centre** on Hesse St displays various old relics from the town's past and opens daily from 2 to 4 pm.

The **Marine Studies Centre** (☎ 5258 3344) on Weeroona Parade (the educational unit of the Institute of Marine Sciences) offers an excellent series of trips and programmes focusing on the hidden wonders of the bay. Its trips include 'snorkelling with the seals' ($35), two-hour canoe trips ($10), marine biology tours, rockpool rambles and lots more – ring to find out what's on.

Next door, the **Queenscliff Maritime Centre** opens on weekends (daily during school holidays).

Places to Stay Queenscliff has four camping and caravan parks. The simple *Queenscliff Recreation Reserve* (☎ 5258 1765) on Mercer St is the most central, and has sites from $14 to $25.

The town has quite a few charming and historic guest-houses. The friendly *Queenscliff Inn* (☎ 5258 3737), 55 Hesse St, has a relaxing old-world ambience, with B&B from $45 for singles and $65 to $85 for doubles. They also have a few budget rooms for travellers, ranging from $15 to $25.

Athelstane House (☎ 5258 1591), 4 Hobson St, has cosy rooms with shared bathroom from $40/60 for B&B, while the elegant *Maytone by the Sea* (☎ 5258 4059) on the corner of The Esplanade and Stevens St does B&B from $70/100.

The oldish *Riptide Holiday Flats* (☎ 5258 1675), 31 Flinders St, are good value starting from $60 a night for up to four people.

At 16 Gellibrand St, the National Trust-classified *Mietta's Queenscliff Hotel* (☎ 5258 1066) is renowned for its fine food and gracious Victorian-era accommodation. Dinner, bed and breakfast packages range from $80 to $170 per person – prices depend on when you come and what you eat. Highly recommended for a splurge.

Point Lonsdale

Five km west of Queenscliff, Point Lonsdale is a laid-back little coastal township centred around its **lighthouse**, built in 1902 to help guide ships through the Heads and into the bay. The turbulent passage of water which leads into the bay is known as the 'Rip', and is rated as one of the most dangerous seaways in the world. The **Rip View lookout** is one vantage point from which you can watch freighters and other vessels negotiating the Rip – **Point Lonsdale Pier** is another.

The foreshore around the headland is a marine won-derland at low tide, when an array of rockpools and caverns become natural aquariums – bring a pair of swimming goggles.

Point Lonsdale has two rocky beaches, the calmer bay beach and the surf beach, which is patrolled by a life-saving club over summer. The town's **cemetery** has the graves of early pioneers, pilots, lighthouse keepers and shipwreck victims.

The council-run *Royal Caravan Park* (☎ 5258 1142) opens between December and Easter. *The Terminus B&B & Lighthouse Resort* (☎ 5258 1142), 31 Point Lonsdale Rd, is a cosy, old-fashioned guesthouse with a tennis court, pool and guest lounges. Tariffs are from $15 per person for budget rooms, from $75 to $150 for B&B, and from $55 to $95 for motel units.

Ocean Grove

This resort on the ocean side of the peninsula has good scuba diving off the rocky ledges of the bluff and further out there are wrecks of ships which failed to make the tricky entrance to Port Phillip Bay. Some of the wrecks are accessible to divers. The beach at the surf life-saving club is very popular with surfers. Ocean Grove is a real-estate agent's paradise and has grown to become the biggest town on the peninsula.

The **Ocean Grove Nature Reserve**, on Grubb Rd to the north of town, is a large area of natural bushland with 11 km of marked walking tracks and lots of native flora and fauna. The 143-hectare reserve is conserved and managed by a staff of volunteers.

Barwon Heads

Barwon Heads is a smaller and quieter resort four km west of Ocean Grove, at the mouth of the Barwon River. It has sheltered river beaches, surf beaches around the headland, and the magnificent **Barwon Heads Golf Course** (☎ 5254 2302) set among rolling coastal hills and sand dunes with inspirational ocean views (green fees $50!). **Thirteenth Beach** is an excellent surf beach.

Hitchcock Ave is the main shopping area. The *Barwon Heads Park* (☎ 5254 1115) has good camp sites, while the *Barwon Heads Hotel* (☎ 5254 2201) has double rooms from $60 to $90.

Torquay

Torquay is one of the most popular surfing and summer resorts on the coast, and the capital of Australia's booming surfing industry. The town itself is no oil painting, but it has a great range of beaches that cater for everyone from paddlers to world champion surfers.

Things to See & Do A popular family beach is **Fishermans Beach**, protected from the ocean swells. The **Front Beach** is ringed by Norfolk Pines and sloping lawns and staffed by members of the life-saving club during summer. **Jan Juc's** sandy beaches are more exposed to the ocean swells, and a couple of km further south-west is the **Bells Beach Recreation Reserve**. Bells' thick and powerful waves are world famous, and the Bells Surfing Classic held annually at Easter attracts the world's top professionals and large crowds of spectators.

There are around a dozen surf shops in town, with the big names like Rip Curl and Quicksilver based at the **Surfworld Plaza** on the Surfcoast Highway – a great place if you're looking for surfboards, wetsuits, surf wear or equipment. Also in the complex is the excellent **Surfworld Australia Surfing Museum**, which opens daily from 9 am to 5 pm (from 10 am on weekends) and costs $5 adults, $3 kids and $15 families. You can also hire surfing gear here or book surfing lessons with the Surfworld Surf School (☎ 5261 2907).

Tiger Moth World (☎ 5261 5100), five km north-east of Torquay on Blackgate Rd, has an aviation museum (open daily 10 am to 5.30 pm; $2) and offers joy flights in vintage Tiger Moths (from $70, or five people can fly to the Twelve Apostles for $300).

The **Surf Coast Walk** follows the coastline from Jan Juc to Airey's Inlet. The full distance takes about 11 hours, but can be done in stages. The Shire of Barrabool puts out a useful leaflet about the track, available from tourist offices in the area.

Places to Stay Torquay has four caravan parks, but over summer and Easter the town is flooded with campers and it can be hard to find a site. The *Torquay Public Reserve* (☎ 5261 2496), the *Zeally Bay Caravan Park* (☎ 5261 2400) and the *Bernell Caravan Park* (☎ 5261 2493) all have sites, vans and cabins.

Opposite the Front Beach at 35 The Esplanade, the *Surf City Motel* (☎ 5261 3492) has double units from $68 to $110, while the *Torquay Hotel/Motel* (☎ 5261 2001), 36 Bell St, charges from $50 to $65.

South of Torquay and close to Bells Beach, *Bells Holiday Cottages* (☎ 5261 5243) have two-bedroom cottages in a rural setting from $60 a double plus $10 per additional person.

GREAT OCEAN ROAD

The Great Ocean Road, running between Anglesea and Warrnambool, is one of the world's most spectacular coastal routes. The road takes you on a journey of dramatic contrasts around the Shipwreck Coast – lush rainforests, sheer and ragged cliffs, idyllic sandy beaches, mountains and forests of towering eucalypts, intriguing rock formations, some great state and national parks and charming seaside settlements.

Things to See & Do

Anglesea is famous for its sheer cliffs and the scenic **Anglesea Golf Club** (☎ 5263 1582), with its large population of kangaroos which graze indifferently on the fairways and greens; a round costs $20.

Aireys Inlet, an interesting little town with a good vibe, is popular with people who find Lorne just a little too trendy. There are some great beaches, and excellent bushwalks through the nearby Angahook-Lorne State Park; there's also a horse-riding ranch nearby.

The **Angahook-Lorne State Park** covers 22,000 hectares of coast and hinterland between Aireys Inlet and Kennett River, with cool-temperate rainforests, blue-gum forests, cascades and numerous well signposted walking tracks. The park has an abundance of wildlife, and seven designated camping areas.

Lorne is the most fashionable and popular town along this stretch of coast, combining great beaches, bushwalks and good food with a wide range of accommodation. Despite the summer hordes it has managed to retain most of its charm and appeal.

Perhaps the most spectacular section of the Great Ocean Road is between Lorne and Apollo Bay, featuring the beautiful contrast of the ocean on one side and the forests and mountains of the **Otway Ranges** on the other. The Otways are an area of great natural beauty and well worth exploring, with their scenic drives, walking trails, waterfalls and tiny hillside townships.

The pretty fishing town of **Apollo Bay** is another popular summer beach resort. It's also a little more relaxed than Lorne, and, in addition to all the fishing folk, quite a few artists and musicians live in and around the town.

The **Otway National Park**, at the southernmost tip of this coast, is another natural wonderland, while farther west is the small and beautiful **Melba Gully State Park**.

The most famous section of the Great Ocean Road is the **Port Campbell National Park**, which features an amazing collection of natural rock sculptures including the Twelve Apostles, London Bridge and Loch Ard Gorge, all carved out of the soft limestone headland by fierce ocean waves. This narrow coastal park stretches through low heathlands from Princetown to Peterborough.

Port Campbell is a small windswept village with one pub and a cluster of motels. It also has a good information centre covering the national park, plus a museum and gallery. Port Campbell Boat Charters (☎ 5598 6463) runs fishing trips (from $40), scenic cruises ($35) and scuba-diving trips ($35 for one dive, $60 for two).

The Great Ocean Road officially ends at **Warrnambool**, the largest provincial centre on this coast, but there are plenty more scenic delights farther along the Victorian coast including **Port Fairy**, an historic fishing village; **Portland**, the site of Victoria's first permanent European settlement; the **Lower Glenelg National Park**; and the **Discovery Bay Coastal Park**.

Places to Stay

Anglesea The *Anglesea Family Caravan Park* (☎ 5263 1583) has sites from $16 to $23 and cabins and cottages from $43. On the main road, the *Debonair Motel & Guesthouse* (☎ 5263 1440) offers cosy, period-style rooms or motel-style units, with B&B from $54 to $89 a double. At the southern end of town, the attractive *Roadnight Cottages* (☎ 5263 1820) provides good, self-contained accommodation from $110 a night for up to four people.

Aireys Inlet The friendly *Bush to Beach B&B* (☎ 5289 6538), a cedar cottage in a bushy setting at 43 Anderson St, has B&B from $60/80. The owner also offers good guided walks. The *Lighthouse Keeper's Cottages* (☎ 5289 6306) are impressive, self-contained cottages costing from $230 for a weekend.

Lorne The Lorne Foreshore Committee (☎ 5289 1382) manages six good caravan and camping reserves in and around Lorne – book in advance. The excellent *Great Ocean Road Cottages & Backpackers* (☎ 5289 1070), in a leafy hillside setting in Erskine Ave, has bunks from $15 and attractive timber cottages from $75 to $125 a night.

Erskine House (☎ 5289 1209) on the beachfront is a 1930s guesthouse with old-fashioned rooms from $95 to $165 a double for B&B. The romantic *Allenvale Cottages* (☎ 5289 1450) are in an idyllic setting and tariffs range from $95 to $150 a night.

Lorne to Apollo Bay In Wye River, the cosy *Rookery Nook Hotel* (☎ 5289 0240) has simple motel units overlooking a pretty bay at $45/60.

Ten km farther south, *Whitecrest* (☎ 5237 0228) has modern apartments from $85 to $125 and an excellent restaurant. And at Skenes Creek is the wonderful *Chris' Restaurant and Villas at Beacon Point* (☎ 5237 6411), with spectacular views, luxurious two-bedroom villa units (from $100 to $200 a night) and one of Victoria's best and most popular restaurants – great seafood!

Apollo Bay The *Pisces Caravan Park* (☎ 5237 6749) has a small backpackers' hostel with bunks from $10 a night. One km inland, the friendly *Lunabella B&B* (☎ 5237 7059) is a bright hillside farmhouse with doubles from $75 for B&B. The elegant *Greenacres Country House* (☎ 5237 6309) has an excellent bar and restaurant, and B&B ranging from $65 to $140 a double.

Port Campbell National Park *Macka's Farm* (☎ 5598 8261), a working dairy farm five km inland from the Twelve Apostles, has self-contained lodges or B&B from $65 to $85 a double. Three km inland from the Twelve Apostles the *Apostles View Motel* (☎ 5598 8277) has good motel units from $50 to $70. In Port Campbell itself, there's a caravan park, a pub and several motels, plus the straightforward *Tregea Hostel* (☎ 5598 6379) with dorm beds from $10 a night.

DAYLESFORD & HEPBURN SPRINGS

Set amongst the scenic hills, lakes and forests of the Central Highlands, the delightful twin towns of Daylesford and Hepburn Springs are enjoying a booming revival as the 'spa centre of Victoria'.

Things to See & Do

The best route from Melbourne up to Daylesford is via the **Wombat State Forest**. The areas around the towns of Blackwood and Trentham are well worth exploring: the scenic **Wombat Forest Drive**, one of the DC&NR's *Great Forest Drives of Victoria*, is a 50-km route through Blackwood, Trentham and Lyonville. A map/brochure of the drive is available from DC&NR offices.

The nearby **Lerderderg Gorge** has some great walks. In Blackwood, the lovely **Garden of St Erth** has four hectares of shaded lawns and stone paths, fragrant flower beds and dappled pools.

North of Blackwood, **Katteminga Lodge** (☎ 5424 1415) is a horse-riding ranch with good self-contained

GLENN BEANLAND

The Twelve Apostles, part of Port Campbell National Park,
viewed from the Great Ocean Road.

units from $75 a double, and horse rides from $15 an
hour.

The health-giving properties of this area's mineral
springs were known before gold was discovered here,
and by the 1870s Daylesford was a popular health resort,
attracting droves of fashionable Melburnians. The
current trend towards healthy lifestyles has prompted a
revival of interest in the area. The **Hepburn Spa Resort**
(☎ 5348 2034) in the Mineral Springs Reserve is an
impressive relaxation and rejuvenation centre with a
wide range of services including heated spas, plunge

pools, flotation tanks, massages and saunas. Daylesford and Hepburn Springs also boast masseurs, craft and antique shops, gardens, galleries, excellent cafes and restaurants, and dozens of charming guesthouses, cottages and B&Bs.

Daylesford's most popular attraction is the **Convent Gallery**, a huge 19th-century convent brilliantly converted into a craft and art gallery and set in lovely gardens (open daily from 10 am to 6 pm; $3 entry).

Also worth a visit are the lovely **Wombat Hill Botanic Gardens**, **Lake Daylesford** and **Jubilee Lake**, the **Historical Society Museum** and the **Central Highlands Tourist Railway** (☎ 5348 3503). There are also some wonderful **walking trails** in the region.

The Daylesford Tourist Information Centre (☎ 5348 1339) is on Vincent St.

Places to Stay

Daylesford and Hepburn Springs have a wide range of accommodation, although budget options are somewhat limited. The *Jubilee Lake Caravan Park* (☎ 5348 2186) and the *Springs Caravan Park* (☎ 5348 3161) both have camp sites and vans. At 9 Lone Pine Ave in Hepburn Springs, *Continental House* (☎ 5348 2005) is a rambling old alternative guesthouse with a vegan cafe; beds range from $13 to $18 a night (BYO linen).

Otherwise, you can choose from a fine collection of guesthouses and B&Bs; double rooms generally range from $80 to $120 a night. Places worth trying in Daylesford include *Ambleside B&B* (☎ 5348 2691) at 15 Leggatt St; *Hillsyde Cottage* (☎ 5348 1056) at 26 Millar St; and the *Lake House* (☎ 5348 3329) in King St, which is part of the wonderful restaurant of the same name. In Hepburn Springs, try *Villa Parma* (☎ 5348 3512), *Mooltan Guesthouse* (☎ 5348 3555) or *Dudley House* (☎ 5348 3033), all of which are along Main Rd. The *Springs Hotel* (☎ 5348 2202) at 124 Main Rd has pub rooms from $50/60 and motel-style cabins from $80/90.

If you're looking for somewhere self-contained, the helpful Daylesford Cottage Directory (☎ 5348 1255) manages more than 50 cottages in the area.

Getting There & Away

V/Line (☎ 13 2232) runs daily buses connecting Daylesford with the train station at Woodend ($4), from where you can continue to/from Melbourne by train. Melbourne-Daylesford takes two hours; the economy/1st-class fares are $11.40/14.40.

BALLARAT & SOVEREIGN HILL

When gold was discovered near Ballarat in 1851, the rush was on and thousands of diggers flooded into the area. Ballarat's alluvial goldfields were but the tip of the golden iceberg, and when deep shaft mines were sunk they struck incredibly rich quartz reefs. The mines were worked until the end of WWI, and about 28% of the gold unearthed in Victoria came from Ballarat.

Ballarat eventually grew into a major provincial town. Today there is a wealth of gracious Victorian architecture, a reminder of the prosperity of the gold-rush era. The town's major attraction is Sovereign Hill, but there are plenty of other points of interest in and around Ballarat, and you could easily spend a few days or more here.

Things to See & Do

Lydiard St is considered one of the country's best and most intact architectural examples of a Victorian-era streetscape. The excellent **Ballarat Fine Art Gallery** is one of the country's best provincial galleries (open daily 10.30 am to 5 pm; entry $4/1). Farther north, **Lake Wendouree** is edged by the **Ballarat Botanic Gardens**. Also of interest are the **Eureka Memorial & Exhibition**, the **Ballarat Wildlife Park** and **Kryal Castle**. The colourful **Begonia Festival** in early March is a great spectacle.

Ballarat's major tourist attraction is Sovereign Hill, a fascinating re-creation of a gold-mining township of the 1860s. It is probably the best attraction of its type in the country, and has won numerous awards – allow at least half a day for a visit. It's a living history museum, with shops and businesses set up in the style of the times and staffed by people dressed in period costumes. There's an old mineshaft, lots of old mining equipment, and visitors can pan for gold in the stream. Sovereign Hill is open daily from 9.30 am to 5 pm and admission is $16.50 adults, $12.50 students, $8.50 children and $45 for families – expensive, but worth it. The same ticket gets you into the nearby **Gold Museum**, which has imaginative displays and samples from all the old mining areas in the Ballarat region.

The Ballarat Visitor Information Centre (☎ 5332 2694) is in the centre of town at 39 Sturt St.

Places to Stay

There are half a dozen caravan parks in town. The *Sovereign Hill Lodge* (☎ 5333 3409) has bunkrooms from $16,

budget rooms from $33/44 and ensuite doubles from
$92. Opposite the main railway station, the *Provincial
Hotel* (☎ 5332 1845) has basic pub rooms at $10 ($15 with
linen).

The *George Hotel* (☎ 5331 1377), 27 Lydiard St North,
has rooms from $35/50 ($50/65 with ensuites). At 10
Lydiard St South, the elegantly restored *Craig's Royal
Hotel* (☎ 5331 1377) has various types of rooms, with
doubles from $40 to $120. Highly recommended is the
stylish *Ballarat Terrace* (☎ 5333 2216), at 229 Lydiard St
North, where B&B ranges from $100 to $130 a double.

Getting There & Away

V/Line trains and buses run regularly from Melbourne
to Ballarat. The 1¾ hour trip costs $12.80/18 in
economy/1st class. Sovereign Hill is three km from the
station, but a direct bus meets the 8.50 am train, or you
can take a local bus or a taxi – station staff will direct you
to the bus stop.

MACEDON RANGES & HANGING ROCK

The Calder Highway takes you north-west out of Melbourne towards Bendigo. The route itself isn't terribly
exciting, but there are quite a few pleasant surprises not
far off the beaten highway.

Take the Tullamarine Freeway and follow the Bendigo
signs. North of Tullamarine airport **Gellibrand Hill
Park** is a flora & fauna reserve, popular with walkers,
cyclists and birdwatchers. Just beyond the outskirts of
Melbourne you come to the turnoff to the pretty and
little known **Organ Pipes National Park**, with a visitors
centre, picnic spots and walking trails. This park features
some fascinating geological structures – hexagonal
basalt columns that look like giant organ pipes and form
a natural outdoor amphitheatre.

Five km east of the highway in the satellite town of
Sunbury are two of Victoria's most historic wineries:
Goona Warra and **Craiglee**, both of which were built
and originally planted in the 1860s. Back on the highway
and 11 km farther on is a turnoff to the historic and pretty
township of **Gisborne**, a former coach stop on the goldfields route.

Ten km east of Gisborne in Riddells Creek is the
Dromkeen Homestead Children's Literature Museum,
with a works-in-progress gallery, original sketches from
Australian classics like *The Magic Pudding, Blinky Bill* and

Snugglepot & Cuddlepie, and gardens with barbecue facilities. It opens weekdays from 9 am to 5 pm and also has open days (last Sunday of each month, noon to 4 pm). Entry is free.

Mt Macedon

Just north of Gisborne you can turn off the Calder Highway and head through the small town of Macedon to Mt Macedon, a 1013m-high extinct volcano. Many of Melbourne's wealthiest families have summer homes up here. There are also several tearooms, restaurants and a pub on the mountain.

The 'scenic route' up Mt Macedon Rd takes you up and over the mountain, past the mansions with their beautiful gardens and into some pretty countryside beyond. At the summit of Mt Macedon is a memorial cross and lookout point. Beyond the summit, the turnoff to the left leads to Woodend, or you can go straight on to Hanging Rock. The nearby Camel's Hump is popular with rock climbers.

The *Mountain Inn* (☎ 5426 1755), an English-style pub, has double rooms from $45 to $95 and good bistro meals *Huntly Burn* (☎ 5426 1411) is a romantic, self-contained getaway cottage costing from $125 a night.

Ten minutes' drive west of Mt Macedon on Shannon's Rd, the **Barringo Wildlife Reserve** (☎ 5426 1680) has emus, kangaroos, peacocks and deer running free. Across the road, Barringo Valley Trail Rides (☎ 5426 1778) offers horse rides through the area's scenic valleys and forests.

Woodend

Woodend is an attractive little commuter town nestled on the fringe of the Black Forest. In the gold-rush days, bushrangers roamed the forest, robbing travellers en route to the goldfields.

Keatings Country Hotel (☎ 5427 2510), on the main street, has simple pub rooms with B&B from $30/60. *The Bentinck* (☎ 5427 2330), a charming English-style guesthouse set in landscaped gardens, offers dinner and B&B packages from $220 a double.

Hanging Rock

The Hanging Rock Reserve (☎ 5427 0295) is 10 km northeast of Woodend. Hanging Rock, made famous by Joan Lindsay's novel and the subsequent film *Picnic at Hanging Rock* about the unsolved disappearance of a group of schoolgirls, has a peculiar and haunting mystique. The rock was formed by solidified lava and eroded over time to its present bizarre formation. It's also a sacred site of the Wurrenjerrie Aboriginal tribe, and a former refuge for bushrangers including the notorious Mad Dan Morgan. It's a popular spot for a picnic and there are walking tracks and good lookouts with superb views from higher up. The ranger's office and tearooms are near the entrance, and admission to the reserve costs $5 per car.

V/Line trains take you as far as Woodend ($7.60/10.60 in economy/1st class). From there a taxi to the rock costs about $10.

Macedon Wineries

Despite its proximity to Melbourne, the Macedon wine region is one of Victoria's best kept secrets. This is a great area for leisurely tours and exploration, with a dozen or so small and picturesque wineries scattered around an often rugged and spectacular countryside.

The area's altitude favours cool-climate varieties like chardonnay and pinot noir, and the sparkling 'Macedon' wine is a regional speciality. Brochures, maps and guides to the region's wineries are available from local information centres and all wineries.

THE YARRA VALLEY

The Yarra Valley, not far beyond the north-eastern outskirts of Melbourne, is a place of great natural beauty and well worth exploring. It's a good area for bicycle tours or bushwalks, there are dozens of wineries to visit, and the Healesville Wildlife Sanctuary is one of the best places in the country to see Australian wildlife.

The Yarra Valley & Healesville Visitor Information Centre (☎ 5962 2600) is at 127 Maroondah Highway in Healesville. The DC&NR's Outdoor Information Centre

---

Horse-Riding Tours
Lancefield Bush Rides & Tucker (☎ (03) 5429 1627) runs good day trips from Melbourne to Hanging Rock which include a walking tour of the Rock (with koala spotting), a visit to a vineyard, a three-hour horse ride through the Black Range State Forest, and a barbecue lunch and bush tucker. Trips operate on Tuesday, Wednesday, Friday and Sunday and cost $75 (10% discount for YHA members). ■

at 240 Victoria Parade in East Melbourne also has a good range of information and maps covering the area.

Healesville Wildlife Sanctuary

The Healesville Wildlife Sanctuary is one of the best places to see Australian native fauna. The sanctuary is in a natural bushland setting, and a circular walking track and boardwalk takes you through a series of spacious enclosures, aviaries, wetlands and display houses. The sanctuary's residents include wallabies, kangaroos, wombats, dingoes, lyrebirds, Tasmanian devils, bats, platypuses, koalas, eagles, snakes and lizards. The staff give regular demonstrations such as bird-of-prey feeds and snake shows. Some enclosures are only open at certain times each day: the platypus from 11.30 am to 1 pm and from 1.30 to 3.30 pm; the nocturnal animals and reptiles from 10 am to 4.30 pm; and the aviaries from 9 am to 4.30 pm.

The sanctuary is open from 9 am to 5 pm daily, and admission is $12 for adults, $9 for students and $6 for children.

Wineries

The Yarra Valley is one of Australia's most respected wine-growing regions, with more than 30 wineries scattered among these beautiful hills and valleys. The region is particularly noted for its pinot noir, chardonnay, cabernet sauvignon and sparkling 'methode champenoise' wines. Wineries that are open daily include **Domaine Chandon**, **Lilydale Vineyards**, **De Bortoli**, **Fergusson's**, **Coldstream Hills**, **Kellybrook**, **St Hubert's** and **Yarra Burn**. Many of the wineries charge a $2 or $5 tasting fee, which is refundable if you buy a bottle.

Other Attractions

The **Warrandyte State Park**, one of the few remaining areas of natural bush in the metropolitan area, is just 24 km north-east of Melbourne. Walking and cycling tracks are well marked, there are picnic and barbecue areas, native animals and birds, and an abundance of native wildflowers in the springtime. Although it's a part of suburban Melbourne, Warrandyte has the feel of a country village. Artists and craftspeople have always been attracted to the area, and there are quite a few galleries and potteries dotted throughout the hills. One

MARK ARMSTRONG

Domaine Chandon Vineyard in the Yarra Valley,
viewed from the tasting area.

of the best ways to explore the river and park is in a canoe; several local operators hire out canoes and equipment and organise canoeing trips.

A couple of km north of Yarra Glen, **Gulf Station** is a National Trust-classified farm dating back to the 1850s. The farm remained in the same family until recent times, and little has changed over the years. With the old slab-timber farmhouse, barns, stables and slaughterhouse, the original implements and the replanted sustenance gardens and orchards, Gulf Station gives an interesting insight into 19th-century farm life. It's open Wednesday to Sunday and on public holidays from 10 am to 4 pm, and admission is $6 for adults, $4 for children.

Much of the valley's early history relates to the timber industry. More timber passed through Yarra Junction than any town in the world except for Seattle in the USA.

Evidence of the old mills, timber tramlines and charcoal plants can still be found throughout the forests. **Powelltown**, 16 km south-east of Yarra Junction, was a busy timber town during the last century, and a collection of excellent forest walks now follow the old timber tramlines and tunnels which were built to transport the timber to the railway line. Walks include the Reid's Tramline Walk, the Ada Tree Walk (past a 300-year-old, 76m-high mountain ash), and the Seven Acre Rock Walk. The two-day, 36-km **Walk into History** track takes you all the way to Warburton. See the DC&NR's *Walks around Warburton 1 & 2* map/brochures.

There are also some great scenic drives. The Warburton-Healesville-Marysville triangle takes you through some great countryside (for instance, along the **Reefton Spur** between Marysville and Warburton). There are several different routes and plenty of great off-the-beaten-track spots to explore. Both the Acheron Way and Woods Point Rd are excellent drives along good gravel roads.

In Yarra Junction, the interesting **Upper Yarra Historical Museum** is open on Sunday and public holidays from 1.30 to 5 pm ($2).

Warburton is a pretty little town set in a lush, green valley by the river, with rising hills on both sides. This area was a popular health retreat last century, when droves of city folk came to Warburton's guesthouses to breathe the fresh mountain air. The township still has a sleepy old charm to it. It's a short drive from Warburton up to **Mt Donna Buang**, which during winter is capped with the closest snow to Melbourne. 'Donna' was where generations of Melbourne kids got their first look at snow, rode their first toboggan and cried as their first-ever Mr Snowman melted and slid off the bonnet of the family Holden as it descended the mountain.

The **Centenary Trail** follows the old Lilydale to Warburton railway line from Woori Yallock to Warburton, and offers good cycling and walking.

The **Yellingbo State Fauna Reserve**, to the south of Woori Yallock on the Warburton Highway, is the last remaining refuge of the rare helmeted honeyeater.

Places to Stay

The *Ashgrove Caravan Park* (☎ 5962 4398) is four km south-east of the centre of Healesville and close to the Sanctuary. Also near the Sanctuary and in a peaceful bushland setting, the *Sanctuary House Motel* (☎ 5962 5148) has singles/doubles from $45/60. *Strathvea* (☎ 5962 4109), nine km north of Healesville, is an Art

Deco guesthouse and gourmet getaway with doubles from $110 to $140 and dinner at $35 a head.

Right in the centre of Yarra Glen, the National Trust-classified *Grand Hotel* (☎ 9730 1230), dating from 1888, is one of the best country hotels in Victoria. Rooms range from $65 to $180 a double.

Magnolia Cottage (☎ 5966 2580), at 33 Blackwood Ave in Warburton, is a renovated 1908 cottage with three charming double guestrooms from $100 for B&B. The cosy *Motel Won-Wondah* (☎ 5966 2059) on Donna Buang Rd has units from $45/55. *Warburton Waters* (☎ 5966 9166), just south of the town, is a popular old-world guesthouse with guest lounges, reading rooms and open fires. B&B costs $95/130.

Getting There & Away

The Met's suburban trains go as far as Lilydale: two bus companies operate services from Lilydale railway station into the Yarra Valley.

McKenzie's Bus Lines (☎ 5962 5088) has daily services from Lilydale to Healesville ($1.50) and Yarra Glen. It also operates direct services to Healesville from the Spencer St coach terminal in Melbourne.

Martyrs Bus Service (☎ 5966 2035) runs regular buses from Lilydale railway station to Yarra Junction ($3.05) and Warburton ($3.85) – fares are cheaper if you show your train ticket.

KINGLAKE RANGES NATIONAL PARK

Situated in the so-called Forgotten Ranges, the Kinglake National Park is the largest national park near Melbourne, and one of the least visited. The park covers a huge eucalypt forest on the slopes of the Great Dividing Range, and was established back in 1928 to protect and preserve the native flora and fauna. There are dozens of walking tracks, good picnic areas and scenic lookout points in the three sections of the park. An admission fee is charged in some areas. For information about the national park or to book a camping site, contact the Park Office (☎ 5786 5351) in National Park Rd, Pheasant Creek.

A scenic way to get here from the city is to drive out through Eltham (stopping to visit the **Montsalvat Gallery**), then up through Kangaroo Ground, Panton Hill and St Andrews.

In the centre of the park, **Kinglake** is a small township with a pub and a few shops and galleries (but no lake!).

Eighteen km east, **Toolangi** was the home of the poet and writer CJ Dennis from 1915 to 1935. He wrote many of his famous works here, including *The Sentimental Bloke*. The *Singing Garden* tearooms and gardens are named after his last published book. Describing Toolangi in autumn, he wrote: 'Earth crammed with heaven and every common bush afire with God'.

Also in Toolangi is the DC&NR's impressive **Forest Discovery Centre** (☎ 5962 9314), with educational displays and videos on the various aspects of forest use. It's open daily from 10 am to 5 pm and entry costs $2 for adults, $1 for children. You can pick up leaflets here for the many bushwalks and scenic drives in the area, which include the **Wirrawilla Walk**, a 15-minute boardwalk circuit through a rainforest, and the Toolangi Black Range Forest Drive, a 44-km route from Toolangi north to Devlins Bridge, with a series of walks to picnic areas, waterfalls and historic sites along the way.

Camping areas in the national park include the *Gums*, on the Eucalyptus-Glenburn Rd 10 km north-east of Kinglake. It's a pretty area with a small stream nearby, and there are eight tent sites and three caravan sites. There's another camping area north of Toolangi called the *Murrindindi Scenic Reserve*, which is on the Murrindindi River and contains some great walks to places like the **Cascades** and the **Wilhelmina Falls**, which are quite spectacular when the snow melts in spring.

THE DANDENONGS

On a clear day, the Dandenong Ranges can be seen from the centre of Melbourne – Mt Dandenong is the highest point at 633m. The hills are about 35 km or an hour's drive east of the city, and their natural beauty has long made them a favoured destination for those wanting to escape the city.

Despite the effects of encroaching urban sprawl and constant droves of visitors, the Dandenongs have managed to retain much of their unique charm and appeal. The attractions include magnificent public gardens and plant nurseries, tearooms and restaurants, potteries and galleries, antique shops and markets, birdlife and native animals, and bushwalks and picnic areas. Things can get a little hectic on the narrow winding roads, particularly on weekends during spring and autumn – midweek visits are usually much more sedate and peaceful.

Dandenong Ranges Tourism (☎ 9752 6554) has an office one km north of Belgrave, and the DC&NR has a park information office (☎ 9758 1342) in the Lower Picnic Ground at the start of the Mt Dandenong Tourist Rd.

Dandenong Ranges National Park

The Dandenong Ranges National Park is made up of the three largest areas of remaining forest. All three sections have barbecue and picnic areas and good walking tracks. The **Ferntree Gully National Park**, named for its abundance of tree ferns, has four good walking trails of around two hours. **Sherbrooke Forest** has a towering cover of mountain ash trees and a lower level of silver wattles, sassafras, blackwoods and other exotic trees, as well a large number of birds including rosellas, kookaburras, robins, currawongs and honeyeaters. The **Doongalla Reserve**, on the western slopes of Mt Dandenong, is not as accessible as the other two areas, and the forest areas there are less crowded.

William Ricketts Sanctuary

The William Ricketts Sanctuary on the Mt Dandenong Tourist Rd on Mt Dandenong is one of the best places to visit. The sanctuary and its sculptures are the work of William Ricketts, who worked here up until his death in 1993 at the age of 94. His work was inspired by the years he spent living with Aboriginal people in central Australia and by their affinity with the land. His personal philosophies permeate and shape the sanctuary, which is set in damp fern gardens with trickling waterfalls and sculptures rising out of moss-covered rocks like spirits from the ground. It's open daily from 10 am to 4.30 pm and admission is $5 for adults and $2 for children.

Gardens

The high rainfall and deep volcanic soils of the Dandenongs are perfect for agriculture, and the area has always provided Melbourne's markets with much of their produce. The gardens and nurseries overflow with visitors who come to see the colourful displays of tulips, daffodils, azaleas, rhododendrons and others. The gardens are at their best in spring and autumn, but are worth a visit anytime.

At the **Olinda Rhododendron Gardens** (open daily 10 am to 4.30 pm, or until 5.30 pm during autumn, spring and daylight savings; entry $6.50 adults, $4.50 kids) on the Georgian Rd next to the Olinda State Forest, giant eucalypts tower over shady lawns and colourful flower

RICHARD I'ANSON

Sherbrooke Forest in the Dandenong Ranges
National Park.

beds. There are groves of cherry blossoms, oaks, maples and beeches, and over 15,000 rhododendrons and azaleas.

The **Alfred Nicholas Memorial Gardens** on Sherbrooke Rd in Sherbrooke were originally the grounds of Burnham Beeches, the country mansion of Alfred Nicholas, co-founder of Aspro and the Nicholas pharmaceutical company. They have in recent years been restored by the DC&NR (open 10 am to 4.30 pm; $4 entry).

A couple of bends in the road away heading east, the smaller and more intimate **George Tindale Memorial Gardens** are also worth a visit (open 10 am to 4 pm daily; entry $4).

Puffing Billy

One of the major attractions of the Dandenongs is *Puffing Billy* (☎ 9754 6800 for bookings, ☎ 9870 8411 for recorded timetable information), a restored steam train which puffs its way through the hills and fern gullies between Belgrave and the Emerald Lakeside Park. Along the way you can visit the historic **Steam Museum** at Menzies Creek and the pretty town of Emerald, with **Lakeside Park** and the **Emerald Lake Model Railway**.

Puffing Billy operates up to four times every day except Christmas Day. The round trip takes 2½ hours and costs $16.50 for adults, $9.50 for children and $47 for a family; lunch specials are also available. The *Puffing Billy* railway station is a short stroll from Belgrave railway station, the last stop on the Belgrave suburban line.

Places to Stay

There are numerous motels, guesthouses, B&Bs and self-contained cottages, but not too many places for budget travellers. One exception is the comfy *Emerald Backpackers* (☎ 5968 4086) in Emerald. The owners can often find work for travellers in local nurseries and gardens. Dorm beds cost $12.

The old *Kalorama Chalet* (☎ 9728 1185) near Kalorama has doubles from $50 to $60, while the nearby *Blue Dandenongs Motel* (☎ 9728 1298) has doubles from $70 to $90.

Opposite the Rhododendron Gardens in Olinda, *Arcadia* (☎ 9751 1017) is an impressive two-storey cedar homestead in a delightful garden setting. B&B costs $110 to $140 a double, or there are self-contained cottages ranging from $125 to $195 a night.

Along the Mt Dandenong Tourist Rd, the old English-style *Kenlock Manor* (☎ 9751 1680) has guestrooms from $95 a double, while the charming *Como Cottages* (☎ 9751 2264) cost from $110 to $170 a night.

Getting There & Away

You really need your own transport to explore the Dandenongs properly – the Mt Dandenong Tourist Rd is the main route through the ranges.

The Met's suburban trains run on the Belgrave line to the foothills of the Dandenongs. From Upper Ferntree Gully railway station it's a 10-minute walk to the start of the Ferntree Gully National Park. Belgrave railway station is the last stop on the line and the starting point for Puffing Billy, and it's a 15-minute walk from the station to Sherbrooke Forest. Buses also run from both stations along the Mt Dandenong Tourist Rd.

MORNINGTON PENINSULA

The Mornington Peninsula, a boot-shaped peninsula of land between Port Phillip Bay and Westernport Bay, is a little over an hour's drive from the city centre. Because of its great beaches and other attractions, it has been a favourite summer resort for Melburnians since the 1870s, when paddle-steamers used to carry droves of holiday-makers down to Portsea and Sorrento from the city.

The narrow spit of land at the end of the peninsula has both calm beaches on Port Phillip Bay (known as the 'front beaches') and rugged, beautiful ocean beaches (known as the 'back beaches'). At the far end of the spit, Portsea has a reputation as a playground for the wealthy, while nearby Sorrento has the peninsula's best range of accommodation and eateries.

Swimming and surfing top the list of peninsula activities, but you can also get your teeth into snorkelling, scuba diving, fishing and sailing. There are excellent bushwalking trails through the Point Nepean National Park, as well as horse-riding ranches, boat cruises and dolphin swims, and several great golf courses.

The coastal strip fronting Bass Strait is protected as part of the Mornington Peninsula National Park, and along here you'll find more stunning coastal walking tracks and some great surf beaches. There are also good swimming and surf beaches in Westernport Bay. Inland, the peninsula is a picturesque blend of rolling hills and green pastures, terraced vineyards and dense forests. It's a great area for leisurely tours and explorations – you can visit dozens of wineries and vineyards, pick your own fruit in orchards and berry farms, shop at craft and produce markets, wander through the bush on foot, or discover one of the many fine local restaurants.

Peninsula Tourism's main information office (☎ 5987 3078) is on the Nepean Highway in Dromana.

Things to See & Do

Mornington to Sorrento If you're not in a hurry, turn off the Nepean Highway at Mornington and take the slower, but much more scenic, route around the coast, which rejoins the highway at Dromana. In Mornington you could visit **Studio City** at 1140 Nepean Highway, with memorabilia relating to TV, cinema and radio (opens daily 10 am to 5 pm), while in Mt Martha is the **Briars Historic Homestead** (open daily 11 am to 5 pm).

Arthur's Seat State Park is just inland from Dromana and signposted off the Nepean Highway. A scenic drive winds up to the summit lookout at 305m, and you can also reach it by the **Arthur's Seat Scenic Chairlift**. The park has good picnic and barbecue facilities, walking tracks, a fauna park and car museum, a kiosk and restaurant, and great views of the bay and peninsula from several lookouts.

In McCrae is the National Trust's **McCrae Homestead**, a timber-slab cottage built in 1846. It houses the paintings and writings of the pioneering Georgina McCrae (open daily noon to 4.30 pm; entry $3).

Sorrento The oldest town on the peninsula, Sorrento has a delightful seaside atmosphere. During the summer silly season it's a frenetic and fashionable resort, whereas during the winter months it's more akin to a sleepy little village. It has some fine 19th-century buildings, constructed from locally quarried limestone, and boasts fine beaches, good accommodation and excellent cafes and restaurants. Dolphin-watching cruises in the bay are incredibly popular, and while you're here be sure to take a trip across to Queenscliff on the ferry.

Local operators including Polperro Dolphin Swims (☎ 018 174 160), Dolphin Discovery Tours (☎ 018 392 507), Moonraker (☎ 018 591 033) and Rip Charters (☎ 5984 3664) offer a combination of sightseeing cruises of the bay (from $25), fishing trips (half-day from $40) and dolphin-watching cruises (three to four hours, $25 to $35 for sightseeing or $50 if you want to swim with the dolphins).

Portsea Portsea has some great beaches. At the back beach there's the impressive natural rock formation known as **London Bridge**, plus a cliff where hang-gliders leap into the void. This ocean beach has good surf and can be dangerous for swimming, so swim between the flags. The front beaches are safer for swimming. If things get too hot wander up to the pub and enjoy a drink in the pretty (and usually pretty crowded) beer garden which overlooks the pier.

Diver Instruction Services (DIS; ☎ 5984 3155) offers one-day beginner's dives (from $75), certified diving courses (from $495 all inclusive), and charter trips for snorkellers and certified divers ($85 for two dives, all gear supplied).

Point Nepean National Park After being off-limits to the general public for over 100 years because it was a quarantine station and army base, Point Nepean National Park on the tip of the peninsula was opened to the public in 1988. There's an excellent Visitors Centre (☎ 5984 4276) near the entrance, and the park is open daily from 9 am to 5 pm (later during summer). Admission fees are $7.50 for adults, $4 for children and $17 for families.

The main track through the park starts from the visitors centre and runs down to the point – a return distance of 14 km. A tractor-drawn 'people mover' runs a shuttle service along here. There are four short walks branching off the main track.

Ocean Beaches – Portsea to Flinders

The south-western coastline of the peninsula faces Bass Strait. Along here are the beautiful and rugged ocean beaches of Blairgowrie, Rye, St Andrews, Gunnamatta and Cape Schanck. There are a series of points and bays and a backdrop of cliffs, sand dunes, spectacular scenery and tidal rockpools – this is the fragile natural habitat of coastal birdlife, surfers and rock-fishing people.

Surf life-saving clubs operate at Gunnamatta and Portsea during summer. If you're planning to swim, head for the patrolled beaches.

At Cape Schanck is the **Cape Schanck Lighthouse & Museum** (☎ 5988 6251), an operational lighthouse built in 1859 with a kiosk, museum and information centre (open Wednesday to Sunday 10 am to 3 pm, to 4 pm on weekends and daily during school holidays; $1 entry, $3 for lighthouse tours). Cape Schanck is a great place for fishing, picnics and bushwalks.

Off the road from Cape Schanck to Flinders is a gravel turnoff to the **Blowhole**, and the rock platforms along here are accessible at low tide.

Mornington Peninsula National Park

The peninsula foreshore along Bass Strait is a protected coastal park all the way from Portsea to Cape Schanck. A series of interconnected walking tracks provide access to the more remote ocean beaches – if you want to get away from the crowds and discover some great coastal areas, start walking.

The walking tracks are accessible from various car parks and from Portsea to Rye they are well marked. From Rye to Cape Schanck the walks are less defined, and you may need to walk along beaches (some impassable at high tide), sand dunes and cliff-tops. Many of the beaches can be dangerous for swimmers, especially during high seas, so don't be adventurous unless you want to get to Tasmania the hard way.

The brochure *Discovering the Peninsula* ($3.50, available from DC&NR offices) has good maps of the coastal walks plus lots of natural and historical information about the area.

Flinders to Hastings

Westernport Bay starts at the town of Flinders, a pretty village with a busy fishing fleet, good rocky point breaks for surfers, excellent ocean-side golf course and views across to Phillip Island from the point at West Head. If the wind is south-easterly, you'll often see hang-gliders launching off the cliff-tops here.

Towns on this coast are not as developed and crowded as those on Port Phillip Bay, and the natural environment on this part of the peninsula is more fertile and 'European', with pine trees and rolling green hills – in stark contrast with the sand dunes and coastal scrub of the western side of the peninsula. There are good beaches all the way along here at Shoreham, Point Leo (which also has good surf beaches), Merricks, Balnarring, Somers and Hastings.

Head inland from Shoreham for some great scenic drives and good exploring around Red Hill and Main Ridge. The hills and bushlands make an appealing change from the coastal scenery, and there are some great craft galleries, produce stores and wineries to stumble across (see Wineries below).

Wineries

In the last decade the Mornington Peninsula has blossomed into one of Victoria's prime wine-producing regions. Wedged between the two bays, the peninsula's fertile soils, temperate climate and rolling hills are now producing consistently good wines, although they tend to be relatively expensive due to the high cost of real estate this close to Melbourne. The region is particularly noted for its pinot noir, but also produces good shiraz, chardonnay and other wines.

There are dozens of wineries, mostly in the elevated central area around Red Hill and Main Ridge. Most of these are small-level producers, and many are individually run. More than 20 of the wineries are open to the public on weekends, and those open daily include **Dromana Estate**, **Hann's Creek Estate**, **Hickinbotham of Dromana**, **Main Ridge Estate**, **Red Hill Estate**, **Stonier's Winery at Merricks**, the **Briars Vineyard** and **T'Gallant** at Darling Park.

A map and brochure is available from information centres and from the wineries themselves, or you can contact the Mornington Peninsula Vigneron's Association on ☎ 5987 3822.

Places to Stay

Rye & Sorrento There are plenty of caravan parks along the bay. The council-run *Rye Foreshore Reserve*

(☎ 5985 2405) and *Sorrento Foreshore Reserve* (☎ 5984 2797) both have sites on the foreshore from $10.

In Sorrento, the YHA-associate *Bell's Hostel* (☎ 5984 4323), 3 Miranda St, is a great place to stay. The facilities are excellent and the owners extremely helpful. Bunks cost from $12. The *Continental Hotel* (☎ 5984 2201) has bunkrooms at $15 ($20 during summer), or ensuite doubles from $60 to $90 for B&B.

Carmel B&B (☎ 5984 3512), 142 Ocean Beach Rd, is an historic and stylish limestone cottage with B&B from $80 to $120 a double, or self-contained units from $80 to $90. *Whitehall Guesthouse* (☎ 5984 4166), 231 Ocean Beach Rd, is a rambling old two-storey guesthouse charging from $75 to $90 for B&B.

Portsea The cheapest option is the *Portsea Hotel* (☎ 5984 2213), which has comfy rooms with shared facilities from $35/60 ($95/110 with ensuites). The *Portsea Village Resort* (☎ 5984 8484) has executive-style apartments ranging from $175 to $410 per night.

The ultimate in luxury accommodation is the *Delgany Country Hotel* (☎ 5984 4000), set in a magnificent old limestone castle on five hectares of private gardens. Rooms range from $215 to $370; dinner B&B packages start from $340 a double.

Flinders & Shoreham The *Flinders Hotel* (☎ 5989 0201) has a few motel-style units behind the pub from $49/59 for singles/doubles, or there's the *Flinders Cove Motel* (☎ 5989 0666) across the road with rooms from $69/89.

The *Black Rabbit* (☎ 5989 8500) on Hillcrest Rd in Shoreham is a modern limestone villa on a bushland property. Doubles range from $110 to $135.

Getting There & Away

Train/Bus The Met's suburban trains from the city to Frankston take about an hour and the one-way fare is $4.50. From Frankston railway station, Peninsula Bus Lines (☎ 5986 5666) runs a service along the Nepean Highway to Portsea every 1¼ hours between 9 am and 7 pm, which costs $6.45 one way.

Ferry Peninsula Searoad Transport (☎ 5258 3244) operates the *MV Queenscliff* car and passenger ferry which links Sorrento with Queenscliff on the Bellarine Peninsula. It runs every day of the year and takes about half an hour to make the crossing, departing from Queenscliff at 7, 9 and 11 am, 1, 3 and 5 pm and returning from

Sorrento at 8 and 10 am, noon, 2, 4 and 6 pm. During the peak seasons (Friday and Sunday from mid-September to mid-December and then daily until Easter Tuesday), there are additional departures from Queenscliff at 7 pm and from Sorrento at 8 pm. Cars cost $30 to $36 plus $3 per adult; a motorcycle and rider costs $17; and pedestrians cost $7 for adults, $5 for kids.

A passenger ferry (☎ 5984 1602) also operates regular daily crossings from Sorrento and Portsea to Queenscliff between Christmas and Easter and during school holidays; the adult fare is $6 each way.

PHILLIP ISLAND

At the entrance to Westernport Bay, 137 km south-east of Melbourne, Phillip Island is a very popular holiday resort for the Melbourne area. The island itself is quite rugged and windswept and there are plenty of beaches, both sheltered and with surf, a fascinating collection of wildlife and several fairly sleepy and old-fashioned townships.

Phillip Island's famous Penguin Parade is one of Australia's most popular tourist attractions. Tourists come by the bus load, and while some people are disappointed by the high degree of commercialisation, the other side of the coin is that the parade and displays are educational and the money contributes towards protecting the penguins' natural habitat.

There is an excellent information centre (☎ 5956 7447) in Newhaven just after you cross the bridge to the island.

Penguin Parade

Every evening at **Summerland Beach** in the south-west of the island, the little penguins which nest there perform their 'parade', emerging from the sea and waddling resolutely up the beach to their nests – seemingly oblivious to the sightseers. The penguins are there year round, but they arrive in larger numbers in the summer when they are rearing their young. The parade takes place like clockwork a few minutes after sunset each day and it is Australia's second biggest tourist attraction. Not surprisingly there are big crowds of up to 4000 people, especially on weekends and holidays, so bookings should be made in advance – contact either the information centre at Newhaven, or the Penguin Reserve (☎ 5956 8300) itself.

To protect the penguins everything is strictly regimented – keep to the viewing areas, don't get in the penguins' way and don't use a camera flash. There's a modern visitor centre, open from 10 am every day, with an excellent souvenir shop and walk-through simulated underwater display. An elevated boardwalk with several viewing stands leads from the back of the visitor centre down to the beach. The admission charge is $7.50 for adults, $3.50 for children or $21 for families, but it's money well spent to see this unique sight. (At least most of the time it is – occasionally the penguins seem to take a day off from fishing.)

Seal Rocks & the Nobbies

Off Point Grant, the extreme south-west tip of the island, a group of rocks called the Nobbies rises from the sea. Beyond these are Seal Rocks, which are inhabited by Australia's largest colony of fur seals. The rocks are most crowded during the breeding season from October to December, when up to 6000 seals arrive. You can view them through coin-in-the-slot binoculars from the kiosk on the headland, as long as it's open. From the kiosk a raised boardwalk gives access to excellent views of the Blowhole, and across to the Nobbies and Seal Rocks.

Wildlife

Phillip Island has always been promoted as a good place to see koalas 'in the wild', which in the last 20 years hasn't really been the case. The resident koalas lived in defoliated trees in badly managed roadside reserves, and through a combination of introduced diseases and road accidents, the population was continually in decline.

However, you can see the little fellas at the newish **Koala Conservation Centre** at Fiveways on the Phillip Island Tourist Rd. The centre has a visitors' area and elevated boardwalks running through a bush setting (open daily 10 am until sunset; $4 adults, $1.50 kids).

Phillip Island also has mutton-bird colonies, particularly in the sand dunes around Cape Woolamai. These birds, which are actually called shearwaters, are amazingly predictable: they arrive back on the island on exactly the same day each year – 24 September – from their migration flight from Japan and Alaska. They stay on the island until April. Your best chance of seeing them is at the Penguin Parade, as they fly in low over the sea each evening at dusk in the spring and summer months. Also try the Forest Caves Reserve at Woolamai Beach.

Other Attractions

The well set-up **Phillip Island Wildlife Park** is one km south of Cowes. Visitors can walk through enclosures and wetlands and see and feed native animals and birds – wallabies, kangaroos, wombats, emus, reptiles etc (open daily 9 am to sunset; $7 adults, $4 children).

Swimming and **surfing** are popular island activities. The ocean beaches are on the south side and there's a life-saving club at Woolamai – this beach is notorious for its strong rips and currents, so swim only between the flags. If you're not a good swimmer, head for the bay beaches around Cowes, or the quieter ocean beaches such as Smith's Beach or Berry's Beach. There are quite a few surf shops on the island which rent equipment.

The old **Motor Racing Circuit** was revamped to stage the Australian Motorcycle Grand Prix for the first time in 1989. It was controversially moved to Sydney in 1991, but is due to return to the island in 1997.

Rugged **Cape Woolamai** with its walking track is particularly impressive. There's a great contrast between the high seas on this side of the island and the sheltered waters of the northern (Cowes) side. **Churchill Island** is a small island with an historic homestead, beautiful gardens and a museum of old farming machinery, as well as some great short walks and picnic spots through the grounds and gardens. It's open from 10 am to 4 pm daily; $5 adults, $2 kids.

Organised Flights, Tours & Cruises

Island Scenic Tours (☎ 5952 1042) runs trips most nights from Cowes out to Penguin Parade ($15, which includes entry), as well as various scenic tours ($20 to $35). Amaroo Park Backpackers also operates an evening service out to Penguin Parade. Phillip Island airport (☎ 5956 7316) operates scenic flights (from $30 to $75 per person). Bay Connections Cruises (☎ 5952 3501) runs cruises to Seal Rocks ($30), French Island ($32) and evening 'shearwater cruises' ($20).

Places to Stay

Phillip Island is a very popular holiday destination, with hostels, guesthouses, B&Bs, motels, holiday flats and camping sites. You'll need to book ahead during Christmas, Easter and school holidays. Unless otherwise stated, the places mentioned below are all in Cowes.

The best backpackers' accommodation on the island is at the very friendly *Amaroo Caravan Park & Backpackers* (☎ 5952 2548) on the corner of Church and Osborne Sts. Six-bed dorms cost $12 ($14 for non-YHA members), doubles are $28/32. It has a swimming pool, bikes for hire and organises trips to the Penguin Parade and

Wilson's Promontory. The owners run free courtesy buses from Melbourne (see Getting There & Around later in this chapter). Other caravan parks in the vicinity include the *Anchor Belle Holiday Park* (☎ 5952 2258) at 272 Church St and the *Kaloha Caravan Park* (☎ 5952 2179) on the corner of Chapel and Steele Sts.

The *Isle of Wight Hotel* (☎ 5952 2301) on The Esplanade has budget pub rooms at $30/35 and motel rooms from $42/52. Further along The Esplanade, the *Continental Resort* (☎ 5952 2316) has modern executive-style rooms from $65 to $100 a double. Also on The Esplanade is the *Anchor at Cowes* (☎ 5952 1351), with modern units from $70 to $120.

Rhylston Park (☎ 5952 2730), at 190 Thompson Ave, is a restored 1886 homestead with period fittings and furnishings, set in two hectares of gardens. Quirky singles/doubles cost from $45/75.

Narabeen Cottage (☎ 5952 2062) at 16 Steele St is a 'gourmet getaway' with five guestrooms and a small restaurant. B&B costs from $140 a double, or $220 with dinner included.

Trenavin Park Country House (☎ 5956 8230) is on an attractive 35-hectare property off Ventnor Rd, about 10 km west of Cowes. This impressive historic homestead has great views and good facilities. B&B is $75 per person ($125 on Saturday nights, which includes a four course dinner and wine).

Getting There & Around

Amaroo Park Backpackers (☎ 5952 2548) runs courtesy buses to the island, leaving from the YHA's Queensberry Hill Hostel in North Melbourne every Tuesday and Friday at 1 pm. Transport is free if you're staying at Amaroo Caravan Park Backpackers.

V/Line has a daily train/bus service to Phillip Island (train to Dandenong, bus to the island). The trip takes 2¼ hours and costs $12.80, and the drivers will usually drop you right where you're staying.

There is no public transport around the island. You can hire bikes from Phillip Island Bike Hire (☎ 5952 2381), at 11 Findlay St in Cowes, or from Amaroo Caravan Park Backpackers.

Index

Maps

RICHARD NEBESKY

Decorative artwork in Brunswick St, Fitzroy.

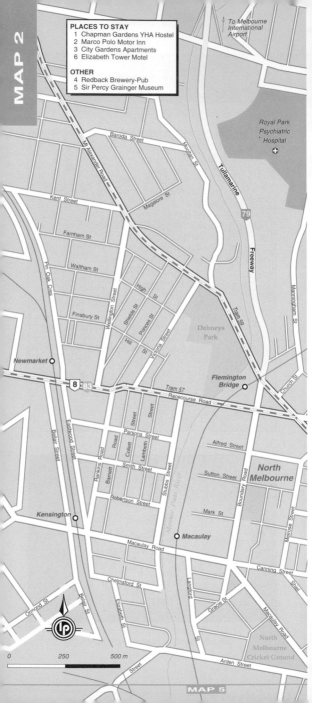

MAP 2

PLACES TO STAY
1 Chapman Gardens YHA Hostel
2 Marco Polo Motor Inn
3 City Gardens Apartments
6 Elizabeth Tower Motel

OTHER
4 Redback Brewery-Pub
5 Sir Percy Grainger Museum

To Melbourne
International
Airport

Royal Park
Psychiatric
Hospital

Baroda Street

Moonah St

Tullamarine

79

Freeway

Kent Street

Farnham St

Magalore St.

Tram 59

Waltham St

High St

Manningham St.

Finsbury St

Wellington Street

Shields St

Princes St

Hill St

Victoria Street

Debneys
Park

Newmarket

8 83

Flemington
Bridge

Church St

Tram 57

Racecourse Road

Pin Oak Cres

Eastwood Street

Bellair Street

Street
Street

Parsons Street

Alfred Street

Collett

Hawkins Road

Road

Lambeth

Barnett

Smith Street

Sutton Street

Boundary Road

North
Melbourne

Robertson Street

Stubbs Street

Mark St

Melrose Street

Kensington

Macaulay

Macaulay Road

Canning Street

Chelmsford St

Langford

Gracie St

Macaulay Road

Shie

Ormond St

Bellair St

Elizabeth Street

North
Melbourne
Cricket Ground

Mooneē Ponds River

0   250   500 m

Street

Arden Street

MAP 5

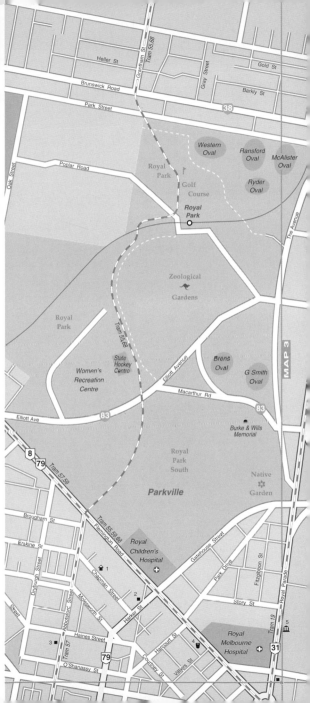

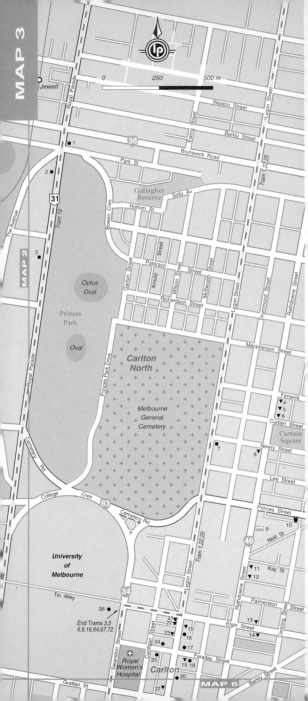

PLACES TO STAY

1. Princes Park Motel
2. Ramada Inn
3. Royal Parade Irico Hotel
7. Lygon Crest Lodgings

PLACES TO EAT

4. La Trattoria
5. La Porchetta
6. Kent Hotel
8. Paragon Cafe
11. Cafe Amritas
12. Wine Bar II
13. Chinta Ria R&B
14. Abla's
15. Trotters
19. Shakahari Vegetarian Restaurant
21. Twins
22. Jimmy Watson's
23. Tiamo's
27. Papa Gino's
30. Cafe Retro
31. Aquarium Bar & Cafe
32. Chishti's
33. Spanish Club (Hogar Español)
34. Kahlo's Tapas Bar
36. La Sangria Tapas Bar & Bar Salona Nightclub
37. Colmao Flamenco
38. Carmen Bar
40. Bakers Cafe & Vegie Bar
42. Charmaine's Ice Cream
43. Joe's Garage
44. Babka Bakery-Cafe
46. The Fitz
47. Rhumbarella's
49. Cafe Cappadocia
50. Mario's
52. Cafe Provincial
55. Thai Thani
56. Sala Thai
57. Black Cat Cafe
59. Cafe Bohemio

OTHER

9. Carlton Baths
10. Dan O'Connell Hotel
16. Lygon Court, Cinema Nova & Comedy Club
17. Johnny's Green Room
18. La Mama Theatre
20. Readings Bookshop
24. STA Travel
25. Carlton Moviehouse
26. Sir Ian Potter Gallery
28. Royal Derby Hotel
29. Fitzroy Baths
35. Universal Theatre & Radio 3RRR
39. Fitzroy Nursery & Artists Garden
41. Punters Club
45. The Evelyn Hotel
48. Gypsy Bar
51. Bull Ring
53. Night Cat Nightclub
54. One-Twenty Bar
58. McCoppin's Hotel
60. The Tote Hotel

MARK ARMSTRONG

Eateries along Lygon St, Carlton.

Fringe Festival Parade, Brunswick St, Fitzroy

MAP 4

Northcote

St Georges Road
Tram 11

45

High Street

James

Street

Waterloo Rd

Brooke St

Charles St

Clarke St

29

Roberts

Street

Mason St

Merri

Merri Parade

Union St

Westgarth
Cinema

High Street

Roberts

Street

38

Westgarth

Creek

McLachlan Street

Tram 86

Ross St

Westgarth Street

Rushall

Walker

Street

Northcote
Park
Football
Ground

Knott
Field

46

Rushall Cres

Queens Parade

Coulson
Reserve

Heidelberg Road

Clifton
Hill

The Esplanade

Dwyer Street

Maria Street

Mayors
Park

Clifton
Hill

John Street

Berry St

Fenwick St

Spensley Street

Walker St

Wright St

Hoddle Street

Ramsden Street

Yambla St

Quarries
Park

Street

North Terrace

Darling
Gardens

Hoddinson

Gold Street

South Terrace

Rodeneath Street

29

Eastern

Alexander St

Maugie St

Dights
Falls

River

Abbot St

Lulie St

Collingwood
Football
Ground

Yarra

Victoria
Park

MAP 3

MAP 7

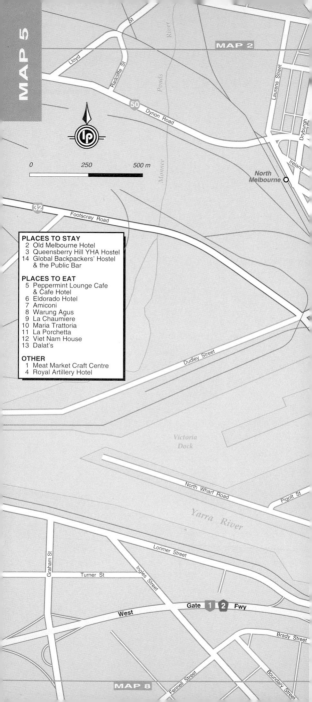

MAP 5

MAP 2

Lloyd

Radcliffe St

St

River

Ponds

50 Dynon Road

Laurens Street

Dryburgh

Ireland

North
Melbourne O

0   250   500 m

Maribyrnong

32 Footscray Road

PLACES TO STAY
2 Old Melbourne Hotel
3 Queensberry Hill YHA Hostel
14 Global Backpackers' Hostel
   & the Public Bar

PLACES TO EAT
5 Peppermint Lounge Cafe
   & Cafe Hotel
6 Eldorado Hotel
7 Amiconi
8 Warung Agus
9 La Chaumiere
10 Maria Trattoria
11 La Porchetta
12 Viet Nam House
13 Dalat's

OTHER
1 Meat Market Craft Centre
4 Royal Artillery Hotel

Dudley Street

Victoria
Dock

North Wharf Road

Pigott St

Yarra River

Lorimer Street

Graham St

Ingles Street

Turner St

West   Gate 1 2 Fwy

Brady Street

Fennell Street

Boundary Street

MAP 8

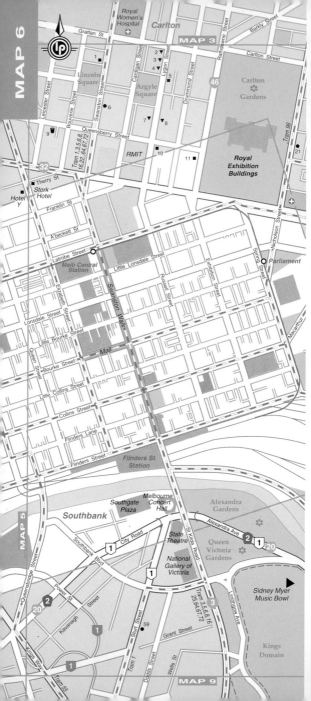

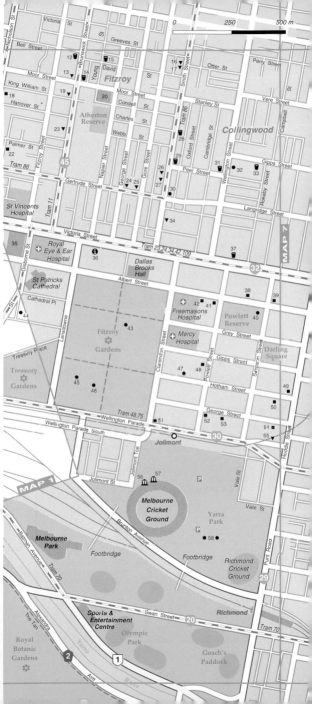

Terrace houses along Nicholson St, Fitzroy.

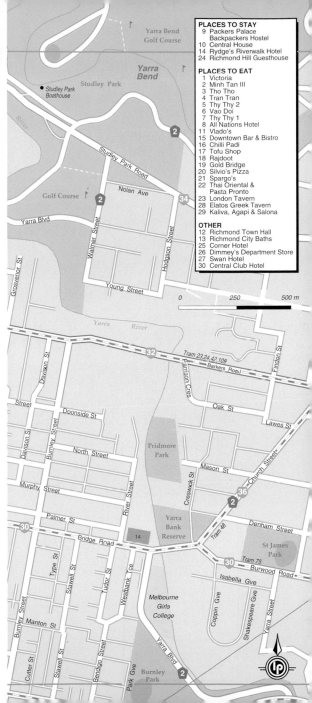

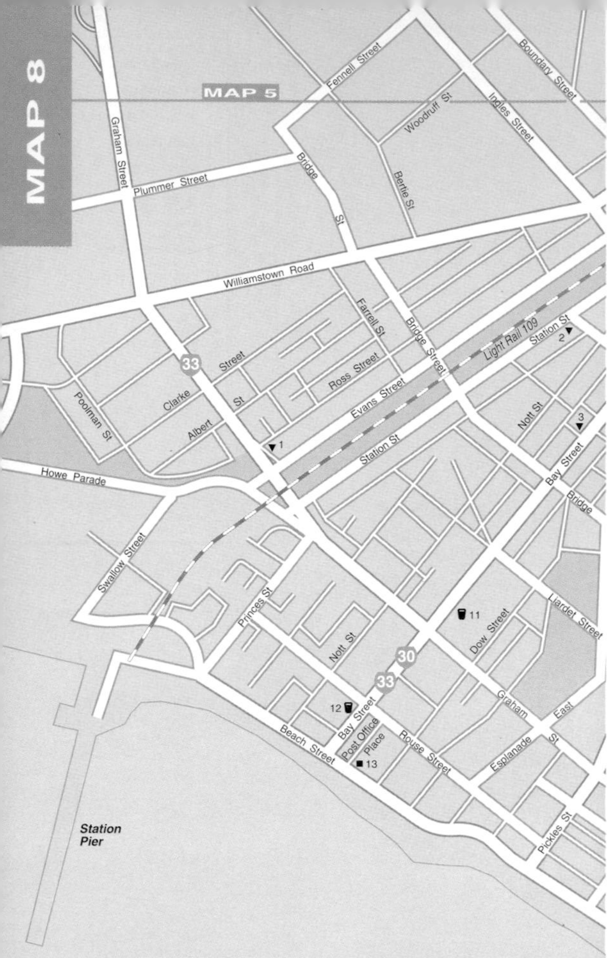

MAP 8

MAP 5

Fennell Street

Boundary Street

Graham Street

Plummer Street

Woodruff St

Indless Street

Bridge St

Bertie St

Williamstown Road

Station St

Light Rail 109

Street

Ross Street

Evans Street

Nott St

Bay Street

Clarke

St

Albert

St

▼ 1

Station St

Bridge

Poolman St

Howe Parade

Swallow Street

Princes St

Nott St

▮ 11

Dow Street

Liardet Street

30

33

Graham

St

12 ▮

Bay Street

East

Esplanade

St

13 ▮

Post Office Place

Beach Street

Bosse Street

Pickles St

Station
Pier

PORT
PHILLIP
BAY

PLACES TO STAY
13 Station Pier Condominiums
21 Hotel Victoria

PLACES TO EAT
1   Clare Castle Hotel
2   Railway Club Hotel
3   Rose & Crown Restaurant & Bar
6   Kobe
7   Centro Cafe
10 Morning Glory Cafe
14 Ricardo's Trattoria
15 Albert Park Deli,
    Villagio Foodstore &
    Dundas Place Cafe
16 Misuzu's Japanese Cafe
17 Avenue Foodstore
18 Vic Ave Pasta & Wine
19 Corey's Cafe
20 Stavros Tavern &
    Albert Park In-Line Skates

OTHER
4   Portable Iron Houses
5   South Melbourne Market
8   South Melbourne Town Hall
9   St Vincents Place
11 The Flower
12 Molly Bloom's Hotel

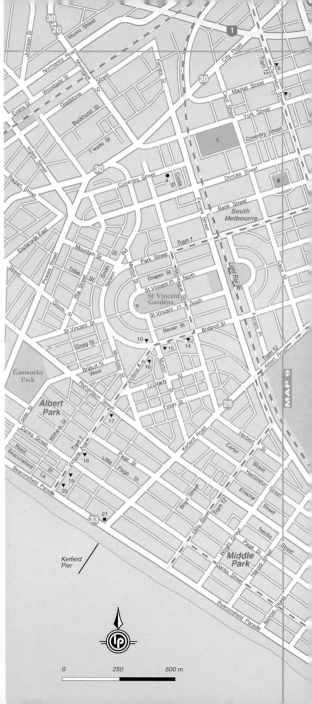

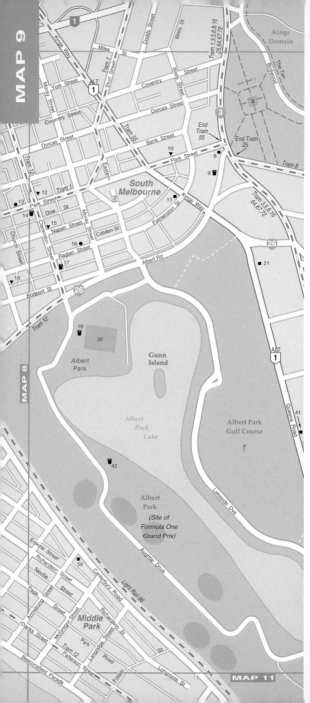

MAP 9

Kings
Domain

Tram 1,3,5,6,8,16
,25,64,67,72

Dodds Street

Wells St

Miles

Kings Way

York Street

Moray Street

Coventry Street

Dorcas Street

Tram 12

Shirt Street

Tram 1

Coventry Street

Bank Street

Dorcas Street

Tram 55

Eastern Rd

Park Street

10

The Tan

Birdwood

3

3

End
Tram 55

8

End Tram
25

Tram 8

9

Tram 3,6,8,16
,64,67,72

South
Melbourne

11

Kings Way

26

Park Street

Dow St

Tram 1

12

13

14

15

Napier Street

Moray Street

Palmerston St

Church Street

Clarendon Street

Cobden St

16

Raglan Street

17

Albert Rd

18

Bridport St

21

26

26

Tram 12

ALT
1

19

20

Queens Road

41

Albert Park

Gunn Island

Albert
Park
Lake

Albert Park
Golf Course

42

Albert Park

(Site of
Formula One
Grand Prix)

Lakeside Dve

MAP 8

Erskine Street

Richardson Street

Neville Street

Page Street

Armstrong Street

Danks Street

McGregor Street

Richardson St

Canterbury Road

Light Rail line

Augtine Drive

59

Middle
Park

Langridge Street

Patterson Street

Park Road

Fraser St

Longmore St

Beaconsfield Parade

Tram 12

MAP 11

MAP 6

Royal
Botanic
Gardens

The Tan

Anderson Street

Yarra River

South Eastern Fwy

Kelso Street

Cremorne Street

1

29

Ave

Domain Road

Bromby St

Domain St

McKaven St

Park St

Marne Street

Walsh Street

Punt Road

Alexandra Ave

Domain Rd

30
31

Caroline St

Avoca Street

Murphy Street

Darling Street

22 23 24
25

Tookak Road

Tram 8

26

26

27

28

29

34

South
Yarra

32

33

40

Caroline St Sth

Macfarlan Street

Fowler St

Davis St

39

38

37

36

35

Fawkner
Park

Alexandra St

Fawkner St

Albion St

Argo St

Osborne Street

MAP 10

St Kilda Road

Tram 72

43

45

46

Moore St

Commercial Road

47

Balmoral St

48 49

Alfred
Hospital

51

50

44

Moubray St

55

Greville Street

Perth Street

Charles Street

Prahran

52

Porter Street

54

53

58
57

56

Tram 6

Punt Road

Alfred Street

Donald Street

Prahran

Lorne St

Tram 3,5,16,
64,67

High Street

24

Windsor

Andrew St

Kent St

Raleigh Street

Upton Road

John St

Green Street

29

Union

Henry Street

Street

0   250   500 m

The distinctive Station Hotel, Prahran.

Melbourne city skyline

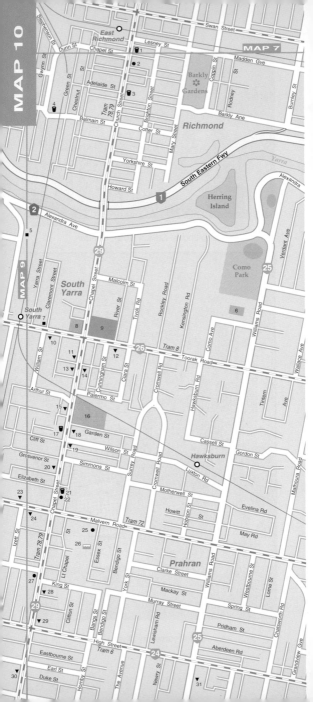

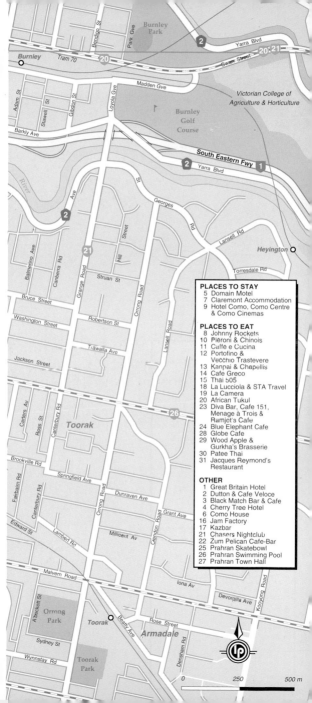

PLACES TO STAY
5 Domain Motel
7 Claremont Accommodation
9 Hotel Como, Como Centre & Como Cinemas

PLACES TO EAT
8 Johnny Rockets
10 Pieroni & Chinois
11 Caffe e Cucina
12 Portofino & Vecchio Trastevere
13 Kanpai & Chapellis
14 Cafe Greco
15 Thai 505
18 La Lucciola & STA Travel
19 La Camera
20 African Tukul
23 Diva Bar, Cafe 151, Menage à Trois & Ramjet's Cafe
24 Blue Elephant Cafe
28 Globe Cafe
29 Wood Apple & Gurkha's Brasserie
30 Patee Thai
31 Jacques Reymond's Restaurant

OTHER
1 Great Britain Hotel
2 Dutton & Cafe Veloce
3 Black Match Bar & Cafe
4 Cherry Tree Hotel
6 Como House
16 Jam Factory
17 Kazbar
21 Chasers Nightclub
22 Zum Pelican Cafe-Bar
25 Prahran Skatebowl
26 Prahran Swimming Pool
27 Prahran Town Hall

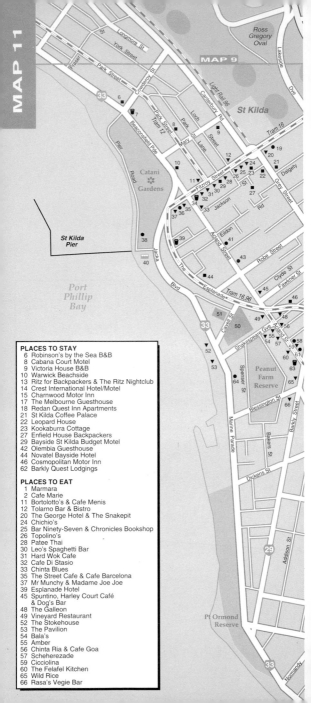

MAP 11

MAP 9

Ross
Gregory
Oval

St Kilda

Catani
Gardens

St Kilda
Pier

Port
Phillip
Bay

Peanut
Farm
Reserve

Pt Ormond
Reserve

PLACES TO STAY
6 Robinson's by the Sea B&B
8 Cabana Court Motel
9 Victoria House B&B
10 Warwick Beachside
13 Ritz for Backpackers & The Ritz Nightclub
14 Crest International Hotel/Motel
15 Charnwood Motor Inn
17 The Melbourne Guesthouse
18 Redan Quest Inn Apartments
21 St Kilda Coffee Palace
22 Leopard House
23 Kookaburra Cottage
27 Enfield House Backpackers
29 Bayside St Kilda Budget Motel
42 Olembia Guesthouse
44 Novatel Bayside Hotel
46 Cosmopolitan Motor Inn
62 Barkly Quest Lodgings

PLACES TO EAT
1 Marmara
2 Cafe Marie
11 Bortolotto's & Cafe Menis
20 Tolarno Bar & Bistro
20 The George Hotel & The Snakepit
24 Chichio's
25 Bar Ninety-Seven & Chronicles Bookshop
26 Topolino's
28 Patee Thai
30 Leo's Spaghetti Bar
31 Hard Wok Cafe
32 Cafe Di Stasio
33 Chinta Blues
35 The Street Cafe & Cafe Barcelona
37 Mr Munchy & Madame Joe Joe
39 Esplanade Hotel
45 Spuntino, Harley Court Café
   & Dog's Bar
48 The Galleon
49 Vineyard Restaurant
52 The Stokehouse
53 The Pavilion
54 Bala's
55 Amber
56 Chinta Ria & Cafe Goa
57 Scheherezade
60 Cicciolina
60 The Felafel Kitchen
65 Wild Rice
66 Rasa's Vegie Bar

OTHER
3 Cha Cha's
4 Astor Cinema
5 Corroboree Tree
7 Beaconsfield Hotel
16 Jewish Museum of Australia
19 The George Cinemas
34 Prince of Wales Hotel
36 Bob's Boards (bike hire)
 & Rock 'n'll 'Skate Hire
38 Royal Melbourne Yacht Squadron
40 St Kilda Baths Complex
41 Theatreworks
43 Linden-St Kilda Arts Centre
47 National Theatre
50 Luna Park
51 Palais Theatre
58 Cosmos Books & Music
61 STA Travel
63 Veludo Bar & Restaurant
64 Apache Junction In-Line Skate Hire

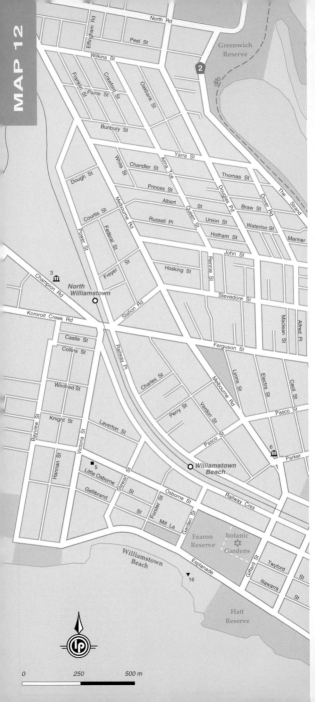

MAP 12

North Rd

Ellingham Rd

Peel St

Greenwich
Reserve

Wilkins St

2

Franklin St

Paine St

Crawford St

Oakbank St

Bunbury St

Yarra St

White St

Chandler St

Alma Tce

Thomas St

Dough St

Princes St

Albert

Douglas Rd

Braw St

Dover Rd

The Strand

Courtis St

Federal St

Melbourne Rd

St

Queen St

Union St

Waterloo St

Mariner

Power St

Russell Pl

Hotham St

Maclean St

Alfred Pl

Freyer St

Hosking St

John St

Rennie St

3

Champion Rd

North
Williamstown

Stevedore St

Kororoit Creek Rd

Station Rd

Ferguson St

Castle St

Collins St

Railway Pl

Charles St

Melbourne Rd

Lyons St

Electra St

Cecil St

Winifred St

Bayview St

Knight St

Victoria St

Laverton St

Perry St

Verdon St

Pasco St

Pasco St

6

Hannan St

Little Osborne

5

Stewart St

Pasco St

Parker St

Gellibrand

St

Forster St

Osborne St

Garden St

Williamstown
Beach

Railway Cres

Williamstown
Beach

Mill La

Fearon
Reserve

Botanic
Gardens

Gifford St

Twyford

St

Esplanade

16

Illawarra

St

Hatt
Reserve

0   250   500 m

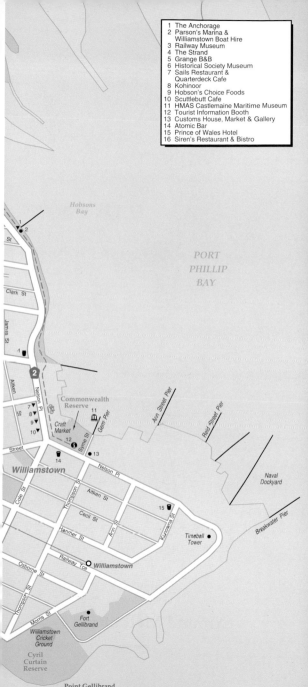

1 The Anchorage
2 Parson's Marina &
 Williamstown Boat Hire
3 Railway Museum
4 The Strand
5 Grange B&B
6 Historical Society Museum
7 Sails Restaurant &
 Quarterdeck Cafe
8 Kohinoor
9 Hobson's Choice Foods
10 Scuttlebutt Cafe
11 HMAS Castlemaine Maritime Museum
12 Tourist Information Booth
13 Customs House, Market & Gallery
14 Atomic Bar
15 Prince of Wales Hotel
16 Siren's Restaurant & Bistro

Hobsons
Bay

PORT
PHILLIP
BAY

Clark St

James St

St

Aitken

Nelson Pl

St

Commonwealth
Reserve

Gem Pier

Arm Street Pier

Reid Street Pier

Craft
Market

Syme St

Street

Williamstown

Nelson Pl

Naval
Dockyard

Cole St

Thompson St

Aitken St

Cecil St

Ann St

Kanowna St

Breakwater Pier

Hanmer St

Timeball
Tower

Osborne St

Railway Tce

Williamstown

Thompson St

Morris St

Fort
Gellibrand

Williamstown
Cricket
Ground

Cyril
Curtain
Reserve

Point Gellibrand

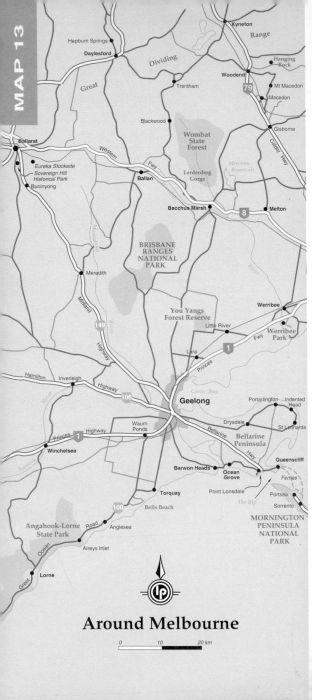

MAP 13

Around Melbourne

0   10   20 km

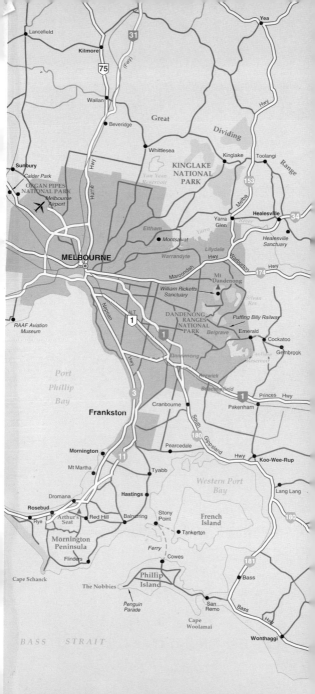

MAP 14

Moonee
Ponds

Cordite Ave

Medway
Golf
Club

Fairbairn
Park

Epsom Road

Ascot
Vale

Hampstead Road

Maidstone

Golf
Course

Western Hwy 8

Mitchell Street

Rosamond Road

Ballarat Road

Showgrounds

Flemington
Racecourse

Flemington

Braybrook

Gordon Street

Flemington Racecourse

South Road

Footscray
Park

Smithfield Road

Ashley Street

Barkly Street

Summerhill Rd

Footscray
West

Footscray

Tottenham

Sunshine Road

Footscray
West

Middle
Foots

Footscray

Paramount Rd

Roberts St

83

Geelong Road

Williamstown Rd

Seddon

Hyde Street

Whitehall Rd

Somerville Road

Yarraville

Francis St

Yarraville

McIvor
Reserve

Westgate
Golf Course

Francis Street

Lorimer Street

West Gate Fwy 1

1

Spotswood

Hudsons Rd

Westgate
Park

Blackshaws Road

Melbourne Rd

Spotswood Scienceworks

2

Todd Road

Port
Melbourne

Altona
East

Newport
Lakes
Parkland

Hall St

Newport

Yarra River

Douglas Pde

White
Reserve

Mason Street

Altona
Lakes
Golf
Course

Newport
North Rd

Market St

MAP 12

Newport
Railway
Works

Melbourne Rd

Williamstown
North

Champion Rd

2

Williamstown
Cemetery

North
Williamstown

Kororoit Creek Road

Victoria St

Williamstown

Altona
Coastal
Park

Williamstown
Beach

Williamstown

Greater Melbourne

0   1   2 km